HIKING THE TRAIL OF TRUTH
Knowing God Through His Creation

2nd Edition (revised edition) by
Mark Stephen Taylor

For since the creation of the world His invisible attributes, His eternal
power and divine nature, have been clearly seen, being understood
from what has been made, so that *men are without excuse.*
(Romans 1:20 NASB)

Mark Taylor
LONG PINE, CA

Unless otherwise stated, Biblical quotations are taken from the following versions of the Bible, and marked as in-text quotations as indicated:

Thompson Chain-Reference, New American Standard Bible,
Copyright © 1993, by, B. B. Kirk Bride Bible Company, Inc.
In-text = (NASB)

New Living Translation Compact Edition, Copyright © 1996, by, Tyndale Charitable Trust. In-text = (NLT)

NIV/KJV Parallel Bible, Copyright, © 1985, by, Zondervan Bible Publishers. In-text = (NIV) or (KJV) accordingly.

New Geneva Study Bible, New King James Version,
Copyright © 1982, by Thomas Nelson Inc. In-text = (NKJV)

Italicized words in text are for emphasis.

If italicized words in the text are direct quotes from Scripture, Scriptural references are in parenthesis following the italicized direct quote. Scripture references in parenthesis following a sentence in the standard text are not direct quotes, but a reference to where in the Scriptures the general subject matter can be found.

Italicized words in parenthesis immediately following and in-text word indicate the Hebrew or Greek meaning of the word(s).

Any graphics in this book are designed by the author. Photos in this book were taken by the author and remain the property of the author.

Any portion of this book may be reproduced for teaching and classroom use. All information is this book is a product of the study, research, notes and personal experiences of the author. Any written references used to enhance this information are super-scripted and indicated on the '*References and Notes*' page, by chapter, in the back of this book. Any statements found within this writing that are similar to other publications not mentioned are purely coincidental.

Note: This 2nd Edition is a 'constructive revision' of the 1st edition (published through Xulon Press), meaning that it contains the *same* material, with *nothing* excluded, however, much more attention was paid to forming paragraphs and choosing certain wording (some sentences added to in various places) that would allow the reader a more meaningful and retainable learning experience along the trail.

MSTaylor Productions, Lone Wolf Limited,
hikemark@hotmail.com

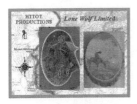

*February 2011 Edition

Dr. Mike J. Mucci, with the author on Mt. Whitney's summit,
August 1998

For The Reader

In seeking to 'display a more appropriate appearance,' this second edition of the award-winning book, *Hiking the Trail of Truth*, has, at our most earnest request, been produced with a 'hiking in progress' picture of its author on the front cover (atop Mt. Whitney). Mr. Taylor is still an avid hiker at age 65, and is also one of those few authors you can reach in person, via his trail phone, should you have any questions for him concerning this writing (909-549-0068).

We believe that his inspiration in the realm of God and the Creation is a spring of significantly refreshing water in an immensely dry and parched land. Within this edition he takes us on an illuminating trek into the wilderness of pure spiritual realities. His particular insight into these things has an unprecedented nourishing effect on most anyone associated with him. He pulls no punches, and the journey on which he can take you into *understanding* is for sure and eye-opener.

To the reader we say, the time you choose to spend hiking into and through this most informative book will be exceptionally well worth your effort. We believe that Mr. Taylor is truly a 'spiritual doctor,' if you will, who operates on the human heart—a professional in his gifted field of teaching. He is a needed voice, crying from the wilderness—one who indeed endeavors to turn the hearts of men and women *back* to God. We sincerely believe he can bring understanding and healing to your spirit through his perceptions of the truth.

*Recent reviews on this book have honored it in several ways:

1. "A book that needed to be written."
2. "An amazing book."
3. "Uniquely interesting."
4. "Life changing."
5. "A magnificent book."
6. "Some of my students have labeled it, 'Life 101.'"
7. "I'll never treat my dog the same—thanks for chapter 11."

May your journey, dear reader, be one of illumination.
Sincerely, *The HTTOT Staff*

Award Winning Edition
May 2009

CERTIFICATE *of* ACHIEVEMENT

SPRING 2009 *Christian* CHOICE BOOK AWARDS

Xulon Press recognizes MARK STEPHEN TAYLOR as a 3RD PLACE winner of the Spring 2009 Christian Choice Book Awards for HIKING THE TRAIL OF TRUTH in the CHRISTIAN LIVING category this twenty-ninth day of May, 2009.

TOM FREILING
VICE PRESIDENT & GENERAL MANAGER

xulon

HIKING THE TRAIL OF TRUTH
Table of Contents

ACKNOWLEDGEMENTS

My life has indeed been full of compassionate people. I would first of all like to thank God for allowing me such a diversity of friends who have influenced my life and occupy a very sacred place in my heart. I could write volumes on these friendships, but for now I will just honor them by listing their names and thanking them for their unforgettable contributions to my well being. I am indebted to each and every one of them...

I offer my thanks to my mother and father of course, long gone but not forgotten. I am grateful to them for the honor of being born in a beautiful country and being allowed to explore *many* of its wonders. Perhaps I will be able to thank them properly after the resurrection. I appreciate their attempts in this life to guide me correctly. I am so glad they taught me also of self-reliance.

I offer my thanks to my childhood friends, especially Russell Everett Greathouse, who was the Tom Sawyer of my youth and shared many adventures with me. Russ is gone now, but his family has many reasons to celebrate.

I offer my thanks to the John McCullouch, John Brandt, and Joe Frankovitch families, the three sets of parents who enlightened my path and gave me the courage to finish high school when times were indeed difficult. They took me in and cared for me at separate times, each as if they were my own family—and so they have become.

I offer my thanks to the entire Copley, Ohio, High School Class of 1963, just over one hundred students, which was the largest gathering of personal friends that I have known to this date. We were a close group indeed, but then the early 60's were indeed a great time in our nation's history, especially in the more rural locations. I will always appreciate this most unique relationship shared with so many.

I offer my thanks to John Brandt, Ken George (Lesniak), Jack Frankovitch, Al Piry, and Harry Brown; the best friends (the rat pack) of my high school experience, who continue to be my close friends, though we are many miles apart from one another. Though varied in our experiences, our lives have been similar in many ways. I hope we can all sit in front of a campfire one of these days and enjoy the pleasure of some great discussions.

I offer my thanks to the United States Army and Major James R. Fulmer, who had no small part in the development of my physical and mental abilities, that I might pursue my destiny.

I offer my thanks to Dan Campbell of Cuyahoga Falls, Ohio, and Charles Cook of Temple City, California, who were the Biblical teachers who laid the foundation for my education in the Word of God. Dan taught me to bring the Scriptures to life, while Charles toiled on me as if with the hands of a sculptor, shaping me into a teacher of truth. What these men gave to me no one can ever take from me, and their tireless efforts I believe have now been vindicated.

I offer my thanks to Edie Mayfield, formerly of Ohio, for her patience and kindness in her relationship with me and my children during some difficult but rewarding times in the early 1980's. I appreciate most of all the inspiration she continually offered my children.

I offer my thanks to the members and former members of the Arcadia Police Department, Arcadia, California, for their endearing friendships and for sharing with me so many memorable wilderness adventures. I especially appreciate their devotion to me as a partner in law enforcement. A special thanks to the following officers for their integrity, their loyalty, and for the honor of knowing their individual, undisputed, unequalled character:

R.S. Sears, Howard Piland, Paul Harrington, Neal Johnson, Dick Honaker, Tim Murray, Rudy Blum, Richard Mauch, Rod Florea, Don Glenn, Ed Winter, Ed Ostashay, David Hinig, Rick Sandona, Bob Sanderson, Ron Bailey, Burton Bernstein, Mike Cervantes, Larry Goodman, Ken Petty, Phil Henry, Chuck Chapman, Steve Gilmore, Richard Prager, Harry Verhiley, Jeff Hudson, Bob McPherson, Raymond Sanchez, David Hunkapiller, John McQuarie, Andy Ballantyne, Ronald Seman, Richard Castro, Kirk Pedersen, Sharleen Wilson, Stephen Delgadillo, Bob Williams, Mitch Wood, Michael Blair, Louise Brandsma, David Campbell, John Pruitt, Joe Bale, Robert Bolduc, Larry Weston, Toni Caylor, Paul Van Der Horn, Billy Walton, Scott Moore, Ken Harper, Don Klock, Clayton Post, Ron Buckholtz, Bruce Smith, Mike Gima, Randy Kirby, Dean Caputo, Steve Fallavollita, Gar Richmond, Steve Crawford, Steve Turner, Tom Le Veque, Scott Elenberger, Vaughn Whalen, Brian Ortiz, Mike Castro, Dave Swearengin, Jim Winstead, Roy Nakamura, Jim Blacklock, Don Wilsterman, Sharon Reynolds, Randy Adams, Don Alcorn, Dr. John Wells, and Tony Minnillo

A special acknowledgment to the following APD staff personnel, who also gave of their friendship, confidence and strength to make my time shared with them significantly memorable:

Larry Morrow, Dennis Hoy, Gloria Freire, Leticia Corral, Sandra Gallegos, Marlene Russell, Nancy Sexton, Lynn Pursel, Emparo Robles, James Coote and Ferdinand Zuletta.

I offer my thanks to Terry Pitts of the Southgate Police Department (Los Angeles County), who on the day that we graduated from the Rio Hondo Police Academy gave me a very special gift—a hardbound edition of Webster's New World Thesaurus. Inside the cover were penned these encouraging words: *Congratulations! Now that you've finished the academy, I hope you will be able to put this to use when you write. To a "good friend" on Graduation Day. Love, Terry, January 30, 1987.* This volume helped me to complete various writings over the years and most importantly this book.

Terry's gift is still the most treasured volume that I own. I appreciate her providential insight into my future.

I offer my thanks to Ken Petty and Sharon Anderson for the important part that each of them played in my life during my years with APD. Without the influence of these close friends in my life and the sacrifices they endured on my behalf, the meaning of friendship would not be completely understood.

I offer my thanks to Sandie Eisenhower, who helped me to launch the *Hiking the Trail of Truth* website, which made possible the writing of this book. I also thank her for her patient assistance with many HTTOT films and for her accompanying me on several inspirational adventures into the Monuments. I appreciate her paintings of the outdoors as well. They continue to be a great source of inspiration.

I offer my thanks to Dr. Mike Mucci, who was my hiking partner for many years. The trails we hiked are indeed numerous and unforgettable. The things we learned are etched on our hearts forever. The things we were allowed to see and the varied paths we were permitted to walk can be pictured at anytime within my mind. This impressive gallery is a gift from God. The Mt. Whitney climb of 1998 with Mike is still the 'summit' of nearly an entire lifetime of hiking. I'm hoping we'll have the opportunity to do it again, before we get to old or one of us takes the final journey. But then, I 'spect we may get to hike forever up there, if it is where dreams come true. Oh—there'll be no hunting up there, Mike. You should find another sport, a hobby or something, and get use to the idea, ol' buddy. Hoo-Haw!

I want to thank Railroad Ron Friend, my good friend from Ohio, who flew to California in 1994 in order to accompany me on a monumental exploration of the Western landscape when I retired from the APD. I also want to acknowledge Hal Deckhert and Thom Hutchinson, who first worked with me at Crystal Lake, California, in 1998, managing the high mountain campgrounds. Raymond Laird was added to that duo in the Eldorado National Forest of northern California. These four were the mountain men— the rare breed—involved in the 'Jeremiah Johnson' experiences that brought substantial meaning to my wayward life.

My final acknowledgment of course is to my family. I am most thankful to Jenny, the wife of my youth, for the time we shared together—for her kind and forgiving spirit. I thank each of my children and grandchildren for their patience with me and their continuing love for The Old Man. I thank my sister, Karen, and her family for their continued thoughts of 'Uncle Mark.' No one sees a whole lot of me nowadays, but they are still there for me…

Some Native Americans say that there are those who hear their own inner voice with great clarity, and they live by what they hear. Such move about with the wind and become legends—I hope when they read this book that each member of my family and each of my friends mentioned in this acknowledgments document will understand more about the real Mark and less about the legendary guy. I am confident that God will open their eyes—hopefully their hearts as well.

Mark Stephen Taylor

From The Author

I welcome you, dear reader, to the pages of this book. I'm nearing sixty-four years of age at this time, and have been creating reading material in some form or another all of my life. *Hiking the Trail of Truth* is my first attempt at publishing a particular writing in book format. I must say however that I do not really think that I am late in life with this endeavor.

In fact, I truly would have never been ready for this without the many years of life experience and grace of God that has led me to this point. Also, as a senior I felt it was now time to allow what I have gleaned from life to flow out, and so I am compelled to write to seniors who may have lost their way—or think they've found their way—who feel that they are approaching the end of the trail.

Now you don't really have to be a senior citizen to learn something from this writing. Not at all. You can be a fountain of youth and still find yourself at the end of the trail. You may have lost your way or think you've found your way. It doesn't matter. The information I am about to give you is indeed profitable at all ages. If you truly pay attention to this writing you will in fact glean much from it. It will be to you like a treasure map, and you may discover riches quite beyond your expectations.

Through this account of my own struggles, interwoven and etched with appropriate insights from God's creation, my hope is that no small amount of profound light might be shed upon *your* personal wanderings along life's trail. My purpose is such that by the time you do reach the end of your trail you will have a deeper understanding of just who you are, and a productive appreciation of what the many wonders of God can teach you.

You will also become aware of just why you are you, and where you may be going from here. You will see things quite differently than what you are accustomed to. Your eyes will be opened—conceivably for the first time.

Perhaps some of you seniors think you already know what life is all about. Most all of the younger folk's think they know. We seniors of course know that they don't know, but many seniors, as experienced as they are, haven't truly understood life either. The end of their trail is a disaster. They are unable to make sense of their life—things just didn't turn out as they had expected.

That's because somewhere along the way they chose an inferior compass and now find themselves dealing with the consequences of poor navigation. And even if they were on the trail of *Christianity*, having wisely chosen the Bible as a compass, then somewhere along their route they missed actually *seeing* God in His creation.

The Bible is a divinely inspired, written compass, which truly points the way, but the creation is a living, breathing compass, which profoundly glorifies the journey. It is impossible for a human being to not know that God exists. We are 'without excuse' if we fail to see Him through the wonder of the things He has made (Romans 1:20).

The creation in harmony with the Scriptures also teaches us that Christianity's God is the one, true God. *Hiking the Trail of Truth* offers profound discovery, romance and adventure along the way to this enlightenment. I will warn you that there are some difficult sections of trail, but it is indeed a journey of illumination—well worth the trek.

Wisdom is a divine gift, and understanding is a product of that particular wisdom. Allow me through this writing to share with you some insights that can bring the gift of wisdom and understanding and peace and satisfaction at the end of the trail, *no matter what sort of a trail it has been.* Allow me to present you with a true compass by which you can evaluate your journey.

Allow me also to take you down some trails of profound illumination that are hard to find—not because they aren't marked on the majority of maps, but perhaps because we've never really learned what the maps are trying to tell us. Believe it or not, at any age, there is still time to get the understanding that will teach you the truth concerning many if not all things.

You can find your spiritual home—your connection with God. Isn't that in reality what each of us the world over is seeking—our connection with God? Many young college students around the world now express that desire. Some old folk's say they have been looking for that connection for the better part of their lives, but have not yet found it.

Then come along and find it—young and old alike. Come along and see it for yourself—the supernatural is indeed revealed through the natural. Come and *Hike the Trail of Truth* along with me...

Sincerely, *Mark Stephen Taylor*
November 2009

DEDICATIONS

This writing is dedicated first of all to my mother, Pauline, who inspired me to write stories when I was just a young lad. She is not here to celebrate with me, but if she is in some way looking down from above, I am sure that she would be most excited about and proud of this first publication. I am looking forward to seeing her again—more than words can express.

This writing is dedicated secondly to Jenny, the wife of my youth. I know that she shares my joy in this endeavor, and without a part of her kind and loving spirit working through me it would have never been accomplished. My hat is off to you, Jenny, and I will see that you get the very first copy.

Thirdly, this writing is of course dedicated to my children, Mike, Mitch, Marc and Carrie, with whom I have shared many adventures over the years—not as many as I would have liked to, but you do what you can do at the time. Now much time has passed and I have nine grandchildren, some of which I have never seen—in person. Perhaps that will change in the near future. Thanks, kids, for your continued love and support for the Old Man.

Fourthly, this writing is dedicated to each of those persons, named or unnamed, in the *Acknowledgments* section. Life is like a river; you keep on flowing where the force of nature takes you, never knowing where it's going to take you. I was fortunate that many beautiful flowers bloomed along its banks. I am eternally grateful for all of those exceptionally good friends.

*Finally, I dedicate this writing to the reader—the brave hiker who begins this journey, with the hope that he/she will make new discoveries along this difficult trail and will indeed find illumination when they reach the summit...

Mt. Whitney, Lone Pine, California
'The High and the Mighty'

Oh these vast, calm, measureless mountain days, inviting at once to work and rest. Days in whose light everything seems equally divine: Nevermore, however weary, should one faint by the way, who gains the blessing of one mountain day. Whatever his fate— long life, short life, stormy or calm, he is rich forever!

John Muir

*Prologue

Mirror, mirror, on the wall—who's the fairest of them all? We've all looked into mirrors—hand mirrors or wall mirrors, door mirrors or floor mirrors, ceiling mirrors or the smaller mirror just above the bathroom sink—some of us do it quite often. For others it's at least once in the morning and perhaps again in the evening, just before going to bed.

We wash our face, brush our teeth and comb our hair. We don't normally spend a lot of time in front of the mirror—a quick look to straighten a crooked tie or to check our makeup. Perhaps we glance to discover a stain on a shirt collar or blouse. We might perhaps check the condition of our nose or look to see if there is food in our teeth from breakfast or dinner. Do we look good or not?

It's a glance here or there at our reflection, for one reason or another. For most of us our appearance seems quite important. Once satisfied with what we have seen we're usually off and running. But wait—slow down for just a moment. Take a few steps with me back toward that mirror. There is a much more urgent need to see your reflection. A truly profound need to see and to understand what's really there.

Hiking the Trail of Truth is a journey into self—a much longer time spent in front of the mirror. Along the way you will encounter the wonders of God's creation—things you see on a daily basis that you take for granted, without really comprehending the significance of their relationship to your life. The fast pace at which most of us race through life tends to obscure what's really there.

True reality can be found within the viewing of the sunrise, in a leisurely walk through the desert or a hike up into the high country. It can be discovered on the wings of an eagle or within the den of the coyote. It echoes back at sunset and is announced all over again among the numberless stars of heaven. True reality is wisdom and understanding—of who we are and why we're here.

Stories are the essence of life and teach us our most valuable lessons. I'm going to begin with a story—a profound story of love, betrayal and sacrifice. A story that mirrors each of us. From there I will take you on a journey through my life, which will allow you to reflect upon your own—to see your true image in the mirror. We will also take an illuminating hike among the wonders of God's creation—the deserts, the mountains and the many formations shaped by water, the sustainer of all life.

You won't need to take much along with you physically on this journey—a few snacks, a canteen of water and a hiking stick will do. But there are some spiritual requirements. You will need both courage and determination. The trail is difficult in the beginning, and the summit (trail's end) is a long way off.

How about challenge—can you handle that? Hikers always face challenges of one kind or another, whether hiking on flatland or negotiating the rugged trails of the high mountains. You will indeed be challenged on this hike. Hiking is a great adventure—trails can reveal many things of which the faint-hearted miss out.

There's a lot to learn on this trek. Male or female, whether you are an artist, a scientist, a doctor, a lawyer, a teacher, a preacher, an executive, an office worker or a laborer of any kind—no matter what your calling in life, you will be both physically and spiritually nourished by this hike. Many profound discoveries await you. Are you ready? Then let's head out...

If you, O Lord, kept a record of sins, who could stand? The sacrifices of God are a broken spirit; a broken and contrite heart, O God, you will not despise.

(Psalm 130:3, & Psalm 51:17 NIV)

Chapter One...First Things First
Knowing Who We Really Are

Once upon a time, a long time ago when the earth was extremely young, a beautiful yet mutinous angel from the heavenly realms made a peculiar choice to entice the very first human inhabitants of that perfect world. Having great spiritual power, he entered into an earthly creature familiar to the humans, disguising himself, and subtly proceeded to deceive them into betraying a trust of the Creator who formed them and who loved them. Their names were Adam (*man or mankind*) and Eve (*mother of all living*).

Adam and Eve were caretakers of a very special garden on the newly formed earth, which contained every tree pleasing to the sight and excellent for food, including the *tree of life* in the midst of the garden. But also in the midst of the garden was a tree that produced a forbidden fruit—the tree of *the knowledge of good and evil*.

Highlighting the garden and all plants of the field was a fine mist that went up from the earth and watered the whole ground (the Lord had not yet caused it to rain upon the earth). This wondrous garden was planted for Adam and Eve in a place called Eden (*delight*), perhaps buried somewhere beneath the sands in the southern area of what is now modern day Iraq.

It was originally a paradise on earth. There are many beautiful gardens around the world today, but I am sure and can certainly picture that none would compare with this original garden. There were also birds and animals and creatures of every sort upon the newly formed earth, which the Creator had earlier brought unto Adam and whom Adam had been allowed to give names. He gave names to all the cattle, to all the birds of the sky and to every beast of the field, and the Creator honored all the names that Adam had given to each and every creature of the earth.

The Creator's entire work was indeed pure and wholesome, as Adam and Eve walked about on the earth in their nakedness and were not ashamed.[1] The Creator, who was the Supreme God (*Elohim, El Shadday, Yahweh*), had told Adam and Eve that they could freely eat of all the trees in the special garden for nourishment and continued life, save the one tree of the knowledge of good and evil in the midst of the garden. He warned them not to eat of its particular fruit—not even to touch it, or they would surely die.

The term, *death,* was unfamiliar to Adam and Eve and meant *separation* from their God, which at the time they could not even begin to comprehend—He walked often with them in the garden, sharing His love through teaching them how to care for the various plants and creatures of the earth. He was their friend. His graciousness toward them was evident as they indeed experienced great freedom through the power of choice. This deep love that God expressed for the family whom He made lords of His earthly creation must have been exceedingly motivating.

But on one particular day, while Eve was alone, the evil angel spoke to her through the mouth of a serpent, enticing her to eat of the forbidden fruit from in the midst of the garden. He assured her that she would not die, but that her eyes would be opened and she would be as God; knowing both good and evil.

Seeing that the fruit was good for food, pleasing to the eye and also desirable for gaining wisdom, she took some and ate it. Suddenly there was strangeness within her body, soul and spirit—an unfamiliar urging. She later tempted Adam and he also ate. As a result of their choice to act upon the serpent's enticement their inherent character became one of shame, deceitfulness and rebellion.

The fruit, which they had eaten from the forbidden tree, quickly 'poisoned' their hearts—their human spirit. They immediately realized that they were both naked, so they sewed fig leaves together and made coverings for themselves. When they heard the sound of their Creator walking in the garden in the cool of the day, the unfaithful couple at once hid themselves among the trees of the garden. The rest of this story is profound.[2]

Adam and Eve had broken their trust with God. Their closeness with Him was shattered. Though they were meant to live pure, unashamed and free forever as the lords of all of God's earthly blessings; falsehood, depravity and physical death became their destiny—the destiny of their offspring as well.

Even the earth itself, in all of its original glory, was ultimately cursed and came under the same bondage of corruption. What was intended to be paradise became a graveyard. The human race, created in the guiltless, immortal image of God, had put on corruption and mortality.

The curse of sin (*corruption*) had entered the world. The hearts of mankind became deceitful and desperately wicked. Depravity, sickness, decay and death, both physical and spiritual, became the way of life. Adam and Eve soon lost their paradise home. One of their eventual children killed his own brother. The curse produced more expectations of pain, suffering and death, which occurrences increased dramatically upon the earth.[3] Why such a terrible curse? We'll deal with that concept and the rest of the story in chapter 2.

In the members of our being there is a natural, subtle inclination toward desire, which can be on the moment both immeasurable and fierce. With overwhelming power desire seizes mastery of the 'flesh'—the human nature deprived of God's Spirit. All at once an unseen, smoldering fire is kindled. The flesh burns and is in flames. It makes no difference whether it is sexual desire, desire for ambition, for vanity, for revenge, for love of fame and power, greed for money, or desire to utter unkind words or to strike out physically against another—at this moment God becomes quite unreal to us.

In fact, He loses all reality and only the desires of the creature are revealed. The only reality at this point in the impetuous process is the devil. The deceiver does not at this time fill us with hatred of God, but subtly overthrows us with forgetfulness of God. We become caught in an intangible net of superficial emotions we cannot even begin to see or comprehend. This lust that has been aroused through desire moves on to envelope the mind and will of man/woman in the deepest of darkness, and in a way casts their reasoning utterly below the roots of the mountains; toward the depths of hell itself.

The powers of clear discrimination and of proper decision are taken from us as egotistical questions arise and cunningly present themselves: "In this situation is what my flesh (*nature*) desires really sin?" And, "Is it not permitted of me now—yes even perhaps expected of me now to appease my desire in this particular circumstance? After all, my feelings are so strong—shouldn't I trust them?"

It is at this time that everything within us rises up against the words of God (remember; He remains quite unreal to us). At this point in time also there is nothing to hold us back and so we plunge ahead in our lust, blinded in our members by the flames of passion against seeking any means of escape—we truly wanted our own way from the very conception of our desire, and so, now we have it—our lust is fulfilled.

The Bible teaches us in times of such overpowering temptation there is but one alternative: *Flee*! Run as far as you can as fast as you can. Do not consider that the evil you are about to do will have a wholesome result in the end—do not even ponder that idea for a second. There is no resistance to Satan (that serpent of old) in lust other than flight.

Every struggle against lust in one's own strength is doomed to failure. If you do not run, you will fall—it's only a matter of time. Lust is indeed more powerful than most anyone can comprehend. However, some people are unable to run—there may be some physical impairment or old age may have taken its toll—if this is the case, one's knowledge of the Scriptures can be their primary defense.

An excellent comparison to the growth of lust in the body's members is like the legend of a man bitten by a wolf. The man begins to take on the passions of the wolf (becomes a werewolf—part man, part wolf), gradually at first, until the rising of the full moon, when the wolf's passions totally consume him and he actually becomes a wolf. At that time all of his passionate aggression is released upon his prey.

This same burning passion can be aroused in the child molester, the rapist or the murderer from the initial bite of desire to full, lustful aggression in less than a minute. This is what can happen in lust—to anyone—so if you *are* unable to run you had better handcuff yourself to a post or lock yourself in a room and swallow the key in either case.

It has been said that temptation is a place bordering the boundaries of behavioral limits set by God. Satan always magnifies the importance of these 'off limit' areas, and if you cross the line just once you will cross it again. Temptation is not sin, but it lives right next door to it. It is also the only address where you are not required to 'love your neighbor.'

There are those who claim that they just don't think about bad things and can escape the downward spiral toward sin, however, temptation can be so unimaginably fierce that the mind goes to places over which we have absolutely no control. You can and will think about bad things and act upon those things, whether you want to or not.

Do not be deceived. *The mind set on the flesh is hostile toward God; for it does not subject itself to the law of God, for it is not even able to do so* (Romans 8:7 NASB). We are fallen creatures. It is not within our nature to do what is right. Our hearts are actually against any rule over us by any type of god.

We are in fact hostile and rebellious toward God and toward one another. If you do not understand this concept or you don't believe the truth of it—or you just don't want to accept it, then it is time you learned both to understand it, to believe it, and thirdly, how to accept it...

Most of us go through life not knowing or realizing and therefore not understanding the depth of depravity within our own, individual human nature. This ignorance is primarily due to the fact that teachers of human psychology have never really taught the truth of it, much less accepted it.

If we are fortunate enough at sometime in life to become aware of it, then we can joyfully thank God for allowing us the privilege of that revelation, and again for allowing us the honor of living long enough to begin an attempt to understand it. This revelation can only take place when an individual progresses into a state of total humility— spiritual humility.

Some form of physical affliction is usually the only condition that may bring about this type of submission. The psalmist wrote: *Before I was afflicted I went astray, but now I keep Your word.* And, *It is good for me that I have been afflicted, that I may learn Your statutes* (Psalm 119:67,71 NKJV).

Only with that selection of attitude can we even hope to begin gaining the knowledge of who we truly are. It is indeed a wise choice of attitude, as you will discover for yourself through this writing. Jeremiah the prophet spoke discerningly with reference to the wisdom in choosing the path of a humble attitude:

The Lord is wonderfully good to those who wait for Him and seek Him. So it is good to wait quietly for salvation from the Lord. And it is good for the young to submit to the yoke of His discipline. Let them sit alone in silence beneath the Lord's demands. Let them lie face down in the dust; then at last there is hope for them (Lamentations 3:25-29 NLT).

The bottom line of humility is that when you put your mouth into the dust of the earth, then there is finally some hope for you. This is the only time when the light of God can dispel the darkness, and you won't fully appreciate the light until you feel the weight of the darkness.

Jeremiah also wrote concerning the natural ignorance of our human nature: *The heart is deceitful above all things and beyond cure. Who can understand it?* (Jeremiah 17:9 NIV)—Is a picture of who you really are beginning to form or take shape? Secondly, have you been somewhat humbled as of yet?

No? Well, there's more to come to assist you through these two processes—if you are willing. We're all put to the test, but it never comes in the form or at the point we would prefer, does it? Knowing and understanding who you are is indeed a *difficult* journey—please continue to bear with me...

Just how utterly wicked and deceitful is this nature of ours? I believe the Apostle Paul wrote the most profound, personal description of it in the 1st century AD. This inspired writing can be found in the Biblical book of Romans, and we'll look into that momentarily.

Depravity is a condition we live with from the time of our birth until the time of our physical death. No matter who we are in the world, each and every one of us is infected with it. Anyone who thinks otherwise is only deceiving himself or herself, having developed no understanding within their heart (1st John 1:8).

As long as our spirit occupies the 'body of our flesh' the deceitfulness of our human nature will be a part of us and usually eludes us. In teaching us *what* we are, the Bible says that we are *fearfully and wonderfully made* (Psalm 139:14 NIV), and it is no

24

wonder, for the very hand of God himself designed and formed us. He weaved together all of our inward parts so that we can function in the miraculous manner that we do.[4]

Our brains control, our ears hear, our eyes see, our limbs move, our hands choose. The precise construction and operative details of each of these things is unfathomable! The theory that we are a product of mere chance and not of intelligent design is preposterous. DNA is just one small reason for believing that we are fearfully and wonderfully made and not evolved from plants, lizards or monkeys.

DNA (deoxyribonucleic acid) contains uniquely coded information that determines what you look like, much of your personality, and how every cell in your body is to function throughout your lifetime. If the DNA (46 segments; 23 from your mother and 23 from your father) in *one* of your cells were uncoiled, connected and stretched out, it would be about 7 feet long. If all of this very densely coded information from *one* cell of *one* person were written in books, it would fill a library of about 4000 books.

You have duplicate copies of this DNA in each of the 100,000,000,000,000 (one hundred trillion) cells in your body. If the DNA in *your body* were placed end to end, it would stretch from the earth to the moon 500,000 times. However, if one set of DNA (one cell's worth) from every person who ever lived were placed in a pile, it would weigh less than an aspirin!

All of this unfathomable construction can be translated *fearfully and wonderfully made.*[5] However, *who* we are, is a different story altogether. We have indeed fallen from the pure faith and are no longer creatures of God's original intent. Our body, soul and spirit have been corrupted or 'poisoned,' if you will. Bottom line is that there is no human being anywhere in the world who is not capable of the most frightful behavior.

We can see this behavior in every country of the world. There are many passages throughout the Bible that teach this truth and that describe just who we are without God—absolutely no one is excluded. Here are just a few examples:

We are filled with all kinds of wickedness, evil, greed and depravity. We are full of envy, murder, strife, deceit and malice. We are gossips, slanderers, God-haters, insolent, arrogant and boastful. We invent ways of doing evil; we disobey our parents, we are senseless, faithless, heartless and ruthless (Romans 1:29-31).

We are also told; *the acts of the sinful nature are obvious: sexual immorality, impurity and debauchery, idolatry and witchcraft; hatred, discord, jealousy, fits of rage, selfish ambition, dissensions, factions and envy; drunkenness, orgies, and the like* (Galatians 5:19,21 (NIV).

All humans from every nation of the earth are under this curse of sin. As it is written: *There is no one righteous, not even one; there is no one who understands, no one who seeks God. All have turned away, they have together become worthless; there is no one who does good, not even one* (Romans 3:10-12 NIV).

The truth of the matter is that *only* when the Spirit of God works through the human heart can any form of goodness proceed outward from that heart (Romans 8:13,14). Let's explore that bold but accurate concept a little further...

It's time now to look at this sin dilemma through an intense, personal description of its power and magnitude. Let us consider the Apostle Paul's struggle with it. Keep in mind that Paul was in fact a Christian (*adherent of Christ*) at the time he wrote to the believers in Rome concerning the personal struggle with the sin nature that the entire human race must endure.

Paul's insight into this matter convicts each of us of the bitter reality of it. This inspired writing is dated approximately 56 AD:

I don't understand myself at all, for I really want to do what is right, but I don't do it. Instead, I do the very thing I hate. I know perfectly well that what I am doing is wrong, and my bad conscience shows that I agree that the law is good. But I can't help myself, because it is sin inside me that makes me do these evil things.

I know I am rotten through and through so far as my sinful nature is concerned. No matter which way I turn, I can't make myself do right. I want to, but I can't. When I want to do good, I don't. And when I try not to do wrong, I do it anyway. But if I am doing what I don't want to, I am not really the one doing it; the sin within me is doing it.

It seems to be a fact of life that when I want to do what is right, I inevitably do what is wrong. I love God's law with all my heart. But there is another law at work within me that is at war with my mind. This law wins the fight and makes me a slave to the sin that is still within me. Oh, what a miserable person I am! Who will free me from this life that is dominated by sin? (Romans 7:15-25 NLT)

It is quite evident through just these few readings I have so far presented that all human beings; Christians and non-Christians alike, are in need of a Savior. The world's increasing moral decay and all things related to it are entirely the result of sin.

Great suffering in the world is also the result of sin, however, an individual may undergo personal suffering that is not a direct result of his/her own sin (Job chapters1 thru 42). Yet, sin in the world is the *root* cause of any type of suffering just the same.

We cannot escape our human nature or the corruption that is in the world by means of our personal thoughts, activities, or moral strength. Sin dwells within us. Everyone is accordingly guilty. Though one may think differently, no one person is better than any other. *All are impure.*

Again, it is only by the grace of God, and through the Spirit of God, that any good emerges in anyone's own particular lifetime. However, when Christ returns, Christians will be filled with His goodness, being made incorruptible at that very moment (1st Corinthians 15:51-54). That in itself is a profound reason for adhering to Christ in this present world.

You might be thinking, 'Hey—wait a minute here—there are a lot of nice people in the world. How can the Bible teach that *no one* is good?'

Jesus Himself said that only God is good (Matthew 19:17). There is goodness in the world because God is good, and He allows these attributes to be demonstrated through the lives of certain human beings. Some people only know goodness through the kind acts or words of others. God's Spirit can produce goodness through a human heart, saved or unsaved, and He does so to display the unfathomable riches of His grace. He leads people to Himself by means of this display. It is only by the Spirit of God that anyone can be led to God (John 6:44).

That Spirit can be identified in His creation, in His word, and through the actions or words of His creatures. We can search diligently all we want to—hoping somehow to find Him, but only God's Spirit acting in accordance with His own will, through any means He chooses, can guide us toward Him. We can claim no personal credit for finding Him, for He is the one who searches so diligently for us.

Someone once aptly said: "We search for God until He finds us." Perhaps His Spirit is using this very writing to draw you to Himself?

27

Behind your reading of this book there is purpose, of that I am confident. God works in mysterious ways that we cannot begin to comprehend. His methods are numberless. Because of sin, our ways are not His ways nor our methods His methods.

Wow! If modern psychology taught these very truths we have explored regarding the deceitfulness of the sin nature—within all humans—this particular knowledge could end the plague of inferiority. It could bridge all cultural gaps. It would highlight without question the absolute necessity for one to become a part of the body of Christ (a Christian—adherent of Christ).

Justice, love and mercy could then rule. Broken lives and broken hearts could be mended all over the world. There could be no more hunger or want. We could be united; for according to Scripture we are all one if we are in Christ Jesus (Galatians 3:29). In Him there is no condemnation regarding the sin nature (Romans 8:1).

However, being in Christ does not *change* our sinful nature—not one bit, for Christian's *do* continue to sin. But it does change one's *position* with God, in that he/she has access to the living Spirit of God, who dwells full time within the Christian without condemnation, and who fights for them and with them against the deeds of the sin nature. The non-Christian does not have this advantage in life and is eventually consumed and destroyed by sin. Their end is both physical and spiritual death, for there is no escape apart from the Spirit of God (Romans 8:13).

You may have heard radio or television evangelists teach that, once you become a Christian, you are a good person—that you are special—above the norm. When one first becomes a Christian, the condemnation of all *past* sins is removed and the Holy Spirit enters him/her to empower their life for good (Acts 2:38). Because of this, Christians are under *grace*—no longer under the law, which condemns.

Under grace, Christians have the duty to present themselves to the Spirit in obedience to the will of the Spirit. Only through their submission to the Spirit of God can they hold back the sin that is still within their nature. When they do sin (and they always do), they have continual forgiveness under grace, through the blood of Christ, by the confession of their sins to God (1st John 1:5-10).

Know also that only the Spirit of God can hold one back from sin (Genesis 20:6). We are completely helpless on our own, and are at all times prone to fall prey to the sin that remains within us (Romans 7:19, 20). Contrary to many 'theological' opinions of today, a Christian is, among other things, a *warrior*. You can't just stand still and do nothing and call it *faith* (more on that in chapter 14).

We're not under condemnation when we fail (Romans 8:1), but we are constantly at war, engaged in a great diversity of battles with the sin nature. The Spirit of God aids that effort and is actually the force that puts to death its (the sinful nature's) deeds (Romans 8:13). That sinful nature however never changes—just keeps on fighting against our attempts to do what is right (Romans 7:18-25).

It is not the individual Christian who is 'good' or 'special,' but the Spirit of God living within them. It is this grace that allows Christians to walk in newness of life. Walking in this newness of life through faith, which is an active (not passive) belief, and being set free from the *condemnation of sin*, they are able to produce goodness from their hearts through Christ, who dwells within them through the Holy Spirit.

Christians are still prone to sin—not 'above the norm'—but they are given the freedom, through grace (*unmerited favor*), of choosing to allow the Spirit of God to help them in dealing with it (Romans 8:13,14). An illustration of this operation is found in the conversation of Jesus with a Samaritan woman at a particular well of water. While there, He engaged in explaining to her the difference between the water in the well and that of a spiritual food called *living water*.

He said to her, "Everyone who drinks this well water will be thirsty again, but whoever drinks the water that I will give them will never thirst again. Indeed, the water I give them will become within them a spring of water, welling up to eternal life." (John 4:7-29)

From her response (her words and subsequent actions) I believe this thoughtful woman had perhaps some understanding of what Jesus was trying to tell her—yet maybe not. However, her drinking the *living water* would enable the Spirit of God to abide within her. The welling or activity of this water would produce in her goodness and eternal life.

The Spirit of God (which *is* the living water) has *everything* to do with what is produced. The well water represents the teachings of the world—they produce nothing but continued thirst and evil. The followers of Christ's teachings are partakers of the living water and are therefore the only folk's in the world who have any hope, and that hope is *certain*.

29

Apart from Christianity there are a host of false gods and unusual beliefs, which are pursued through sensuality, vain religions and ill-supported philosophies. This is the work of Satan, who lives to consume and destroy the lives of men and women all over the earth. He has done his work well.

Whether you are a person of religion or not makes no difference to Satan. He is out to consume and destroy you—no matter what your philosophy. No matter what you think you may know, he indeed knows more. In fact, he has committed to memory every single word —every dot and tittle—in the Bible. No matter who you are you will never accomplish that, but there is *no reason* for being ignorant of his devices (2nd Corinthians 2:11).

There are hundreds of false 'religions' throughout the world as well. Each of them proclaims a different way to approach God. Some of them teach that their god cannot be approached—that their god has instead made certain men his representatives, and that you must adhere to them. Some believe that their god wants them to kill everyone who is not of their culture.

You will come to learn through this writing, if you don't already know, that Christianity is indeed the only way to the one, true God (John 14:6), who made all things, is compassionate, can be approached by the individual, and is not the author of death. The God of the universe is a God of love, which most people find difficult to comprehend.

Darth Vader of the Star Wars saga was a fictional character in a remarkable story about the forces of good and evil. If you are familiar with the story you may remember that he warned his son, Luke: "You don't know the power of the dark side." As fictional as Vader was he was absolutely right! Most people don't know the power of the "dark side." Satan is actually the ruler of this world (Matthew 4:8,9), controlling all kingdoms (governed realms) of the entire world, save one, which is the spiritual kingdom of Christ (Matthew 16:18), His church.

With the trace bit of light that has just been shed on *your* dark side, I am sure you can now know and understand how vital it is for you to truly become aware of who you are, what you are capable of, who governs you, and to learn how to do something about it. No matter who you are, you were sent into the world at this particular point in history for a reason. You did not just 'happen'—you are more important than you might think. Light is coming into your world. Don't be unresponsive or apprehensive—stay with me here...

Among the best selling self-help books today are those that deal with the human heart. People want to know that their hearts are *good*, and so they purchase these books to be encouraged in that direction. Usually the authors of these writings are quite learned, according to human standards, and very sincere. Unfortunately, they have been cleverly deceived and will remain so until the light of God's truth opens their eyes—no personal offense to the authors themselves. I have written several of these renowned authors over the years, but as of yet have received no response.

(An important note here: If an author does not have a mailing address where you can reach him/her, or does not list their personal phone number within the pages of their book(s), I would say that their books are probably not worth reading. This would apply mostly to Christian authors, whose *duty* it is to be responsible and to help those with questions concerning the truths of God. This is their reasonable service. Anyone unwilling to discuss personally what they've written shouldn't be writing in the first place.)

As a result of these writings many other people are also deceived. Don't be deceived! Nothing good dwells within the human nature. We are fallen creatures, impure in heart. *Only* when the Spirit of God works through the human heart can that heart produce what is good. I've said that previously and will repeat it again: *Only* when the Spirit of God works through the human heart can that heart produce what is good (Romans 7:18, 8:11).

Satan does not want you to be made aware of your fallen condition —your need for God. He wants you to feel that apart from God there is still a measure of good within you. God, on the other hand, is gracious and has given us His truth:

Jesus himself said: *...apart from Me you can do nothing* (John 15:5 NASB). The Apostle Paul also proclaimed: *For I know that nothing good dwells in me* (Romans 7:18 NASB). Don't forget Jeremiah: *The human heart is most deceitful and desperately wicked. Who really knows how bad it is?* (Jeremiah 17:9 NLT)

Moreover, Jesus told a rich young ruler: *No one is good but One, that is, God* (Matthew 19:17 NKJV). There are a host of other Scriptures concerning this matter. If there is *any* form of goodness in your life; thank God, for He is where it comes from and the One who has allowed it to be so.

Satan was once a beautiful angel, ambitious to place his reign above that of God himself. He did not honor the position of God nor did he stand with truth. He brought his deceitfulness and wickedness to the young earth and polluted it. As a result of his rebellion he was cast out of heaven. In his fall from the heavenly courts he drew an immense number of celestial creatures (angels) with him. The Bible refers to them as demons, evil spirits, principalities, powers, world rulers of darkness and spiritual hosts of wickedness in the high places.[6]

The nature of our daily struggles in life is therefore not at all physical. Not one bit! It only appears that way because of Satan's ability to disguise it as such. He is the author of your deceitful heart. He is the ruler of this evil world as well, however, he continually masquerades as an *angel of light* and has done so from the very beginning.

He makes evil to appear as good and good to appear as evil—darkness to appear as light and light to appear as darkness (2nd Corinthians 11:14, Isaiah 5:20). He will deceive you as long as you continue to allow him to do so. Satan's battles with God and mankind are spiritual. Every human heart is a part of his battleground. He is assured of victory over your heart unless you choose to allow the Spirit of God to dwell there.

We do have choices in this world—as did Adam and Eve—we were formed as creatures of choice—made in the image of God. We must choose wisely. Understanding one's total inability to protect and cure the heart on his/her own should make that particular choice easier.

*

I believe you must now know, based on God's immutable truth, that we *do* have a sin nature, which is entirely against us. If you believe and accept that concept, then God has begun a work within your heart.

The sin nature is a seemingly unbearable curse. Death has always surrounded it. Everyone dies as a result of it. Yet, there is a way to live with it. It can actually be quite enlightening. Part of that illumination comes from a better understanding of the original curse (*judgment of sin*) itself. If you can begin to understand the rational behind the original curse you will become a much stronger warrior in your battles with temptation.

This is because you will come to understand more about God and His greatest of attributes—that of love. This particular love is extremely motivating and can put you on the narrow path to eternal life. Nothing in this world—absolutely nothing—can compare with the good fortune of your ending up on that trail. Let us then hike on toward that end, shall we?

Chapter Two...Understanding the Curse
(Genesis 3:9-24)

You have just hiked through the most difficult terrain along the *Trail of Truth* (chapter 1). I am glad that you've made it this far—it shows that you've got some sand in you, and that's a good thing—you'll need it.

Most folk's who come to know, understand, believe and accept their condition of depravity usually continue to ponder the following questions: Why such a terrible curse? Why has it lasted some six thousand years? Will God ever relent?

There are many books out there that attempt with all sincerity to answer these important questions. However, the majority of their authors seem to have just not dug deep enough—it's really a question of excavating down to the *heart* of the matter.

We're going to do that. I would like you to first consider, as I go forward with this, that God had *no pleasure* in the curse, and still doesn't (Ezekiel 33:11). God is certainly not pleased with depravity, sickness, disease, decay and death, nor any consequences related to those conditions, which are all obviously results of the curse.

34

The Hebrew word *curse* or *alah*, *me'erah*, and *qelalah*, on the human level, means to wish harm or catastrophe. On the divine level, it means to impose a judgment. Psalm 19:9 tells us:

The judgments of the Lord are true; they are righteous altogether. The Psalmist praises the infinite wisdom of God's heart in Psalm 119:75: *I know, O Lord, that Thy judgments are righteous, and that in faithfulness Thou hast afflicted me* (NASB).

The Psalmist had reasoned within himself that the curse, which resulted in his personal affliction, was actually beneficial to him. Does that seem strange? We will consider the curse itself and its prevalent benefits for us momentarily.

To help understand the curse, you first need to know something of the adversary, who is the *primary reason* for the curse. The name, Satan, literally means, an *adversary*. He is the chief of fallen spirits, the grand adversary of God and man. He is the ruler of a powerful "kingdom of darkness," which stands in opposition to the power of God in this world. He is "the mighty prince and power of the air" and skillfully directs a host of wicked spirits ("his angels") in the heavenly realms as well, who do his bidding.[1]

Spirited by an unrelenting hatred against God and all goodness, Satan is engaged in a worldwide, age-long struggle against Him, ever seeking to defeat the divine plans of grace toward mankind through cleverly seducing men and women to do evil, ultimately kindling their ruin.

As the "deceiver of the whole world" (Revelation 12:9), his primary method is that of deception—about himself, his purpose, his activities and his upcoming final defeat. The whole world, not offering a truly conscious resistance, is in the grip of and yielded to his power (1st John 5:19). This power over mankind he holds by virtue of his ability to capture (2nd Timothy 2:26), to devour (1st Peter 5:8), and to literally possess (Luke 8:30) the hearts and minds of the human race.

However, his fiercest conflict is with the Christian, his most targeted prey (Revelation 12:17). He first and foremost subtly distorts the Word of God (Genesis 3:4), and he hinders the work of God's servants (1st Thessalonians 2:18). He will blind the minds of potential believers to the truth of God's word (2nd Corinthians 4:3,4), and persuades them to believe his lies instead (2nd Thessalonians 2:9,10).

If they do come to know the truth, he is able to snatch away what they have learned before they come to believe in it (Matthew 13:19).

He also cunningly (with great strategy) places counterfeit Christians among true Christians (Matthew 13:25,38,39 & 1st Timothy 4:1). These are referred to as wolves in sheep's clothing—and there are many out there!

Satan can also cause great physical disasters upon the earth and has caused death and grief among families, both of which for generations we have labeled and continue to *mistakenly* label, *acts of God* (Job 1:13-19). He can plunge men into war (James 4:1). He is the absolute author of sickness and holds the power of death (Luke 13:16, Hebrews 2:14).

However, Satan masquerades as an angel of light: Though he is limited as to what God will allow him to do, he has indeed great power of deception and influence, far above and sometimes* beyond the comprehension of any human being (2nd Corinthians 11:14, Job 1:12, Luke 22:31, *2nd Corinthians 2:11).

Again, I want to emphasize as I did in the previous chapter that the nature of our daily struggles in life is not of physical origin. In reality, as a child of God, our individual lives are a very tiny but notably significant part of a great spiritual warfare with the unseen evil rulers of this world, and with those wicked spirits in the heavenly realms.

We are not therefore put on earth to fulfill our own agenda. We are here to attain to daily spiritual victories within our lives, each one being a part of an infinitely larger victory for the Creator of the universe. Our individual lives are indeed important to the One who formed us.

I also mentioned your personal importance to God in chapter 1. Bear with me and I will continue to enforce this concept for you as we hike along in this chapter. Let's take a look now at the curse (judgment) of Genesis 3: 9-24. The reading is from the New International Version of the Bible, which is a more readable translation than some of its predecessors. We will continue the story from where we left off in chapter 1. If you recall, Adam and Eve had sewn fig leaves together to cover their nakedness, and had hidden themselves from God among the trees of the garden:

The Lord God called to the man, "Where are you?"
He answered, "I heard you in the garden, and I was afraid because I was naked; so I hid."

And God said, "Who told you that you were naked? Have you eaten from the tree that I commanded you not to eat from?"

The man said, "The woman you put here with me—she gave me some fruit from the tree, and I ate it."

Then the Lord God said to the woman, "What is this you have done?"

The woman said, "The serpent deceived me, and I ate."

So the Lord God said to the serpent, "Because you have done this, cursed are you above all the livestock and all the wild animals! You will crawl on your belly and you will eat dust all the days of your life. And I will put enmity between you and the woman, and between your offspring and hers; he will crush your head, and you will strike his heel."

To the woman he said, "I will greatly increase your pains in childbearing; with pain you will give birth to children. Your desire will be for your husband, and he will rule over you."

To Adam he said, "Because you listened to your wife and ate from the tree about which I commanded you, ' you must not eat of it,' cursed is the ground because of you; through painful toil you will eat of it all the days of your life. It will produce thorns and thistles for you, and you will eat the plants of the field. By the sweat of your brow you will eat your food until you return to the ground, since from it you were taken: for dust you are and to dust you will return."

Adam named his wife Eve, because she would become the mother of all living. The Lord made garments of skin for Adam and his wife and clothed them.

And the Lord God said, "The man has now become like one of us, knowing good and evil. He must not be allowed to reach out his hand and take also from the tree of life and eat, and live forever."

So the Lord God banished him from the Garden of Eden to work the ground from which he had been taken. After he drove the man out, he placed on the east side of the Garden of Eden cherubim and a flaming sword flashing back and forth to guard the way to the tree of life.

God first pronounced judgment on the serpent and on Satan. The serpent would from that day forward crawl on its belly and eat the dust of the earth. Dust is the symbol of abject humiliation, an indignity lasting forever. Some biologists and zoologists believe that the serpent at one time in history had legs, like the lizard.

Whether or not this is true I am not certain, but if it is, it certainly agrees with this event. I do know that; as the rainbow remains a physical sign of remembrance for the great worldwide flood; the snake remains a physical reminder of what took place in the garden—a warning for people of all generations to be mindful of Satan (that old serpent) until the end of time.

God graciously converts the depraved Eve's affections from Satan to Himself through pronouncing enmity (hostility) between her and Satan. The judgment on Satan is a warning to him of his final defeat under the heel of her offspring (Jesus, the Messiah), but is delayed so that God's program of redemption through this promised offspring of Eve may be accomplished.

That Jesus suffers and dies for the sins of the world is a strike at His own heel by Satan, however, by His resurrection from the dead, Jesus gives Satan a crushing blow to the head from which he will never recover.

The woman is to be frustrated in her natural relationships within the family; experiencing painful labor in bearing children and subordination toward her husband. However, pain is experienced at a point of great fulfillment for the woman, and in her role of bearing and raising children of promise the woman is privileged to participate in God's plan to create a people for himself.

The relationship between Eve and her husband is also corrupted by sin; being marred by domination and forced submission. However, the restoration of a proper attitude regarding this relationship can take place through new life in Christ (Ephesians 5:22-33).

The man is frustrated in his activity to provide food. His natural relationship to the ground, to rule over it, is reversed; instead of submitting to him it resists and eventually swallows him up. Though his labor itself is a blessing that reflects the activity of a creative God, the object of man's labor—the ground—is cursed and becomes a source of frustration.

Both Adam and Eve experience pain by these reversals. In less than two thousand years from Eden the earth will undergo another radical change, which I will elaborate on in chapter 9 of this writing. Man's earthly body of dust makes physical death possible. It is interesting to note here that modern science now tells us that all the chemicals needed to make up the human body are found in the very dust of the earth (Genesis 2:7).

Though this judgment comes upon Adam and Eve as a result of their response to the evil Satan, the Creator cares for them by making clothing for them of animal skins. How grieved the Lord must have been in slaying the first animals of His Creation! This was the very first sacrifice of life for the sake of mankind. Yet, it was also the beginning of the greatest and most tender of love stories, foreshadowing the sacrifice of God's own Son on the cross.

Unfortunately, true love could not allow mankind to live forever *in their fallen condition.* The fact that a perfect plan to redeem them had already been set into motion (Genesis 3:15), God had to expel Adam and Eve from the paradise garden. This was part of the plan. Without continued access to the tree of life on a daily basis, the couple will begin to age.

The effect of their having eaten of the tree of life while in the garden, of having its nutrient within their bodily systems, will lengthen their lives somewhat, as well as that of their offspring, but this effect will gradually wear off in time and mankind's earthly life will be reduced to an average of seventy years (Psalm 90:10).

Protecting them from an eternal bondage to sin and misery, God kept humanity from entering the garden and continuing to eat of the tree of life by placing *cherubim* at the east side of the garden, and a flaming sword which turned every way to guard the tree. The cherubim are living heavenly creatures—servants of God in judgment, whose features are both animal and human, with the faces of each creature usually being four-sided—of a man, a lion, an ox and an eagle. Primarily the cherubim are the 'living chariot' or carriers of God when appearing to men—His throne or the bearers of it.

Two golden cherubim were later placed on the mercy seat above the Ark of the Covenant, and were also embroidered on the curtains of the tabernacle at the entrance to the Holy of Holies, where the Ark was kept. God was said to have dwelt in the Holy of Holies between the cherubim. This was His earthly throne. The tree of life is later restored again, at the heavenly throne of God (Revelation 22:2). Whether the tree is spiritual (Jesus Himself) or a physical tree is uncertain. Some believe that the physical tree is a spiritual representation of Jesus, which is conceivable.

It may fairly be claimed that the Fall narrative alone gives convincing explanation of the perversity of human nature. Though the doctrine of original sin seems an offense to reason, once accepted it makes total sense of the human condition. It is apparent that the issue was whether Adam would let God determine what was good and bad, or would seek to decide that for himself, in disregard of what God had said.

Adam, led by Eve, who was herself led by the serpent, defied God by eating the forbidden fruit. As a result, the anti-God, self-aggrandizing mindset expressed in their sin became a part of them and the moral nature that they passed on to their descendants. Though the story is recounted in a somewhat figurative style, Genesis asks us to read it as history.[2]

Why such a terrible curse? As we look at the history of the world since the Fall in the garden we see an increasing depravity in mankind. There is ongoing warfare, expanding throughout the centuries; beheadings and physical torment, murders of women and children, annihilations of entire countries and cultures, merciless rule and dominion.

There is also ever-widening natural destruction and a decaying process in the earth itself; earthquakes, extreme draught, extensive flooding, hurricanes, tornadoes, a decline in natural resources, crop failures and the threat of global warming. These things are just on the surface of the consequences related to the Fall. Paradise is indeed lost —for now.

Consider also the personal plights of the human race; sickness, diseases of various kinds, birth defects, starvation, mental problems, suicides, vile passions, sexual perversions, wickedness, covetousness, maliciousness, envy, murder, strife, deceitfulness and complete evil-mindedness.

They are backbiters, violent, proud, boastful, inventors of evil things, undiscerning, untrustworthy, unloving, unforgiving, unmerciful, practicing things that are deserving of death, and not only do they do these things but also approve of others who practice them as well (Romans 1:32). It's a mad, mad, mad world—almost impossible to comprehend. Sin is not just what we do—it is *who we are*.

Because of these terrible conditions many people do not believe that there is a God. If they somewhat believe in Him, they consider Him to be unjust. If their belief is a little stronger than somewhat, they blame Him for the failures of their lives. If they have about a halfway belief in Him, they still continue to question His methods and complain about human disaster. And if they have a substantial belief in Him, many of them suggest ideas created by their own imaginations of who and why He is, and why all these aforementioned things have happened and continue to happen.

But the truth is: no one can know the mind of God (Romans 11:34). Yet, they *can* know the heart of God (Matthew 11:29). Our minds are finite, and that means that we can only look at things in the here and now for the brief time that we live on the earth. God, however, has infinite knowledge and sees all things, both small and great, from beginning to end (Revelation 1:8).

God is an *eternal* being. He not only has to deal with mankind, but also has to deal with all creatures in the heavenly realms. This responsibility is like no other. We cannot even begin to fathom this responsibility. We therefore need to drop the questions, acknowledge His sovereignty (as Job did), and give Him the benefit of the doubt:

Consider that Lucifer (*Day Star*), one of the most beautiful angels in the universe, whom we now know as Satan, somewhere in time, chose to rebel against the most high God (Isaiah 14:12-14). Consider also that he came to earth to corrupt the new paradise that God had formed, and eventually brought a third of the angels with him. How in the name of heaven and earth was the Creator going to deal with these catastrophic events?

Let us consider that all of the heavenly host (occupants of that realm) know both good and evil (Genesis 3:22). God had constructed this vast universe in which we live, choosing to form the human race on a planet He created and placed, theoretically, in the center of that universe.

God's newest creation, mankind, made from the earth, did not originally know both good and evil. What special privilege He gave them above the rest of His creatures, in that mankind was not to know any evil! Mankind was therefore at the center of the Creator's heart. It is my belief that mankind was and is the love of His life.

God is in the business of creating. The heavens and all the host of them, including this earth, declare that very glory of God (Psalm 19:1), which is obvious to *anyone* who lives on the earth and has eyes to see with and looks around at what has been made (Romans 1:20). What a paradise this was! What a beautiful world it was meant to be. Mankind was to live uncorrupted on this newly formed planet—*forever*. God would walk with mankind and be a friend to them and share with them all the glory of His creation! The very thought of this concept overwhelms the human imagination with awe.

But on one fateful day a rebellious angel, who in his pride had attempted to corrupt the heavenly realms, brought corruption to the earth and upon the earth. At some time a third of the heavenly angels also joined forces with him. In dealing with these rebellious events, God, whose heart is incorruptible, had no choice but to judge Satan, the angels who followed him, the human race and the earth, in order that the wages or consequences of rebellion would become evident— that the horrible end result of sin's devastation could be clearly seen and understood.

The only way to stop any future rebellion would be to insure that the consequences of this particular rebellion were fully known and understood by the entire creation. Seeing is believing. To never entertain thoughts for repeating such a catastrophe is grace. Due to this rebellion, death was now reigning over the human race. God's love demanded that He put His plan of redemption, which was beforehand known by Him, into action. He would not at this time destroy all that He had made, but would allow the host of heaven and all creatures of the earth to witness the madness and folly of rebellion.

God would allow that mankind, Satan and the fallen angels would exist long enough to see the climax of sin's horror. He would allow the earth itself to stand for some time, demonstrating His patience, in order that those in future generations would also have an opportunity to see and believe the absolute senselessness in any acts of rebellion against their Creator. This plan demonstrates God's unfathomable love for everything He has made. It also proves that He will never take the freedom of choice away from any of His creatures.

At this point some of you may wonder; if God so loved all that He had made, why did He deluge the earth in a flood, destroying all animals and mankind, save the few that were aboard the ark of Noah? I will discuss the Great Flood with much detail in chapter 9, but for now will offer the following explanation for the rationality behind that event (at least from a human standpoint):

Approximately 1656 years after the birth of Adam the earth's population had reached an estimated 900,000,000 (nine hundred million), and that is a conservative estimate.[3] The Bible teaches us that the thoughts and imaginations of men's hearts at that time were only evil continually (Genesis 6:5,6), and it began to grieve God in His heart that He had made them.

I don't blame Him—they were worthy of destruction—yet He still grieved. The Great Flood was God's judgment upon that evil generation, but in keeping with His promise to bring a Savior into the world, He extended grace to a man named Noah and his family, providing a way of escape for them.

God also provided an escape for many creatures of the world, aboard the ark of Noah, which would serve to repopulate the earth after the flood. However, the ecological condition of the earth would be vastly different after the flood, not allowing certain species of God's creatures to maintain life. And so, they were buried in flood sediments along with the human population. We know that all things needed to be done at that time were very grievous to the Lord—but they had to be done just the same.

Yet, God's plan at the beginning of creation was so perfect that it will eventually bring fallen humanity into a state of *total incorruption* and *immortality* (1st Corinthians 15:52-54), and will even provide for them new heavens and a new earth, where only goodness dwells (2nd Peter 3:13). There will be many beautiful birds and animals there as well, I am sure. There may even be creatures there that were here before the flood—no one knows exactly what the new earth will consist of, but it will undoubtedly be paradise restored—and more.

The consequence of sin is death—eternal separation from God. God does not lie and cannot go back on His word, therefore the sin debt incurred in the garden had to be paid. The heavenly rebellion had to be exposed. A time of testing was at hand. God's entire creation would have to 'stay the course' until all of the events He had pre-determined would come to pass.

As a result of God's divine understanding and consideration for all that is involved in His plan, the entire creation waits and we wait—both in eager expectation to be liberated from the bondage of corruption and brought into the glorious freedom of the children of God (Romans 8:18-25), which will be revealed when Christ returns.

Though the curse prevailed after the Fall, God's deeply committed love for mankind would eventually allow His only Son to become the sacrifice for their sins, through whom humans could be saved from the final destruction awaiting Satan, his angels, and those of the human race who insensitively choose to reject that sacrifice.

His only Son would pay the death penalty for those of the human race who would choose wisely to believe in Him—from Adam and Eve until the last man/woman standing. God's son would be conceived by His Spirit and born of an earthly woman. In this way, He could taste of death for the entire human race. He was the perfect sacrifice, whom the heavenly host would declare victorious.

Again, all of these things would take time. God would have to let history take its course until the proper time for Him to bring this brilliant plan to a close. He would allow the earth to remain until all those destined for salvation were born, even if it took several thousand years awaiting the birth of the very last one!

This is because God determined the individual lives of men and women from the very foundation of the world. The saints that were to be born to Him, whose lives would give glory to His name on the earth, were and are the love of His life. He was unconditionally committed to His word, to His saints and to His dream. He would wait.

You, dear reader, living in this twenty-first century, were in God's mind before the world was formed (Ephesians 1:4). He knew each day of your life before you were even born (Psalm 139:16). In a way, God has actually waited all this time just for you. And He did this knowing that He must endure the onslaughts of the wicked for several thousands of years—until the day that *you* were born, reached an age of accountability, and were saved.

His love for each individual is just like his love for you—unfathomable (Romans 5:8). Is the implementation of the curse starting to make *some* sense to you now? The Apostle Paul wrote this to the Roman Christians, that they might make some sense of God's unfathomable yet glorious ways—that they might be encouraged in hope:

What if God, although willing to demonstrate His wrath and to make His power known, endured with much patience vessels of wrath prepared for destruction? And He did so to make known the riches of His glory upon vessels of mercy, which He prepared beforehand for glory, even us whom He also called, not from among Jews only, but also from among Gentiles (Romans 9:22-24 NASB).

We can add up all the pains and sorrows in the world and they would not be equal to the horror that God has endured and continues to endure for us. Each moment He bears up under the evil that rules our world. Each moment He is subject to grief over the angels who rebelled. Each moment He suffers the painful loss of human life. Each moment He endures the iniquity of the wicked.

He sustains the adversity of all these things only because of the glory He has prepared for those who truly believe, love and obey Him —those who want to be with Him and share in the riches of His holiness, which He has kept in store for them since the very foundation of the world (Matthew 25:34).

When I personally consider the ills of our current world; religious wars in the name of God, the homeless in America, malnutrition in India, starvation and genocide in Africa, the overthrow of a struggling government by radicals in Mexico, protests and riots in France and England, children in all nations with deformities and diseases and the majority of the world's indifference toward them—for each of these things I am both frustrated and quite angered.

I do not have the patience that my Creator has. I do not always remember that His patience is my salvation—that His patience endures for each of us, all of which are sinners, including the salvation of some yet unborn. So, I've been known to hike up to the top of a hill or climb a mountain to a place of solitude, and do the 'dance'—the Native American chant.

"Hey-ah, hey-ah, hey-ah, hey-ah, hey-ah, hoi-yah-oooh—Oh, Grand Father, Why do the nations rage and the people plot worthless things? The kings of the earth prepare for battle; the rulers plot together against the Lord and against His Anointed. But the One who rules in heaven laughs, and rebukes them.

"How great are Your judgments and Your ways past finding out! Now therefore, oh kings of the earth, show discernment. Do homage to the Son, lest he becomes angry, and you perish in the way. Ah-ho, ah-ho, ah-ho, ah-ho, ah-ho." (Lyrics from the book of Psalms)

I'm actually quite sane, well, pretty much. The dance is a great outlet for frustration, anger, depression, expressions of joy—you name it, and it's a healthy way out—great physical and vocal exercise, and you do honor God through using His inspired writings in your prayers. You can use any tune for the chants; of course a Native American tune is best (more on this 'dance' in chapter 12).

It was a Native American who taught me, on one of my treks into the Arizona Desert—literally out in the middle of nowhere; 'When there is doubt, there is hope. When there is fear, there is love. When there is hate, there is peace. When there is suffering, there's the dance.' You can bet that I *will* climb a mountain and do a dance of joy the day this book is published!

As I was saying before I interrupted your train of thought, there is absolutely no doubt that the God of the Bible loves us, and endures moment by moment for us the onslaughts of the wicked. God is the essence of love itself (1ˢᵗ Corinthians 13:4-8). There are no other gods worshiped by various human religions who possess this quality. Religions that claim to honor the true God and don't recognize this quality—their rituals, personal behavior and demands upon one another bearing witness to their ignorance—honor Him in vain (Mark 7:7).

Jesus, whose love of mankind was demonstrated on a cross, is the only way to the one, true God. Anyone who does not adhere to His living example and His recorded teachings will *never* know the love of God (John 14:6). The God of the Bible is Christianities God. He is a God of love, not willing that any should perish—He does not want anyone to be lost (2ⁿᵈ Peter 3:9).

The Son of God is the only spiritual leader[4] in any period of history who has risen from the dead, which proves beyond any doubt His supreme power over all things—including death (Ephesians 1:19,20). All leaders of various world religions who have died are still in their graves—Jesus is not. His tomb is empty!

Jesus (the God of our spirit) is the light of the world. Those who follow Him will not walk in darkness, but will have the light of life (John 8:12). Our knowledge into the mysteries of Christ is one of the greater benefits that have rained down upon us through the curse (Ephesians 3:5).

Note: *Christian* was a name given to any first century follower of Christ (Acts 11:26) and rightly so, as the Greek word means *adherent of Christ. Religion*, on the other hand, is the adherence to ceremonial practices, which constitute man's relationship with other powers and principles of the universe. It can also refer to superstition.

Belief in Jesus involves neither ceremonial practices nor superstition. It involves *obeying the living truth.* Many have made ceremonial practices out of Christianity, but that is in keeping with the traditions of men. True Christianity is found in imitating the attitudes of the person of Jesus, not in ceremonial practices regarding Him (James 1:27).

Your life is indeed very important, as I pointed out to you both in this chapter and the previous one. There is great joy in heaven when you acknowledge your sins and choose to turn from them (Luke 15:7). This acknowledgment of sins and your turning from them is *repentance*, which can give birth to great spiritual victories.

Choosing to believe and obey the word of God can lead to your salvation. God is not the author of confusion, but of peace. It doesn't matter who you are or what you have done. He is the author of eternal salvation to all those who will obey Him. (1ˢᵗ Corinthians 14:33, 1ˢᵗ John 5:3, Hebrews 5:8,9)

*

I hope you now have a better understanding regarding the curse of Genesis 3. There are two basic *external* reasons for the curse as it relates to mankind. First of all, it was because God was *not honored as God* among mankind, and secondly, mankind was *not thankful* for their inexhaustible blessings (Romans 1:21).

This mindset (refusing to acknowledge God as God and being unthankful for His many blessings), first revealed in Adam and Eve, leads to futility and a further darkening of the heart (Romans 1:28). This is what happened to the generations before the Great Flood.

All of us have held this mindset at one time or another, and many, many still do. It's evident all over the earth. This attitude is the source of all of our problems, no matter where we are in the world. Not respecting who God is and not being truly thankful for what He has done—both these things are like chasing after the wind.

I call this particular vanity, *pursuing the hawk*—running after something that is fleeting—an attitude that refuses to accept, whether in ignorance or not, the *reality* of God. We are either unaware (just plain stupid) or forgetful of His sovereignty. This is the moral dilemma that envelops our world, and the result is utter chaos.

God chose a nation for Himself thousands of years ago, but they rejected the freedom they had in Him, desiring instead to be governed by earthly kings (1ˢᵗ Samuel 8:7). It is our nature to think externally, our nature to want to become our own god. When we look into the mirror we don't really observe who we are, we merely see what we appear to be—what's on the outside. However, beautiful flowers bloom from the inside out. They are a divine example of how beauty develops—of how things are to mature—an illustration that God has painted for us, revealing to us the way of the natural order.

47

The plant kingdom was created before man, as were the birds and animals, that they might give us wisdom and understanding. God shared this principle with the prophet Job many years after the creation.[5] Though we were delegated the authority to rule over each of these things, we have a hard time discerning that we need to learn from them as well. Only God can give us this discernment, and He works through the heart—from the inside out. His desire is that we allow Him to reign over us, that we might truly be free.

The wind and the elements, the mountains and the deserts, the waters, the plants, the animals of the field, the birds of the air and the fish of the sea can teach us so much, yet we fail to apply the lessons available from these external wonders of God to our inward being. We fail to see the wisdom of God in everything that He has made—all that is around us. We don't take it all in and grow from the inside out, as we should. We fail within ourselves to see the supernatural through the natural—we just don't look for it.

Our rebellious hearts are made of stone. We listen, but we do not really hear. We look at things, but we do not truly see. We rule in pride, but we do not practice discernment. We spend our lives outside of ourselves. We chase after the things of this world because we have no concept of the *real* part eternity plays within our being. We are as far from our true selves as a hawk is from the moon.

We pursue the hawk because we do not truly comprehend how he flies, nor do we more importantly stop to consider *why* he flies…

Chapter Three…My Pursuit of the Hawk, Part 1
The Early Years

You've hiked a short way into this book—hiking on one of the most difficult sections along the *trail of truth*. It reminds me of my climb up San Gorgonio—old 'gray back'—the highest peak in southern California, in 1997.

It was about an eight-mile trek to the 11,499-foot summit, and the first mile was indeed the most difficult. It was exceedingly steep—a nearly 'straight up' climb from the trailhead at Mill Creek Canyon. I had to take several breaks to catch my breath along that route and was so exhausted at one point that I nearly turned back.

My thighs hurt, my back and shoulders ached under the weight of a pack, and I didn't think I was going to make it. But I hung in there with much anticipation, hoping the grueling ascent would level off somewhat. It eventually did, and I was able to chill out a little bit, hiking with contentment among lush fields of manzanita near the 7000-foot level.

When I reached the summit, nearly five hours later, I was elated to say the least. I found great exhilaration up there on that peak. What a rush one has when he/she is able to complete a difficult hike! I was glad I didn't quit down below where it took all that I had and then some to continue the journey.

I liken that hiking experience to your journey through the pages of this book. The initial ascent is difficult, is it not? You'll begin to level off some now, hopefully gleaning some insights into your own life while hiking leisurely through mine. The difficult early ascent you will find was worth the effort as the hike continues. I may take you through some stretches of my life's trail that are very similar to your own.

This may help you to more readily accept what the difficult part of the ascent has taught you. There's much to see along the way here. I've hiked a lot of trails in my life—lots of miles on my hiking boots. As I reached each destination I was always well rewarded by the journey—no exceptions. I hope you will keep that in mind as you continue this hike.

There's an Apache Indian story about a man who woke up one morning and saw a hawk on the wind. He walked outside and never returned. After he died he met his wife in the spirit world, and she asked him, "Why didn't you ever come back home?"

The man replied, "Well, that hawk kept flyin'—there was always the next somethin', my dear, and that *will* take a man away. I told myself I was protecting my family; that they would be better off without a whimsy, wanderin' fool like me, who never stayed put. Yet, stay or go I learned that there's nothin' a man can do to protect his family from himself. I guess I do realize now that I made people's lives more difficult by the things I have done, and by the things I have not done—people I did love—mostly."

The Apache Indian story that I've just related to you indeed parallels my own life and times; that hawk kept flyin' on the wind and I always pursued it—there was always the next somethin'—always some new thing that had to be experienced. The joy and spiritual value of genuine contentment was for a long time unknown to me.

God forms each of us in a different fashion. The discovery of DNA is now of course infallible proof of that difference. We also have many similarities, which DNA is also a proof of. Our personalities of course vary, but can be similar, and the way we journey through life varies, yet can also be similar. The way we adapt and function is what usually determines who we are—throughout life.

I've always been a drifter—like a wisp of smoke. My wandering ways in life have hurt many people—people that I loved, yet I have to assume that God made me this way for a reason—for a purpose. Because of my wandering spirit I've also been allowed, through the many things I've seen and learned, to help a few folk's. There's not much I can do this late in life but to accept who I've been and who I am—a strange mixture of good and evil. Jesus taught us that humans are basically evil (Matthew 7:11). But many of us, for reasons only God knows, have been allowed to be this 'strange mixture.'

I want to emphasize something related to the story I'm now about to tell you—something that I talked about in chapter 1: Only when the Spirit of God works through the human heart can that heart produce what is good (Romans 8:9). It takes a long time to grasp the truth of that concept, and an even longer time to allow it to really take hold.

Long before I discovered the error of my ways, her second husband once asked the wife of my youth, "What ever happened to Mark—why did he turn out the way he did?" I now know that in my youth I paid attention to the wrong things—and I lost. I did not allow the Spirit of God to dwell constantly within my heart. That was unintentional, but it makes no difference. We do not function well in life unless at some time during our journey we learn to focus our thoughts on God and His creation—to understand who we really are, the time allotted to us, and the spiritual struggles we face along the way.

These are the things that we truly need to pay attention to. His creation is a most profound teacher. One tries to walk a straight path in life, but when you get to be my age you find yourself looking back at your footsteps to see where you went wrong. With great remorse for many failures, yet now with a greater hope through the illuminating journey that I have been allowed to hike, I present you with a fittingly detailed overview of my story—my pursuit of the hawk:

*

I was born in June of 1945, just as World War II was coming to a close. My very early years were spent in a small town in Ohio. I was the only son of Steve Taylor, an industrial engineer who worked for the Goodyear Tire and Rubber Company of Akron. My mother, Pauline, was an executive secretary for the Summit County Board of Education.

My only sister, Karen, was five years senior to me. She was a great student in school, intellectual like our father and attentive like our mother. I was intelligent as well, but quite 'ornery,' as my grandmother put it. "You're a rolling stone, Mark," she would say. "Can't you ever sit still?"

I was quite impulsive in my youth, unable to hold my attention on any one thing for an extended period of time and truly unaware of it. Nowadays they call it an *attention deficit* in children and treat it as a medical problem. My first grade teacher wrote on my report card: 'Should work more carefully and neatly, and should make better use of time.' However, at that young age and in those times I saw very little abnormality with my own behavior. After all, I was just doing what I thought was best for myself—acting in accord with my limited knowledge—just living life the best I knew how as a kid.

Public schools at that time did not teach us about our indwelling sin nature. They still don't, at least not accurately. I therefore had no boundaries that I was aware of. I had no knowledge that each and every desire proceeding from the human heart required true awareness, some higher form of understanding, and a persistent effort at control.

I now long to undo those years—I want to go back and talk to that young Mark—to tell him how things would turn out, but I cannot. Yet, I have learned that without the failures of life, I may never have discovered who I was or who God is. Life is indeed strange, but worth the living. And, life must be lived forward, but I believe it can only be truly understood backward.

Grandma was right; I could not sit still. I had watched too many Lone Ranger and Zorro episodes. I was Robin Hood also—I even shot a suction-cup tipped arrow at a jogger one time. My bicycle was my horse and oh how I loved to ride like the wind! I spent hours riding alone on the many wooded trails that surrounded our residential neighborhood. I was Huckleberry Finn as well—that being the very first book I ever read—I spent much time in playful adventures along the Cuyahoga River, which flowed near our home. I even 'borrowed' a canoe once and camped on a small island for three days and nights. I smoked a corncob pipe while I was there, just like Huck.

My parents had no idea where I was at that time and I later paid the price that children must pay. I had a couple of good friends too, just like Huck, but was a loner for the most part, living in the world of my imagination a lot more than I did in the real world, or should I say, what most of us call the real world? Either place, I was always acting out the part of someone other than me—I suppose like Adam and Eve did after the Fall, when they disastrously lost the sense of who they were really supposed to be—who they were created to be.

My father and I did not get along very well. I was such a free spirit and he was such a stickler for law and order. He was quite well organized and carried that work habit home with him. His rules were his rules and if I didn't do the household chores properly; if I didn't keep my room neat or make my bed or take out the trash on time, or I didn't hold my silverware properly when eating and keep my napkin on my lap, then I ended up with a severe scolding or even a whipping.

I was most likely afraid of my father during those early years, for I was somewhat nervous in his presence and had to sneak around quite often to fulfill my own agenda. It's a sad thing when a young boy (or girl) has to live under a halo of fear for what their parents might say or do to them. Many parents are guilty here, with no concept of the damage their choice of words can inflict.

I was mechanically inclined at a young age and my father did allow me, with reservations, to work on my own bicycle. He was disappointed, though, when he discovered that I had taped a plastic bottle full of water to the bicycle frame and punched a hole in the bottom of it, so that the water would drip slowly out onto the ground as I peddled along.

I told him it was my gas tank, and that I had to fill it up each time it went empty. He removed it from my bicycle, and said that I was destructive and an idiot. He called me, 'Mr. Daydreamer.' He wasn't one to give encouragement, nor did he take the time to build a relationship on the foundation of my own personal creativity. I don't recall that he ever did.

In those early days of my youth I remember having a little dog who was the pride and joy of both my sister and myself. We failed to clean up his doggie mess one day, my father stepped in it, and that was the last we ever saw of that little fellow. My father took little Blackie away in the car and dropped him out somewhere along a rural road. That was quite hard to understand—difficult to live with.

I never got close to animals for many years after that—I threw stones at animals and shot birds with a BB gun. Shot a friend's hamster as well. Now, thank God, I am very respectful toward animals and have learned much about myself through them. Animals can serve to keep an individual or a family focused on the simple things in life; teaching us the values of tenderness, loyalty and other ingredients of love. We'll talk much more about animals in chapter 11.

I learned to forgive my father for his hard to understand behavior when I was much older—when I found that I had become like him in many ways. We become who we are, firstly, through our teachers (by example), and secondly, because of our own lack of understanding about ourselves. We usually remain blind to the character habits we form, and if we are fortunate enough to regain sight it usually comes at great cost. Understanding can come late in life, but not necessarily *too* late. When it does come it changes one's entire perspective on things. We are then more careful with each step and most concerned about the direction in which we walk when we look back at where we've been.

My father and I had some contact over the years, yet we never got really close and he died nearly a stranger to me when I was thirty-five. I gave the eulogy at his funeral in 1980, at his brother's request. It was a great honor to be able to do that, being at that time free of any ill will toward him. God had shown me great mercy in the formation of that particular attitude, but I understood very little in those days about the favor or grace of God. An in-depth perception of God's grace (*unmerited favor*) takes both time and experience to develop.

My mother on the other hand was quite a different person. She was kind to everyone and had a host of friends. The neighborhood women came to visit and care for her daily after she became ill. She adored all of my friends through the early years, especially the more mischievous ones. She had a big heart toward the less fortunate as well.

She would feed the hobos who wandered by now and then during difficult times. She sang in the choir at church, visited sick folk's and shut-ins each week, worked diligently and very artistically in a community garden, and I rarely saw her without a smile on her face. Mom would also stand up for my sister and I when our father's anger was aroused. He had quite a temper and so she became our shield of defense on many occasions.

She was also there when I was baptized in our local Christian church at age twelve. She was a monumental encouragement throughout my youth. She taught me that God existed and encouraged me to seek Him. Sadly, she passed away after a courageous two-year battle with a lymphatic disease, when I was just turning fourteen (there's a cure for it nowadays). She died on the day before my birthday in June of 1959. My grandmother informed me that her last words had expressed a deep concern for me.

I have visited the resting places of both my father and my mother many times over the years. I have spent time with them and have 'talked to them,' if you will, about my successes and failures, mostly my failures. My life has been in past times a combination of their personalities. I have been both kind and cruel, both patient and quick-tempered, both merciful and heartless.

Yet, because of unmerited grace on my heart, I now hold the memories of my parents in equal honor. For that I am grateful. I've learned that *all people fail* in one way or another, many times, parents or not parents, and so there is *no excuse* for personal resentment against anyone. We're all sinners—perfection is something that we will *never* attain in this earthly life. To be merciful should be our greatest pursuit.

Shortly after my mother passed away my sister left home. She stayed with relatives and friends while she attended college. She eventually ended up working in communications for the State Highway Patrol. Her road was indeed difficult; a marriage went sour and her children strayed a little, yet in my opinion she has traveled well. She recently retired from a long and successful career. We are in contact often and I keep encouraging her to move out West, however, she stays involved with her children and grandchildren in Ohio and I don't think she'll ever venture out on her own again.

Not long after she had left the nest, late in 1959, I ran away from home. I ended up in some mischief (which I later learned we are prone to) and in trouble with the local police. I was what they labeled, 'incorrigible' and a 'runaway.' My father was somewhat indifferent to my actions and I eventually ended up a resident of the county juvenile detention home. The police picked me up minutes before I was to get on a bus that would have taken me to California.

I often wonder how life would have turned out had I made that getaway. I was just fourteen years old at the time, but I now know that the California adventure was just not meant to be—not then anyway. I spent nearly six months in the county detention facility, learning some invaluable lessons while residing among other boys of misfortune, before friends of my late mother came forward and had me released into their custody.

I spent some time with them, some time with an aunt, some time with my father, and some time with the family of a fellow student until I graduated high school. When I turned eighteen, about a month after graduation, I joined the United States Army. I was truly out on my own then and at the time glad to be so. Life during the high school years had indeed been a struggle; living here and there, subject to differing standards and various weights of measure.

Sometimes I look back and wonder how I ever made it—how on earth had I even graduated? God was watching out for me of course; His angel encamped around me constantly (Psalm 34:7), though I was too occupied with my daydreams and my somewhat fast pace of life to take genuine notice. In fact, in those days I wasn't even aware that I had a guardian angel.

Most of us do not consider that God is involved in our daily lives —that is why we don't pray more often and also why we have a hard time finding our way. I now believe my guardian angel allowed me to have lots of friends and indeed some very close friends during those high school years, which was probably the reason that I *did* make it through them.

I was allowed over a hundred good friends (the entire senior class) and had my own rat pack as well—Ken George, Al Piry, Harry Brown, Jack Frankovitch, and my best of friends, John Milton Brandt. John and I were inseparable. We cruised the town in his '57 Chevy convertible our senior year and were quite popular among our classmates and envied by the underclassmen. We also lifted weights together on a regular basis, and talked often about many things.

As I look back I now realize that we were actually one another's personal counselors, but we never thought of it in that way—too full of piss and vinegar to have any psychological insight. The thoughts and ideas we shared were actually what kept us going during the ideological explosions of the early '60s. (John was a writer most of his life, and worked for a time as a publisher. He passed away early this year.)

Though I was acquainted with the Bible and had become a baptized believer through my parents' earlier influence, I was not at that time a student of it, nor did I always behave as a Christian should. The ignorance of youth is the worst of our ignorance! And I have learned that, when you're young and quite gullible, which includes one's high school years, the polluted mindset of the world is the very foundation of that ignorance.

The Bible warns us of the world's condition, yet even the most faithful to God sometimes ignore those warnings. The results are deceitful—evil many times takes on the appearance of good and proper discernment is obstructed. Poor discernment allows many high school students to make fun of their more serious Christian classmates. I was fortunate that someting within me would never allow me to do that, thank God.

In July of 1963 I left Ohio on a Greyhound bus, feeling like a free man, though bound for some difficult military training in the deep woods of Missouri. I wasn't worried in those days; I looked at the Army as the adventure of a lifetime. They indeed took me to some far away places that I had never been. My family and I had vacationed in Florida in 1955 when I was just ten years old, and that, though a grand adventure, had been my only experience far from home (in excess of 1000 miles) until I enlisted in the Army. Hopefully you can understand my enthusiasm.

I think I began to get my head together somewhat at that time, in that I was away from Ohio and the painful experiences of my youth. The rigorous military training I encountered was a good thing—a needed thing. I had no problems with the discipline. Though 'be all that you can be' had not been invented as of yet, I gave the Army all that I had. The military experience eventually brought out some better qualities in me that I didn't know existed.

We just have to be in the right place at the right time to gain any insight into ourselves—into our potentials. Our qualities and potentials are, of course, a gift from God, and He chooses both how and when we are to become aware of them. My father had always told me that I was a 'Hollywood actor,' and that I would end up being 'a nobody.' I suppose that's partly true, being the drifter that I am, but he later changed his mind about me and I'll get to that part, yet, I think the Army changed *my* mind about me long before my dad considered doing so.

However, that military education was both a good thing and a bad thing; I found out that I had the guts to try anything I chose in life, and that I had within me the ability to succeed at most endeavors. But, pride raised its ugly head in those days and worked against me for many, many years after that. It all started when I became a 'good soldier.'

Pride is Satan's worst problem. He wanted to be above God in majesty and still does, though he has been advised that he just won't make it. God's blessings in any form are to be used in His service and for no other reason. In the Army I earned several honors and promotions during my three-year enlistment. Pride allowed me to feel very special.

After I went through basic and advanced training with honors, I shipped overseas and spent a year in Korea in 1964. While there I made Post soldier of the month in September, in competition with over 600 other soldiers. I also received two promotions that year, ascending to the rank of Specialist E-4, working in the Intelligence section of an artillery battalion.

Near the end of that overseas tour I voluntarily signed up to jump out of airplanes. I eventually became a participant in a total of thirty-three military parachute jumps by the end of my enlistment, twenty-two of which were nighttime jumps. When I shipped back to the States I was trained as a parachutist in Georgia, but was then permanently stationed in Kentucky. I had the good fortune of being assigned to the 101st Airborne Division—that was in the spring of 1965. I was a gung-ho trooper—all the way *Airborne.*

My continued success in the Army was indeed a blessing from God, yet I had no idea of my need to *take the time* to truly honor His friendship, or to take the time to sit down and consider, within my heart, His many blessings and how I was to use them. Naturally my human, military heart was quite gung-ho—always on the move and prone to wander.

When I should have been on my knees in thankfulness, I instead continued to enjoy the pursuits of the world I was a part of. I was all puffed up with who I had become—Mr. Airborne, defender of the realm. That's what pride does. I did not then know that the heart is deceitful above all things, and incurably sick (Jeremiah 17:9).

Again, God's blessings are only to be used in His service. He gives us physical abilities, talents and spiritual blessings, and these three in varied measures, for particular reasons. We are to use them according to their measures to serve others in one way or another and not for self-satisfaction or personal gain. The Scriptures teach us that these gifts, being freely given to us, are to be freely given to others. This 'love' we have been given is to be used to both edify and encourage others in one way or another. Use your imagination—if every human in the world embraced this principle, then paradise would be restored!

When I wasn't soldiering I was off Post with my band of brothers, drinking beer and seeking willing women—the kind you have to pay for. This of course is a common practice among soldiers and a frequent practice among other young men most everywhere as well. The lust for sex is a powerful adversary when unrestrained or undisciplined. It can lead to decisions of madness that cripple or destroy one's life. It certainly did mine.

Many men and women dangle by the cords of these particular sins, some sinking into the mire of shameful sexual passions that have disastrous outcomes. My very first sexual encounter, while still a high school student, uncovered but did not help me to understand or learn to control this particular burning lust within. I was but fifteen, she was twenty.

Prior to this first contact I was like most young boys; I played with my privates now and then, while having thoughts of fondling the pretty mothers of some close friends in those days. Grown women in shorts or revealing clothing were indeed a temptation to a young, unrestrained mind—a mind without an unwavering focus on God—a mind absent of an in-depth understanding of self and the purpose of sexual fulfillment in a God ordained relationship.

Some of you may be thinking here: 'I never had any thoughts like that—no desire for any kind for immoral sex or other things that are morally wrong.'

Let's get real—everyone has *secret sins*. God sees everything that you do and knows everything that you think. You may presume that you can get away with a lot of things, because other people don't actually see what you're doing or cannot listen in on your thoughts. But the Psalmist has said, *Who can understand his errors? Cleanse me from secret faults. Keep back Your servant also from presumptuous sins; Let them not have dominion over me* (Psalm 19: 12, 13 NKJV). God knows *all* things—you need to keep that in mind when you look into the mirror and profess your innocence.

Again I warn you of the destruction that proceeds from ignorance. Know that sexual sins among humans are the most dominant of sins along the road to total depravity. Anyone is capable of them, but fortunately this particular 'thorn' seriously infects not everyone. Our 'thorns' are as varied as our fingerprints. We will deal with 'thorns' in one form or another our entire lifetime.

I was visiting my sister when my first immoral sexual encounter took place. At the time she was rooming with two young ladies in a rented house. During that visit I was given my own bedroom to occupy. In the middle of the night, my first night there, I was awakened by one of my sister's roommates. She had actually crawled into bed with me, clad only in a nightgown, and began fondling my private parts and whispering at me to "take" her.

She was quite an attractive lady and well built. She instructed me in everything that took place that night and kept me up all night. This went on for two or three consecutive nights, all other occupants in the household being completely unaware. She truly lit my fire—I believe that wild encounter aroused my passions for the rest of my life.

The sexual ones dominated. When I even looked at attractive women from that point on my desires were easily stirred and lust from the heart usually crept into my thinking. We wrestle with lusts in one form or another throughout our entire lifetime. My friends of course were no different in these attitudes, and so I shrugged them off at that time as being, 'okay.'

As I mentioned in chapter 1 of this writing, when our passions become inflamed our need for God becomes unreal to us and the mind and the will then proceed forward in darkness. While in the military, in the U.S. and in Korea, I spent nearly every available weekend furlough with my band of brothers in the company of immoral women. I don't know how I managed to escape disease—some of my brothers were stricken with it in one form or another. Yet, immoral sex was just one of the natural passions I had in my late teens and early twenties.

Sin does not stop at just one passion. It progresses into many deceitful transgressions that give birth to evil thoughts, harsh words and unbelievable actions. It is a consuming fire that rages out of control and brings the spirit of a man/woman into captivity, making them a prisoner of the sin that is within them. At the time however I never thought of any of these desires as lustful passions, which required knowledge of moral restraint and point-by-point consideration of their consequences, nor did I know how to consider or take into account how my thoughts, words and actions could and would affect my future.

Again, the ignorance of youth is disastrous! And, *because everyone around us in infected with sin, we are blind to its deceitfulness and therefore shrug of its wrongfulness.* Sin runs a course over the lifetime of every human being and each, individual person is infected in a different way with passions as variable as fingerprints. Only God can open our hearts to this particular understanding at any age. Some parents endeavor to open our minds, but I didn't have that luxury at that critical time. My mother would have jerked a knot into my tail, that's for sure! It would be some time however before the things she did teach me about God would begin to take hold.

In another realm, both my parents and the Army had taught me the importance of being neat and organized physically. I was brought up with the truth that everything has its own place. As a result, my living quarters were always spotless. Drawers of socks and underclothing were folded quite neatly. Jackets, shirts and pants were hung in seasonal order. My desk and bookshelves were uncluttered. Even the shoes at the base of my closet were lined up. I was about as organized as one can get.

I kept the trees, bushes, plants, flowers and lawn trimmed on the properties I occupied over the years. My personal and work vehicles were clean inside and out. The clothing I wore was always coordinated. The various jobs I worked at were done neatly with much attention to detail. I have continued these practices to this very day. Yet, in those days and for many years following, the man on the inside of me—the spirit of me—was in complete disarray. I never thought to look on the *inside*—I didn't know how.

My first grade teacher's words, 'should work more carefully and neatly,' and, 'should make better use of time,' should have been applied there (on the inside)—instead of on the outside. What a difference it would make in the world in which we live if our teachers were permitted, from the very first grade onward, to educate us spiritually, according to truth—to teach us how to do the math on the *inside*. Things would be much 'neater' within our lives and we could certainly find 'better' and more productive ways to make use of our time, could we not?

In those days I did not comprehend the disarray on the inside—as I said before, I was unaware of the power that my indwelling sin nature had over me. It is a blinding force that we remain totally ignorant of until we are given the grace to become aware of it. This force was in complete control. I believed in God and thought of Him on many occasions, throughout life, but it was a superficial belief—a mind-only belief.

Deceitfulness of the heart does this to us and we fail to truly come to know God because of it. Again, the fallen world around us prevents

61

us from learning the real truth. Knowing God is an active, wholehearted belief and takes some time to develop. When God finally becomes a part of one's inner being, only then is there any hope of facing up to and winning battles against the dark forces of the sin nature.

As I look back on 'the early years,' I see a young man of great ignorance and one in almost constant turmoil. Through the eyes of present knowledge, I see a young man who was caught up in worry, fear and doubt, loneliness and despair, yet, completely unaware of these particular wilderness wanderings. Due to his lack of knowledge and ever-present anxieties he made impulsive decisions. Each morning he looked for some new thing to which he would occupy himself. He did not force his thoughts or will upon others, and he rarely considered what others said or advised in any given matter. He lived like the words in the song by Frank Sinatra: "I did it my way."

Young Mark did things his way, and that attitude of course is the 'wrong way' for anyone. Some of these traits my father had, but it was many years later that I learned; regardless of the attitudes and actions of my parents, I was the one ultimately personally responsible for my own attitudes and actions. Those things came from within my own heart, not the heart of someone else.

We choose our own attitudes, so there is no one else to blame for one's own sin except one's own self. Don't pin the tail on the wrong donkey. Sin runs a course in all of us over time and *each* of us are infected in a different way. I mentioned that once before. I also mentioned that sin is profoundly deceitful and as variable as are our individual fingerprints.

Yet, in any form, it is still sin at work—depravity in motion— standard equipment within the human, no matter what the modern day psychologists' label it or interpret it to be. Your counselor, if you have one, cannot help you if he/she doesn't know or teach you the absolute truth, and you surely can't help yourself if you don't know the truth.

Human knowledge, or knowledge of the world, is not really knowledge at all. And, since we are inherently evil, it is against our nature to develop trust in the God of heaven for true knowledge. So, until He allows us the light of grace, which enables us to trust in Him and not in ourselves, we remain in darkness, without true knowledge, ruled by the sin nature—that's just the way it is.

Your counselor, if you have one, is just as guilty as you are—commits sin just like you do—so I wouldn't count on getting the help you really need, unless of course the counselor embraces and practices the truths of God (Romans 8:7). Those practices are *Godly* psychology. Human psychology is deceitful. A counselor educated in and practicing human psychology will deal with you as if you have some type of problem that he/she does not have.

They will scan your brain, so to speak, to find it. That's because, hc/she doesn't understand the depravity of his/her own nature. Psychologists would be exceedingly more careful and then indeed helpful if they understood this most important truth—you can't remove the speck of sawdust from someone's eye until you take the plank out of your own (Matthew 7:3).

To fear or to truly respect God is the very beginning of knowledge (Proverbs 1:7). If you are, dear reader, just starting out in life from high school/college, I kindly encourage you to please slow down and take some needful time to meditate on what the first three chapters of this writing have endeavored to teach you. Knowing these things can help you to avoid many destructive consequences throughout your lifetime.

So, go ahead, sit down now and think deeply about all the things that you have just learned. I can guarantee their authenticity. Many plagues can come upon you, but there is always a way out if you make the right preparations ahead of time. At this time the rest of us will hike ahead on the trail, which is going to take us out of the Army and into California.

You high school/college students can catch up with us later, after you've had a chance to consider what you've learned up to this point. Most of you older folk's should not be in 'shock and awe' concerning the truth of those things. Most of you have encountered similar experiences and have made your own discoveries. Hang on though and stay alert—there is some ground coming up upon which you may have never before tread...

Chapter Four...My Pursuit of the Hawk, Part 2
California Dreamin'

During the last nine months of my military service I was assigned as a sergeant with the special honor of training new troops for Vietnam. I was one of three soldiers in the entire 321st Artillery Battalion of the 101st Airborne Division who were not sent from Fort Campbell to Vietnam in September of 1965.

Each of us had already completed a hardship tour in Korea, and each of us had somewhere in the neighborhood of nine months remaining on our active enlistments. Vietnam was a minimum one-year tour of duty at that time and the push was on. With the estimated troop build up in that far away jungle, they opened up Fort Campbell to basic training and assigned the three of us (promoting us to sergeants), along with other non-commissioned officers remaining on the Post (who were not paratroopers), to the training and managing of several platoons of raw, new recruits.

It went quite well. We went through several cycles of bright, young men with various backgrounds who were willing and eager at learning to work together as a team. At the end of the very first cycle the recruits from all training platoons voted me their number one instructor. I was indeed honored by their kindness. They threw a party for me and bought some gifts on their meager pay. Being an airborne sergeant I had become their idol—a for real, living example of the 'Screaming Eagles.'

Paratroopers were big stuff in those days and the 101st were considered the elite of America. Though most of those young men were not pre-paratrooper recruits, I had allowed them to experience the challenging leap from the 25-foot tower at the jump training area. For this they were extremely grateful. It was a rewarding experience for all of us.

At the end of that first training period I was allowed a well-earned furlough. I hitchhiked 500 miles to visit my sister (I didn't own a car), who was at that time living in Marietta, Ohio. My first ride took me all the way there. Life was indeed kind in those days, especially if you were in the bold and polished uniform of a U.S. Paratrooper.

Not having seen my sister in nearly three years it was for sure a grand reunion. She about fell over when I walked onto her porch in that bold uniform. She told me that she was very proud of me—that our mother would have been quite proud as well. My sister has always had an attitude of encouragement—no matter what personal difficulties she herself has gone through or may be going through at the time.

That's a rare find nowadays. It was also on this particular furlough that I met my future wife, Jenny. She too was a most encouraging individual—rarely speaking a negative word. She and I met in December of 1965, and were married the following February. I wrote her a letter each day from December through February while I was back on Post. The rest of my pay went for long distance phone calls. It was indeed a joyous time in my life.

Again, all of this success and happiness was God's doing. Though unworthy, I have tried not to forget to thank Him in the years that have since gone by. Forgetfulness of God's blessings will draw us away from Him, and without a constant mindfulness of this forgetfulness we are prone to wander. If you forget about your blessings it won't be long before you actually lose them. Remember that any goodness comes only from God, and comes in many forms. It's wise then to develop and hold onto an attitude of gratitude.

Jenny had a two-year-old son, Michael, and following our marriage in Ohio on February 20th of 1966, the three of us returned to Ft. Campbell to finish out my enlistment. We were indeed quite happy.

We rented a two-bedroom duplex, just off Post. It was a nice, clean little place with a big yard. Jenny had a sharp looking '59 Ford that became our family vehicle.

Those were probably the happiest days of my early life. If I could relive any time in my life those tender days of 'love' in bloom would be my very first choice. How I've truly missed them! How I wish I could have at that time understood the *value* of them. As I look back I could now write a book on the should-have-said's and should-have-done's that perhaps would have allowed those times to physically endure forever.

If you don't live life moment by moment, and we'll talk about that some more, then you are missing the fullness of what God can offer to your life, what you can offer to your life, and what others can offer to your life as well as what you can offer them—moments of peace that literally exceed understanding but reveal the treasures of contentment.

It wasn't long until I adopted Mike and he legally assumed the Taylor name. What an honor that was! Life was so good that I couldn't wait to get home each day after work. Once, when I was camped in the field for a week with my recruits, I snuck off post on a rainy night and walked several miles to get home. What pure adventure! Jenny dropped me off quietly the next morning, before I was missed. It seemed that all the difficult years of my childhood had vanished away and that I had some real purpose in life.

It was motivatingly different—sharing my life with someone. Nothing else seemed very important. I know that I endeavored to make my family happy, but that endeavor I later learned was based on the subtle condition that things went my way. It is always difficult to abandon 'self.' Unaware of the sin nature within, I failed to develop the attitudes and the patience that make a marriage the *partnership* that God intends it to be. I was indeed impulsive. In my haste to do all things I failed to truly learn how much the little things really matter.

I failed to take precious time (moment by moment) to listen in depth and to communicate with my wife, who was about as loyal, tender and soft-spoken as one can get. I failed to think things out before I acted. I focused not only on self, but also on acquiring material possessions, rather than desiring spiritual knowledge and wisdom. My spirit had been deceived in the woods of humanity, unable to see the forest for the trees. I was hiking the trail of pride on a hopeless course that would eventually cause me to lose touch with my family.

Time went by quickly. I turned twenty-one in June of 1966. Upon my separation from active service early the next month, Jenny, Mike and I returned to Marietta, Ohio. We rented a small apartment there and I worked construction for nearly a year. It was nice to be out of the Army, but working at various construction sites wasn't the most inspiring of civilian careers, and Jenny wasn't really too happy about being back in her hometown.

In late April of 1967, after a long winter, we determined that we should put some adventure into our lives and move west—to California. Even young Michael was excited about the idea of it. "Cal-for-nee," he called it—talked about it all the time. We started forming some plans and determined that we would be out of Ohio sometime in late May.

That old '59 Ford became a trade-in on a new, '66 Mustang. I bought the car one day, drove it home and surprised Jenny with it. I told her we could go to California in style. I know she was excited about the Mustang, but I don't think she ever appreciated me making the deal with her '59 Ford without consulting her first. Yet, this was who I was in those days. She said nothing that day and rarely challenged or questioned me on anything at anytime. She was just happy that our "little family," as she called it, was indeed a family— that we were together and had a vision for the future.

I was 'in charge' of things and as I mentioned before, they had to go my way. I guess I thought I knew it all. This was not intentional, and I was fortunate to have such a submissive wife, yet if she had stood up in my face a time or two, perhaps I would have begun to learn something about mutual partnership before it was too late. However, I can happily say that Jenny wanted California probably more than I did.

I have always been glad about that joint decision, even though just four years later I robbed her of my share in it. That part of the story is forthcoming (chapter 6), but the original move to California has been a big influence in my life; both good and bad have come from it, and mostly good these last years. I've been allowed to live the California dream, that's for sure.

The American West is indeed the marrow of the world, and California, largest of the western states, is true to the various meanings of its name, one of which is translated, *earthly paradise*. We left for the Golden State in mid-May of 1967, pulling a little U-Haul trailer behind our new '66 Mustang. It was at this time that Jenny, Mike and I were allowed a most scenic vacation.

There wasn't much traffic along old routes 40 and 66 in those days. We'd never experienced the raw West before, and those old routes hit some of its best parts—they still do—winding through old towns, heavily brushed desert terrain and picturesque buttes—it was so much more than we had ever imagined it would be, and all formed by the waters of the Great Flood, some 5000years ago.

We marveled at the grandeur and majesty of the high and mighty Rocky Mountains. We saw endless canyon formations throughout New Mexico and Arizona, stopping to walk among some of them and touching their numerous rock outcrops—pinnacles of red rock and an untold variety of sandstone monoliths. We beheld impressive varieties of desert plants as well, the likes of which we had never seen before. We gathered bark and twigs and rocks of various sorts—it was breathtaking!

The American West is truly a heaven on earth. You can learn endlessly about God and his attributes in that part of the country. I have spent much time these last years in the wilderness areas of Colorado, Utah, Arizona and California. We will devote much time to these captivating and illuminating wilderness areas in a few chapters down the trail.

However, in the earlier days of my ignorance, the West became a place to fulfill the gusto of my carnal, earthly appetites. My sinful nature was indeed pitching its tent toward Sodom and Gomorrah and the cities of the plains. The exquisite inner beauty of the mountains and the deserts was unknown to me initially, and their enthralling outward beauty became overshadowed by the lure of deceitful lusts from within the metropolis.

I was definitely no Abraham—no shepherd of the flock; content in the fields. I wish I had been, but I was at that time more irresponsible in spirit, much like Abraham's youthful nephew, Lot (Genesis 13:10-13), who ended up for a time wandering among haunts of the exceedingly wicked. Those haunts exist today in most of our major cities—unfortunately in some rural towns as well.

Jenny on the other hand thought of California as a great place to raise a family. She could do that anywhere. It was her goal. It was her passion as well, and she did a superb job of it. Her spirit always seemed unaffected by the troubled world around her. She was radiant like the sun.

I so wish my spirit could have at that time discerned the great depth of her inner beauty (she read the Bible quite often). I could have been just like her in those days. Like-mindedness is a very special gift from God. Those who develop this quality in a wholesome manner are prone to experience much more happiness in this difficult life as a result of it.

She was a true shepherd. She was the 'helper' whom God had given me, which I so desperately needed. But, most of us are self-centered; we seldom realize our need for examining the good qualities in others for the purpose of adopting those qualities into our own heart, and then displaying them through God's Spirit by our patterns of living. Again, like-mindedness is a Godly virtue (Philippians 2:2).

Without understanding that the true nature of the marriage relationship is to establish *spiritual union*, we forsake that noble endeavor of becoming 'one' through like-mindedness and instead concentrate on our individual needs and desires apart from our spouse. This attitude is incorrect. After all, God made the first woman from the rib of the man. The two are indeed one.

Not realizing the significance of this union ignores God's purpose for us, and is the destroyer of marital unions all over the world. We need to change our attitudes regarding this matter. God's word, the Bible, is actually a book about *attitudes*, which makes it relevant in any generation throughout all generations. When one brings to life the stories within the Bible, he/she discovers that attitudes are the foundation of any relationship—with others and with one another.

Even though our nature is sinful, through the Spirit of God we can *choose right attitudes*. This is a freedom unlike any other. It all starts with an attitude of gratitude. Your world can indeed be a better place through the positive and truly right attitudes that you choose to develop and embrace.

When we finally arrived in California, we first visited Paul and Kitty Lesniak, in the city of Arcadia, Los Angeles County. I knew Paul and Kitty through a furlough I had spent there with their son, Ken, when I was on my way to Korea in 1963. I had graduated high school with Ken, who moved to California to live with his father following that event.

Ken had more recently completed a military tour in Germany, not long before we had arrived. He was one of my best friends in high school (chapter 3), a member of the rat pack, two more of which (Jack Frankovitch and John Brandt) were I believe still in military service, and at the time both serving in a foreign land.

The Lesniaks were no small help in our endeavor to establish roots there. Paul treated me like his own son and honored Jenny and Mike as family. The Lesniaks helped us to find and furnish our very first apartment in the nearby town of Monrovia. Through Paul's influence I became manager of that little apartment complex. We received a partial reduction in rent for gardening work and other small chores. I've always loved gardening, and that quality is inspirational, for God loves gardening as well. If you enjoy gardening, consider yourself blessed. Believe it or not, you can learn much about yourself while cultivating and tending a garden. Think about it.

I found a position almost immediately with the California Institute of Technology Seismological Laboratory of Pasadena. I had been proficient in map reading and chart plotting while in the Army, so Cal-Tech hired me as an assistant on an earthquake study project, which involved jeep travel into wilderness areas to record and chart temperatures below the earth's surface.

This was done by core-drilling deep holes into the earth's crust, removing and examining the core samples, then measuring with an electronic probe the temperatures at various levels from where the core had been extracted. Cal-Tech had drilled these holes on a perpendicular line, at long distances from one another across the San Andreas Fault, both in northern and southern California.

This specialty science was called the Heat Flow Project, which was just a small part in the overall study of earthquakes throughout California in those days. I was quite honored to land that position. It required at least two years of college level geology, which I did not have at the time. Dr. Roy, my supervisor, told me that my map and chart work made up for my lack of geological education. He was one of those educated folk's who had the wisdom to appreciate the value of experience. He said that experience was indeed knowledge in itself.

When I later attended college, sometime after my Cal-Tech employment, geology became one of my favorite courses of study, thanks to Dr. Roy's influence. I later learned however that the study of geology truly begins and ends with God. As a college student I was a little confused about things, but when time moved on from that institution and I experienced some time wandering about in remote areas of the West, true knowledge increased and I eventually became unconfused. Confusion ends when one begins to understand that God originally created almost all things full grown.

Dr. Roy was right—experience is knowledge. Unfortunately, most college professors formally educated in geology continue to confuse students as to the true origin and age of things, namely, the earth and all of its wonders. An incorrect understanding of origins has a disastrous affect on any of the sciences. The resulting 'scientific' theories (*speculations*) passed on to high level educational institutions have, over the years, become known to the majority of the world as fact, and are the curriculum handed down to most all lower levels of education. This curriculum is actually 'false' science (1st Timothy 6:20) and only enforces the concept of absolute depravity.

The higher education level ignorance (or confusion), regarding what will later become *obvious* to you through this writing, serves to emphasize the truth of Satan's dominion and rule over the entire earth. We see it all the time on so-called educational television—Science Channel, Discovery Channel, History Channel, etc. Their explanations regarding geological and even Biblical events, for the most part, do not truly consider God and reflect disregard for His sovereignty.

There is indeed a shortage of true knowledge, of truly scientific knowledge, and most importantly, a shortage of knowledge regarding what's going on in the spiritual realms. The Native Americans, who many folk's consider to be primitive, know far more about the spiritual realms than most of us can comprehend. Their wisdom far exceeds that of those whom we label the 'educated' in our society.

During the year that I was under government contract with Cal-Tech I had been allowed to travel into many wilderness areas of California, Arizona and Nevada. The line of core holes stretched eastward from both north and south perimeters of the San Andreas Fault into these neighboring states. I was gone from home sometimes with my work for two or more weeks at a time.

Jenny was so patient with me. She had some girlfriends, with whom she worked at crafts, and of course Michael kept her occupied most of the time, yet, my absence from the home was still a hardship. While traveling and working in the wilderness I was also able to live out the fantasies of my youth, which were still a part of me—a part of all of us, if we will but make the admission.

If you can recall from chapter 3, I was never me. I was a mountain man, exploring the vast landscapes of the West. I was a cowboy, stopping by a rural Nevada tavern on occasion to sip on a beer or to fondle a prostitute now and then. I was always everybody except who I was supposed to be; a child of the Most High, an ambassador of His truth, and a married man named Mark Taylor, responsible for the love and nurture of a growing family in a world full of subtle evil and deceitful ambitions.

I was a poor steward of what had been given to me—a somewhat profane man who thought himself responsible and benevolent. I was indeed a blind guide—naïve to the world's pollutions. How I despise the ignorance of my youth! The remorse is sometimes more than I can bear. The sin nature is indeed as deceitful as it is wicked; stealing from us true peace and happiness, which has no part of pride, immoral sexual behavior, the pursuit of possessions or greed for wealth and/or fame, or any other form of ill-chosen self-indulgence. Only God can snatch one from the flames of these fires.

In early 1968 my second son, Mitchell, was born. I was allowed to be home that particular week. After I brought Jenny and the baby home from the hospital, she smiled at me and asked, "Do you want to hold your son?" Indeed I did—I still remember to this day the indescribably tender emotions I experienced while he was in my arms. I sobbed then and I still sob when I think about how I felt. I was holding a part of Jenny and me there in my arms. I remember looking up and thanking God for His incomparable gift. Little Mike loved him dearly as well and wanted to hold him all of the time.

These affections for a new child should remain within a father's or a mother's or a brother's or a sister's heart each day of their lives, all the days of their lives. If they did, no child would ever suffer the horrors of the absence of love. These deep affections originate with God. This is just one more illumination for you, dear reader, regarding His character. I have mentioned God's attributes throughout these first few chapters and there are many more 'mentionings' on the way. Understanding the depth of God's love can reconstruct your entire perception of God, which will indeed serve to change your life for the better.

I have learned through the years that patience and trust are the greatest of virtues. True patience looks to God and trusts in Him for all things, both great and small. True patience is *having patience*—a willingness to wait. False patience trusts in one's self or in others when choosing his/her paths in life. Without God we are always in a rush, which results in our failure to allow Him to participate in our decisions.

In March of 1968 my employment with Cal-Tech came to an end. There were no available research funds to allow the continuation of an assistant's position on the Heat-Flow Project. Fate would have it however that the city of Arcadia was at that time looking for police officers. I immediately put in an application and then took a temporary job as a security officer for a small outfit in Pasadena.

I knew it could take some time to land a police department position, and the odds were against me—there were three openings on the department and over two hundred applicants. My fate was indeed in the hands of a loving God. Don't ever think for one minute that you are somehow responsible for your own good fortune. God oversees all things—both good and bad.

Through the providence of God it turned out that I was one of the three selected to fill the positions. They told me that, since I was a former military man with honors, I had been moved to the top of the list. This was obviously a blessing from above, however, my pride would dominate the handling of this windfall and, without seeking God's will, I would make decisions down the road that would seem to indicate that what I had been so graciously given at this time was not all that important to me.

I would continue to trust in myself and not in the God who formed me. One's career or chosen profession in life, along with everything else in one's life, has to be put into its proper place. I may have become a 'good policeman' over time, but I still didn't know how to stop and smell the roses—how to get my nose right down in the pedals and take a grand sniff.

I didn't stand still for any length of time to admire, with a deeper understanding, the picture God had painted of me and for me, which was my family—His work of art. That is what God wanted me to put into first place—alongside Him. Instead, I was irresponsibly ignorant in the leadership of my family. I didn't know how to be a role model for one thing, because I didn't know anything about love in those days.

I didn't know how to slow down—how to take the time to recognize any failures—to examine myself and correct them. I was blind—I didn't 'get the picture.' Anxiety in the wrong direction literally stole away many hours, days, weeks, months and years of my life. Natural affection eluded me as well. It wasn't a part of my life's experience. Achieving worldly success had been instilled in me from my youth. The self-seeking desires that evolve through that particular mentality became my passions.

Being a police officer in southern California was indeed a great honor. The State offered the best training in the country, and at that time was the only State that 'State Certified' each phase of the training. After eight weeks at the Pasadena Police Academy I then trained and worked in the city of Arcadia with an elite group of men and women.

There were quite a few former military men on the department and so I fit right in. I still wasn't Mark Taylor though; I was now Matt Dillon of Gunsmoke, Marshall Jim Crown of Cimarron Strip, and Qui Chang Kane of Kung Fu. In 1969, when Butch Cassidy and the Sundance Kid came out, I was Sundance—blond hair, mustache and all. We want to be like other characters/people because we don't really understand who we are. Or, perhaps we don't like who we are and want to be someone different.

We cannot understand ourselves at all—that's our nature. But, when you begin to know (understand) God through His creation, you can at the same time begin to truly discover who you are and who you are not. Once you make that important discovery, you can then learn to *accept* who you as well as who you are not. The earlier you accomplish this in life, the greater chance you have at living—choosing the proper attitudes, making the right decisions, and avoiding many of the should-have-said's and should-have-done's that always catch up to us in the later years. You older folk's are in agreement here, I'm sure.

My best friend, officer Tim Murray, was Butch Cassidy. We were like two peas in a pod. Tim was single and like Butch, loved the women. It's not wise for a young married man to run in the wrong direction with a single man or crowd after work. I soon developed a growing desire to be like Tim in my personal life; free of family responsibility. That lust continued to flourish. It was one of many attitudes of self-love that would eventually cause my downfall.

Though we always assume the grass to be greener on the next slope, we usually find it to be quite contrary to that assumption.

In those days we worked a six-day work schedule with two days off. They called this arrangement 'rotating days off.' I was on the swing shift, from 3 to 11 pm., which didn't leave much time for quality evenings at home, and the rotating schedule made it somewhat difficult to live a normal life.

My family was in bed before I got off work, so Butch and I and other officers hit the local taverns when work ended, to play pool, eat shelled peanuts and sip draft beer. Sometimes we hit the topless bars —no table games there; only raw entertainment and pocket pool, if one was so inclined. A man needed to unwind from the stress of police work, and pool halls and topless bars were two of the ways I chose to unwind.

Of course these were poor choices, but when you live life on the edge you don't always take the time to develop the understanding that considers whether a personal choice is a good one or a bad one. You just do what you want to do or feel you have to do at the time, and that's just the way it is. Police work of course is not the only occupation that pulls against the family unit, and our Creator still maintains, even in this crazy, modern age in which we live, that family unity should be our number one priority no matter what our occupation.

Nowadays I see star NFL athletes, most of them married, laughing and talking about their nights at the topless bar, and I just cringe. I want to call them up and warn them of the terrible consequences that can result from their visiting those kinds of places. Lions on the hunt become lambs to the slaughter—whatever you do that's immoral will catch up with you, sooner or later. There is no escape.

Jenny and I were able to buy our first home in 1969. What an absolute blessing it was! We were much more than excited. I spent a little more time at home then, working a graveyard shift. During the mornings I was involved in yard work on the property, indeed a more productive way to unwind. Jenny loved yard work as I did and had a developing artistic interest in crafts, as I mentioned earlier. Together we worked on many projects, decorating and improving both the exterior and interior of the home. It was *so much* fun!

We made a few trips to a distant beach in a borrowed pick-up, where we gathered truckloads of smooth, gray rock for our rock garden. We picked out those rocks one at a time, loaded them into a bucket, carried them off the beach, and then unloaded the bucket into the bed of the truck. This activity was repeated again and again for most of the day. It was a full days work each time we went, but it was a great family outing. Mike helped out with the chore while Mitch watched it all from a stroller.

It always took a while to get home with all that weight in the truck —we got 'honked' at a lot as folk's passed on by us, shaking their fists and 'flinging the bird.' We just shook our heads and laughed—it got to be a routine. Of course I wanted to 'flip the bird' right back at them and accompany that with some swearing, but with my being an officer and all, that reaction really wasn't a proper way to deal with their ignorance, especially in front of my children.

We planted mostly desert type plants and poppies within the rock garden, and it was a beauty. We painted the house inside and out, bricked the whole inside wall around the fireplace, fixed the garage up a little bit, and within a few months had a real nice place where we could enjoy our life n' labors and proudly entertain any guests. I had all my toys and trinkets in the garage, and Jenny had a special place to work on her crafts and plants. We were living the American Dream, together, under the California sun.

In December of 1969 we took a needed vacation, driving clear back to Ohio to visit Jenny's parents and family. They were all so happy for Jenny that they could barely contain themselves. They loved looking at our family pictures and talking about the things related to our 'Western' projects.

She had quite a large family and I had always enjoyed being among them when we lived in Ohio that year before we moved away. They were genuine folk's. They always treated me like I was somebody special when indeed I was not. It turned out to be a great Christmas that year. Christmas is such a special time. If we could just hold onto those feelings and attitudes year 'round we'd all be much better off.

We saddled up shortly after the New Year for the return trip, making room for Jenny's sister, Lula, who rode along in the car with us for some western sightseeing. We took the central route and were able to visit many interesting sites in Colorado and Utah. We gathered various twigs and rocks as we had on our first journey into the West, only this time we had a home where we could artistically display them in one way or another.

Lula thoroughly enjoyed her journey with us and remarked constantly about the scenery. She was so inspired that she actually ended up spending quite some time at our home in California. She and Jenny had some great times that winter and I was glad that Jenny had familiar company. Jenny was always an encouragement to all the members of her family.

Lula was slightly older than Jenny and was going through a difficultly sad divorce—is there any other kind? Though inspired by her California experiences and motivated by each day's rising of the sun, she also had her times of grief. Jenny and I both encouraged her as best we could during those dark moments, but I personally didn't spend that much time at home following the vacation.

In January of 1970 I was attending college in the evenings and working patrol afterward on the graveyard shift. When Lula went back to Ohio in early spring, I started in on the morning yard work, which occupation helped to keep me more focused on family life, but I didn't remain active for long in that attitude—couldn't stay put.

I was so preoccupied with self; with police work, its related agenda and with night school, that I just couldn't stop long enough to smell the roses, as I mentioned earlier, even though I had a beautiful line of them down the driveway and possessed an even more exquisite group of flowers—Jenny, Mike and Mitch—who bloomed in all seasons.

Again, my family was actually a part of God's painting of *me*; His artwork that He loved—I didn't stare at it, and I should have. The fact was that God's precious artwork was being destroyed through my lack of knowledge—my inability to establish *family oriented* priorities. I was a man with no lasting perception or control of my many anxieties —a flip-flopper.

Not only was I spiritually adrift, but also was as dumb as a post when it came to common sense with regard to family matters. Jenny had a good laugh when she first pointed that out to me. On the other hand, I was meticulous at police work. I bloomed there—smart and productive, and was always involved in the most interesting of cases. I received several types of commendations, which had flowered *that* work into a passion. I remained continually fruitful at my job and though I surely overdid it in those days, that attribute later helped me in life to understand more about myself.

There was however another passion that I must entitle *pure passion*, and one great personal event that would eventually change the course of my life forever, *truly* for the better. Sometimes God takes something or someone that we really, truly love and uses it or them to draw us to Himself.

He can also do the same thing—draw us to Himself—through something or someone that we hate. Seem strange? The methods God uses in fulfilling His purposes for us are unfathomable. His ways are past finding out, but I believe that, over time, He used my particular pure passion to draw me to Himself because I *did* love it so much.

That pure passion was hiking. On my human side, the military was partly responsible for that desire—their sometimes daily 20-mile forced marches were common in all types of weather—I ate them up! Prior to the army, I was always off hiking somewhere amidst the Ohio woodlands. And so, I did a lot of hiking in California from 1967-71, mostly in the local mountains.

The great personal event of late 1970 was a more notable adventure in California's High Sierras; at that time the most esteemed adventure of my life—an ascent of Mt. Whitney, highest mountain in the contiguous United States.

Chapter Five...Monuments
The Whitney Climb

Just West of Lone Pine, the towering granite crest of the Sierra Nevada is one of the most majestic sights in California. Mt. Whitney crowns the escarpment; its 14,497-foot summit is the highest peak in the contiguous United States. It has been the mountain backdrop for many motion pictures filmed in the area for over six decades. Three local fishermen made the first recorded climb to this elusive summit from Lone Pine on August 18, 1873.[1]

Explorer Clarence King climbed to the summit in mid-September of that same year. This was his fourth attempt to climb the mountain, the previous three having failed due to his inability to find the right peak. King explored the Sierra for quite a few years after his triumphant ascent and wrote about many of his exploits. As it turned out, he was more successful as a writer than a route finder, and later became one of the Sierra's best-known historical figures.

Another Sierran climbed the mountain in early October of that same year. His name was John Muir, the famous conservationist and founder of the Sierra Club. Climbing all day he eventually reached the summit 'Needles' about midnight, however, tired and weakened from that journey he was forced to retreat the very next morning, without

79

having reached the actual summit. He had camped overnight just a few hundred feet below it! Muir kept a diary of the difficult journey and later wrote that he was forced to "dance all night to keep from freezing." (It appears that he and I are kindred in that 'dancing' thing.)

He returned to Mt. Whitney within a week from the town of Independence and started his climb, spending the first night camped among sagebrush at a low elevation. The next day he hiked up the North Fork of Lone Pine Creek and spent that night camped at timberline. On the third day Muir started out quite early and climbed the chute just north of the east face, now known as the 'Mountaineer's Route,' reaching the summit at about eight o'clock that morning. It was October 21, 1873. He returned to the town of Independence the next day.[2]

Muir was indeed an exceptional hiker. He climbed the mountain in three days, having left the first morning from the town of Independence, some fifteen miles away. Today, most hikers take an average of three days to ascend the Mountaineer's Route, starting from the trailhead at Whitney Portal, some 8000 feet up on the mountain—not from the town of Independence fifteen miles away.

Muir also explored much of the Sierra Nevada and formed the Sierra Club in 1892, which was to insure protection for the mountain range, and still does (I'm a happy member of it). He also helped to establish Yosemite as a National Park by 1906. Legend says that he shouted for joy when he first laid eyes on the High Sierras. Do I know that feeling? Oh, my goodness!

The Whitney peak was originally discovered in 1864 and named after Josiah Dwight Whitney, who was at that time the chief geologist for the California State Geological Survey.[3] Some believe Native Americans may have made the very first ascents. Hieroglyphics have been discovered in the high crags along the summit Needles. The 'Needles' are the two high points just south (left) of the grand summit crest (refer to the photograph at the beginning of this chapter). Storms atop Whitney are frequent, usually accompanied by extremely violent bursts of lightning. Local Native Americans call it *the rock of thunder*.

In 1970, ninety-seven years after the first recorded ascent, a group of determined young men arrived at the Whitney Portal just after sunrise. The wind was fierce that September morning, the temperature just at freezing, yet the constant gnawing of an ever-present wind put the chill in the air quite a bit below that mark. It didn't really matter, though—our purpose was pretty much set in stone. Cold weather in effect wasn't an obstacle, but that long, winding trail up that high and mighty mountain would indeed be.

There were five of us who ended up being a part of that most memorable adventure—five young idiots at the time—I think. We had parked the trucks along the road somewhere near the 8000-foot level. We then unloaded our gear and went through the process of harnessing, shouldering and checking one another's backpacks; final prep stuff. Our conversation at the portal was somewhat brief. It was cold and definitely time to get a-hikin' on up the trail. We had an approximate eleven-mile trek ahead of us—and that was just one way along a somewhat primitive route; originally constructed in 1904.

The goal was the renowned and historically elusive summit of Mt. Whitney, highest mountain in the contiguous United States—he's a big'un. The trail ahead appeared to be extremely rugged and steep. One thing sure—the climb would certainly generate some body heat. It was just too cold for September 1st. We were hoping the wind and cloud cover would soon disappear—hoping the intermittent sunlight would become more stable and begin to warm things up a bit. Cold weather menacing a hiker is harder to deal with than the trek itself.

The 1970 climb to Whitney's eminent summit was the first for each of us. We had conquered a few other California peaks in the preceding months, but this was the big one—the high and the mighty. Our hiking group consisted of two thirty-five year old's and three twenty-five year old's, all male. I was among the latter, just under three years a police officer at the time, out on a weekend adventure with some of my peers. I was young, energetic and curious, but with absolutely no concept of what this particular climb would mean to my understanding in the distant future. None whatsoever.

Far down the mountain I had it made; a loving and caring wife, two young children at the time, a new home with an adequate yard to cultivate and maintain, two cars, a motorcycle, a motor scooter and a garage full of pending projects—all the toys and trinkets I would ever need. Add to that the pat-on-the-back mentality that goes with an extremely responsible and good-paying job at a young age. Of course the credit card bills came right along with all of the above. I was attending college too, majoring at that time in criminal justice and public relations, with minors in geology and psychology.

I thought of myself as a man of adventure. My first love was indeed yours truly. Prior to Whitney there had been many other escapes into the wilderness. I was a very passionate fellow; an early riser for duties in the yard, an afternoon through early evening-shift patrol officer, an after work late night pool player and beer chugger, from time to time an ignorant-of-the-consequences womanizer, and a somewhat my-opinion-is-usually-right know it all. Human nature was completely in charge. Get the picture?

I attended church occasionally, a church of the world. I was, for the most part, just like everyone else my age at that time, but of incredibly free spirit. We are something, aren't we? Well, at least we think we are. We get involved in this and that and the other thing, busying ourselves with worldly pursuits, thinking we've discovered the fountain of youth. Thing is, with this line of thinking, we become shortsighted. The reality is that we just get old and die, and are no more—we're just a handful of dirt or a puff of smoke in an eternal wind.

Our Group hiked that first day for about six hours, ever so slowly, until we reached a place called *Mirror Lake*, at an elevation of about 10,600 feet. The wind had completely subsided. The sun was shining full time and we leisurely soaked up its warmth as we rested atop some rather large granite boulders, dispersed around the lake.

It was a most impressive area; clothed in stout pines and manzanita, the lake itself mirroring the high cliffs and rocky crags just above it. The serenity of the place indeed put our bodies to a much needed rest, and having worked up a little appetite, we thought it time to build a fire for cooking. Unfortunately we were right at timberline— above the taller pines, oaks and various bushes, where scrounging for dead wood became quite wearisome. Everyone was too tired to climb down to a lower level, search for the dead wood and then have to carry it back up.

We were however able to manage enough kindling for a small fire and we took turns sawing through some old timber stumps we had found just before the lake, which allowed us some larger pieces of wood with which to stoke up the fire. It actually turned out to be a *good* campfire. If a campfire is built properly it can be more than exquisite. A properly built campfire is as follows:

You start by digging a small pit in the earth, circular, about three to four feet in diameter. If rocks are available you can place them around the edge of the circle as a firebreak. Rocks also absorb and reflect heat, which ultimately produces a warmer fire and allows hotter, longer lasting (all night) embers, ready to stir at breakfast to heat up the morning 'trail coffee.'

Wad up about a half dozen pages of newspaper (one page per wad) and place them in the middle of the circle. Toilet paper or facial tissues do not work well. Writing pad paper, napkins or paper towels are okay, but newspaper works the best. Sprinkle some twigs or small kindling atop the wadded newspaper. Find a medium sized forked branch to use as a support for the next phase—building a *teepee.*

A teepee generates a lot of heat in a short time and produces quick coals for heating up hot dogs or marshmallows. Construct the teepee's center support over top of the kindling you have just prepared; brace the forked branch by angling another branch or two into the yoke of the fork itself. Add branches on all sides, forming a *teepee* around the kindling and newspaper. Use small branches initially, then add a circle of larger logs, as your teepee will support.

Now, light the kindling inside the base of the teepee in three or four places and you'll have a nice fire almost immediately, soon producing ample good coals for cooking or barbecuing. You may continue to stack wood in the teepee formation, or choose to knock down the teepee to place a grill over the coals for barbecuing. The grill may be supported by placing rocks under each of its corners, or in any manner that renders it sturdy enough to support your food. You can reconstruct the teepee later by removing the grill after you've done your cooking.

The teepee formation is best for the evening campfire and marshmallow roast. A teepee fire is uniquely elegant. It is particularly nice to stare at; its embers are affected by the slightest breeze and give a most radiant performance with their varied intensities. The teepee fire also displays exquisite shadow formations on the surrounding terrain. Most important, it is adequately warm and eminently inviting —a truly *Native American* campfire. I can now also inform you at my age that a good campfire is better than anything.[4]

We placed some foil-wrapped meat and potatoes into that fire, but the altitude somewhat hindered our cooking efforts. It took nearly two hours on what remaining coals we had just to boil water for coffee. Nevertheless, we ate what we could for nourishment and we did sleep well that night, having a little alcohol to relax us. We rolled out of our sleeping bags at O-dark-thirty the next morning (before sunrise; just after 0530 hours), eager to begin the final ascent of that granite wonder.

We left the majority of our gear at Mirror Lake and set out with just our individual canteens and snack packs, which made the rough ascent of high-stepped terrain above the lake less burdensome. Just above and a little beyond that difficult ascent, the trail offered a superb view of the Owens Valley and the town of Lone Pine far below. We took our first break of the day at that vista, taking some time to appreciate its magnificent panorama. You can yourself experience that view from the photograph at chapter 8.

A short time later we hiked through Trailside Meadow (11,395 ft.), then continued on to Trail Camp at 12,039 feet, where we passed by a few other trail hikers. Some were gearing up to go back down, and a couple brave-hearts were headed up. Whitney wasn't crowded in those days like it is now. There were only about two hundred folk's a year who reached the summit. Nowadays there are about two hundred fifty a day who make the attempt, and that number just from July through October of each year.

We reached Consultation Lake within the Trail Camp area at about 10 am, and then began an arduous ascent of the ninety-six switchbacks that wind up to Trail Crest, at about 13, 777 feet. It's a steep climb up those switchbacks—no bowl of cherries. Along the way the trail was iced up. We stopped to help some folk's who were struggling to get back down and managed to pull them safely across the ice.

We crawled about fifty feet ourselves on hands and knees to make it through that somewhat dangerous area, which itself boasted of a sheer drop off just to the east. You can't cheat a mountain—you have to pay attention to it at all times. A mountain's got its own way. The arduous trek up the switchbacks and over the Crest put us on the backside of Whitney, where we journeyed along a hair-raisingly narrow portion of the John Muir Trail before reaching the Whitney Summit Trail.

The Summit Trail proceeds up from the John Muir and begins the final two-mile ascent to the summit. We were almost there! The trail winds among great boulders until it passes along the west side (backside) of the Needles, which bold, rugged pinnacles are a breathtaking sight from the Owens Valley far below and to their east. As we began to tire in the thin air, our group, grade by grade became separated, each of us continuing upward at our own pace atop loose shale and rocky terrain.

Stopping to rest and catch my breath for just a brief moment, within every three to five minutes of wearisome, onward plodding; for nearly an hour from the John Muir junction, I became the first of that group to reach the summit block. Tim Murray arrived forty-five minutes later. Ron Bailey, Burton Bernstein and Chuck Poe joined us within the hour. Tim and I had waited on the others to arrive before making the final assault. We then moved along together atop the summit ridge, eventually standing proudly, yet with great exhaustion, over a geologic benchmark that had been erected in 1909.

The elevation read: '14,496.811 feet; highest point in the contiguous United States.' It was after 2 pm. on a sunny day, the sky a deep blue and cloudless. The temperature was at about seven degrees on top—just a bit chilly. There was some gusty wind up there as well and we had to keep our faces covered. Fortunately we each carried a cowboy bandanna, thanks to the packing expertise of Ron Bailey. Packing for any extended hike is both a trial and error, live and learn adventure. Ron Bailey (ol' Jed), a man with a variety of wilderness experiences, was well aware of those things that one cannot do without.

None of us said too much in the way of appreciation when we looked, for 360 degrees, over the summit's edge toward the distant peaks and valleys both near and far below us. It was more of a, 'we did it, we're tired, let's go back down before dark,' type of thing. None of us took the time to acknowledge God—to thank Him for creating that magnificent, lofty view we had encountered. We didn't thank Him for the life nor the health He had allowed us, that we might experience such a wonder, nor did we ponder the many sacred steps upon His granite rock, which we had taken to get up there.

To each of us, at that time, God was somewhere in a building labeled, 'church'—that place where many believers go on Sundays to hear the words (from the Bible) of the One who formed them. They don't necessarily hear God's words, as some preachers are inclined to promote their own philosophies, yet most folk's continue to attend the services anyway.

However, most people who attend church services, on any given Sunday, feel free to indulge in their own personal lifestyle, with all of its godless pleasures, during the other six days of the week. We become our own individual gods during those six days—in spite of the good intentions by many, *only* a few live to honor God in spirit and in truth at all times. We were our own individual gods on the top of the mountain that particular day.

After we honored ourselves for the climb, we started the journey back down the trail. We reached our camp at Mirror Lake just after dusk. We slept well that night—we were pretty much played out. The next morning we packed up and hiked back down to our vehicles and left the mountain.

I remember looking back at this granite wonder as we increased our distance from its base. I did not know that in twenty-eight years I would climb all the way to its summit once again. Life would change —wisdom would increase and I would come to understand that Mt. Whitney is one of the *true monuments*. Whitney is one of several true monuments I will talk more about later on in this writing.

From the standpoint of human definition, according to Webster, monuments are works of art and/or scholarship, etc, regarded as having great significance or enduring value to us. Most folk's then don't consider Mt. Whitney to be a monument (it's not man-made), nor do they consider any of the other creations of God that I will talk about to be monuments.

In reality, there are three types of monuments in our world—true monuments, monuments of men, and personal monuments. The second and third types of monuments are usually found along the road of *pride and ignorance*—a road that every human being, save one, has traveled. Many have traveled quite some distance further on that road than others. Yet, it is a common road, whether traveling just a short distance or surviving a lengthy one.

At various points along its descending route are exit signs, labeled, *understanding*—get off here, fool! Exiting the road of pride and ignorance at any of these points, in order to proceed upward on the road of understanding, is of course a matter of choice. *Personal monuments* are more responsible for keeping us on that road of pride and ignorance than are the monuments of men. *Monuments of men* are actually created through the continued pursuit of personal monuments. Let's take a look at each of these that you might understand their formation and individual significance.

Personal monuments are as follows: our attitudes, our families, our homes, our jobs, our friends, our activities, our trucks, our cars, our boats, our recreational vehicles, our hobbies and all that sort of stuff. What occupies *your* thoughts? Where are *your* morals? Are *your* attitudes God-centered? What family member or friend controls *your* thoughts and life? What earthly possession do *you* have that *you* honor the most? What thing do *you* do in life at which *you* spend the most time? What are *your* short-term and long-term goals? Are *you* a planner? If so, how far ahead do *you* plan and what do *you* count on?

How do *you* feel about *your* neighborhood, *your* social status, *your* power, *your* position or *your* authority? What about *your* self-confidence—or self-esteem, as the psychologists call it? Do *you* consider *yourself* to be sovereign—number one and/or above others? Are *you* one who refuses to move or even budge from *your* purposes? How do *you* feel about *your* appearance or *your* health—*your* handsomeness or beauty, personality, energy or fitness? What about *your* losses, *your* pain, *your* sorrows?

So, what's wrong with any of the above—or all of the above? *Anything* can become a personal monument. The Bible teaches: *For where your treasure is, there will your heart be also* (Matthew 6:21 NASB). Yet, most of us fail to realize when something or someone becomes a monument, or is or has been a monument.

Since people or things or conditions all around us appear to be 'normal' in this present world, it is our nature to fail at recognizing that the *attitudes* we have formed concerning those people, things or conditions, can be subtly detrimental to the correct forming and maintaining of the more just attitude of heart within us that is desired by the One who formed us.

What about music? Do *you* listen to music? It can also have an influence on our lives. Music can create various moods within us. It can be a good influence or a bad influence, depending on how it is dealt with. People who sing songs or listen to songs can actually become a part of them. The rock fan many times gets involved with the drug culture. The country music fan can buy a pick-up truck, leave home, cheat on his wife, beat on his dog, start a fight in the tavern, or fall off the bar stool from intoxication.

Music in a play or in motion pictures serves to involve us in the story. It can cause us to get angry, to hate, to fight and to even want to go to war. It can make us proud and arrogant. But, it can also give us courage and strength. When the going gets tough it can seemingly make you tough enough to get going. Music can motivate us to climb mountains, to pursue adventure or do something difficult that we may not normally attempt to do. Music can affect our emotions in a number of ways.

Music can inspire us to fall in love—the downside of this is that we can fall in love with someone whom we don't even know. Music can give us a false assessment of one's appearance or character. Our imaginations can run wild and become out of control through the motivation of music. Music can also overwhelm us with loneliness, sadness and despair, and in some of these instances has driven people to the very edge and even over the cliff of suicide.

However, sad music properly dealt with is good, causing us to examine our actions and ourselves, inspiring and motivating us to turn away from past behaviors or things not in our best interest. It can motivate us to do good for others—to offer kindness and gentleness in place of bitterness. Music can also be medicinal—ease our physical or mental pain, teach us to forgive, or inspire us to turn failure into success or despair into joy. The bottom line however is that music in any form should ultimately result in our honoring God and His creation, in one way or another.

Remember that we live in a world both dominated and ruled by evil (Ephesians 2:2,3), and since we fail to understand the great depth of that evil, we may indeed be asleep—blind to the cunningness of the evil rulers in this dark world. We need to wake up and open our eyes to the reality that there is great *spiritual* warfare going on—all around us and within us. It can have a profound affect on our attitudes. We must be transformed by the renewing of our minds (Romans 12:2), and learn to give God, our creator, an absolute first place in our hearts.

We need to exit that road of monumental pride and ignorance through changes in attitude, and proceed both boldly and patiently upward on the road of *understanding*. It is there where we can allow our senses to be trained in discerning good from evil, so that we may become more familiar with the unique artwork and enduring value of the *true* monuments—God, His word, and His creation. These true monuments should become our personal monuments. They should be allowed to consume our thoughts and continually influence our actions.

Monuments of men are those things erected by men that give glory to mankind and their accomplishments, in one way or another. One of the largest in the United States is Mt. Rushmore, in South Dakota.

Another is the Great Wall of China. The tallest buildings of the world are also among the monuments of men. South America is full of the ancient ruins of monuments erected to men, as are the sands of Egypt, with its great pyramids. Italy contains the distinguished ruins of the Greek and Roman cultures. Monuments of men fill the entire earth, from country to country and even from city to city.

Mankind has continued to erect monuments of a myriad of sizes and shapes for thousands of years. They are everywhere in the world, a part of every culture of the world. These things are not good or bad in and of themselves. What is *not* good is that when the works of mankind dominate the land, then the works of God and the truths concerning Him are not retained in their knowledge. They begin to pursue things that are earthly, sensual, devilish, and not at all in their best interest. God and His monuments are forgotten.

Because of this the hearts of men and women are thrust into darkness, separating them from the God who formed them. This separation caused the destruction of the old world by the Great Flood. Separation from God is also why this present earth has been reserved for fire by the word of God, being kept for the Day of Judgment and destruction of ungodly men and women (2nd Peter 3:6,7). We need to stay alert to the fact that this promise *will be fulfilled*.

Everything we've built in the physical realm will be destroyed— ashes in the wind. Personal, earthly monuments and the monuments of men are therefore unimportant. Giving God first place in one's heart is extremely important, and a monumental accomplishment of a different nature. Recognizing that He does not have first place is the very first step—a big first step.

We are so accustomed to the world we live in that it becomes difficult to make the mental changes required to first of all recognize that we need to make a change. We can scarcely even fathom that the 'normal' things I mentioned in the preceding paragraphs *can* become our personal monuments. But they do and they will continue to be, if God is not placed in the foreground of the picture.

I grew up in an era when most of this country's population attended a church of one faith or another. Again, for the majority, there was a lack of faithfulness after hours. They still yelled and screamed at one another, they still got drunk, they still remarked grossly about other races, they still argued about sports, mouthed off to officials and booed at the athletes. They were still rude in the grocery line, they still honked with impatience in traffic, they still let their dog do his business in the neighbors yard, they still built fences to isolate themselves, and they still cheated on their income tax.

Moreover, they still, within their families, harbored resentment and ill feelings toward one another and toward outsiders. They still committed adultery. They still lied, defrauded and stole from one another or destroyed one another's property. They argued, fought, maimed and killed. They did what they felt was right in their own eyes. (Judges 21:25)

No, God did not have first place in their individual lives These are just a few examples of the results of *attitudes* built on the foundation of personal monuments. We construct them from within on a daily basis, never realizing what we are building, and then we attend a church, cathedral, synagogue, mosque, temple or tent of meeting, and act as if nothing's wrong? What hypocrites we are!

We all fail in many ways (James 3:2). We are totally rotten within, as was pointed out in chapter 1. The tongue spews prime examples of the rottenness that proceeds from within—such a small part of the human body, yet no one can tame it. This very small member of the body is examined and described as follows:

It is a restless evil, full of deadly poison. With it we praise our Lord and Father, and with it we curse men, who have been made in the likeness of God. From the same mouth come both blessing and cursing. My brethren, these things ought not to be this way. Does a fountain send out from the same opening both fresh and bitter water? Can a fig tree, my brethren , produce olives, or a vine produce figs? Neither can salt water produce fresh (James 3:8-12 NASB).

The human tongue, though quite powerful and unable to be governed, is only *one* example in *hundreds* of ways that we are prone to failure. Our throats are an open grave, the poison of asps is under our lips, and with our tongues we keep on deceiving (Romans 3:13). How can we dare say that we have God in first place? As I mentioned earlier, one needs first of all to accomplish that *monumental task* of realizing that God is *not* in first place.

Don't get frustrated here—you are still going to make many mistakes in life, even after you have put Him in first place. Thinking about Him all the time should be your initial goal, for by nature and habit we are prone to pay attention to the wrong things—prone to build our own monuments through the corruption that is within us.

Learning to think about God all the time will get you spiritually oriented atop the right hill as you hike on toward the mountain of putting Him into first place. It is a high and difficult mountain, and you will encounter a diversity of setbacks along your journey. Yet, as you hike upward, personal monuments can be either put in their proper places or destroyed, depending on their value as it benefits your personal relationship with God, and/or benefits your dealing with other humans, who are made in the image of God.

This divine consideration needs to become a habit, for the natural heart is deceitful above all things and incurably sick (Jeremiah 17:9). Along the route of thinking about Him you need to learn that the Bible itself is our *only* written revelation from God (you'll learn how we got our modern day Bible in chapter 14). It is the spiritual map and compass that keeps us oriented upon the trail of truth—His truth, which is the only *absolute* truth. It may take some time for you to learn to accept this most important concept—that He *is* the absolute truth.

Nevertheless, He is—this acceptance will enlarge as you study and apply the Bible's life-giving teachings to your own life. Actually, you may find that particular task not as difficult as one might consider it to be. You will continue to be enlightened when you have a better understanding of His creation, which is the purpose of *this* particular writing; *Hiking the Trail of Truth*.

This writing is likened to a map and a compass, and was created with that concept in mind. An illuminating journey has been mapped out for you through the latter chapters here (9 through 12), and you can truly begin to both see and know (understand) God through the things He has made—see the supernatural through the natural.

When you reach the final three chapters on this hike (13 through 15), the compass will guide you among outcrops of solid granite—profound Biblical discoveries rarely encountered by hikers seeking enlightenment. This compass will also direct you to the map that can lead to your understanding the mysteries surrounding the knowledge of salvation. You are without a doubt hiking toward a truly monumental summit—*the Mountain of Believing*—well worth your continued effort.

*

Within that group of Whitney climbers in 1970, I went on to become a chief of sinners, ranking up there with the Apostle Paul, although I 'feel' that I was much worse, even though he claimed to be

91

the greatest sinner of sinners. I should have just jumped off the mountain back then and saved others a lot of trouble. I eventually lost everything I previously mentioned that I had, including my family. During my lifetime I have broken all of the Ten Commandments. I believe I was unlike Paul in that respect.

I know that he was partly responsible for the death of many Christians, but I am not convinced that he broke all of the Ten Commandments, for an entire record of his life is not available. He may have. God however was indeed merciful to him, and to me—both sinners—like all of mankind, unworthy of any type of pardon or reconciliation.

Yet, God seeks many of us out, finds us, and then uses us in a variety of ways for His good purposes. I'm no Paul and neither are you —we never will be. He was an astounding teacher! There's been no one exactly like him since. But, though we're all unworthy, God can use us, as He did Paul, in special ways and for specific purposes (even tiny little ones) that ultimately glorify Him. Our like-mindedness with Christ is then established, as was Paul's.

The Lord has allowed me over the years, through various afflictions and illuminating experiences, to lie face down in the dust of the earth, and to rub my face deeply into it in grievous remorse. He has also, through time, lifted me up from the dust and mire, extending to me the grace that has allowed me to come to know much about Him through the things He has made. I have had many adventures in discovery through His generosity! You can too, if you are willing. You can learn also to speak only the truth, for he/she who speaks the truth, speaks what is right (Proverbs 12:17).

When I evaluate the 'action' of the many Hebrew and Greek words that describe the character of God, I find that, in summation, the English word, *generosity,* is about the most fitting translation there is. He is indeed generous to have allowed little ol' me to live long enough to share my discoveries with you. It is a *great* honor.

Naturally I am still human, just like you are. My human nature has not changed, however, my *position* has. Under His grace I have been allowed understanding that has served to open my eyes and my ears to a profound reality. It is my desire, through Him, to share with you these things, to allow you to see them with your own eyes and to hear them with your own ears.

I am a nobody. I am merely a voice, crying (or writing) from the wilderness. There are others out there and have been others from the very foundation of the world, who have proclaimed God's truth with the utmost sincerity. Yet, in truth, we cannot influence you; only God can do that. He is the one who, through truth and His Spirit, operates on your heart—they are *His* words and *His* creation.

He is the one who skims away the dross and refines you over time, as choice silver is refined. He is the one who can build your faith in a truly *monumental* fashion. Continue this hike with me, and you'll see...

Chapter Six...My Pursuit of the Hawk, Part 3
The Fall

In December of 1970, my father and my stepmother, Florence, came to California from Ohio to visit Jenny and I and our two sons. My father had never before seen his grandchildren. I had talked to him once or twice after we arrived in the West, but prior to that I hadn't talked with him in length since before I went into the Army, back in 1963. I had finally contacted him from California in mid '70 at Jenny's request.

When he learned of my military accomplishments and found out that I was now a city police officer, well respected in the county, he decided to spend Christmas with us that year. They flew out a couple weeks before the Holiday and we met them at the L.A. Airport. It was great to see them, and the enthusiasm expressed through their words and actions was no small amount. We brought them to the house, where they were even more thrilled. I don't recall ever seeing my dad that happy. He took to his grandchildren right away, capturing their attention in the way that grandparents do.

We got along extremely well during his stay. He regularly expressed deep admiration for Jenny and the boys. He wanted to buy us a useful gift for the holidays, so he purchased a new washer and dryer at Sears and had it delivered to our residence. It was indeed kind of him to do that.

We went to Disneyland while he was there, and I gave him a special tour of the police department and the city where I worked. He was most impressed, and I was certainly humbled by his attitude. It was indeed a good Christmas, rating up there with the previous Christmas, when we visited Jenny's folk's. Both Christmas seasons were indeed the best I'd had in a long time.

Dad and Florence left just after the New Year, and I would think of them often. There were some changes in the police department's pay structure at that time, which all of the employees seemed more than a little upset about. I used that as an excuse in pondering the impulsive idea that I would rather be back east, working construction, and within a couple months put it firmly in my mind that I actually wanted to move back to Ohio.

In fact, I had my mind made up even before I discussed the idea with Jenny. It was really a stupid decision, but there are times when we close our eyes to considering what's best, build an impenetrable wall, and then allow our emotions and/or daydreams to rule over us. I thought I wanted a normal job with normal hours. I wanted to live along the old river. I wanted to experience all four seasons and remember Christmas as it was in my early youth.

I wanted to visit my mother's resting place more often—to sit near her and tell her how difficult life's journey has been without her. I wanted to be closer to my father. I wanted to spend more time with Jenny's family. These are normal thoughts for most anyone who lives far from the nest, but instead of putting these things into their proper place and looking toward the future, I dwelt on the past, blindly imagining that things could be better.

The grass would not really be any greener in Ohio. For one thing the winters are long and brutal and the job market has always been depressed. Things only seemed like they would be better back there because more than my innocence had been lost in California. My off-duty activities had at times taken me into topless bars and occasionally into strange bedrooms.

My impulsive, live-for-me lifestyle blinded me to any clear understanding of or focus on what should have been done—what actually needed to be done, to both preserve and strengthen the here and now. That urge to run had taken over—it's always easier to turn and run than to stay the course and kick against the goads.

Jenny and I had a wonderful start in life. We had built a foundation for our future with our own hands. The American Dream was indeed ours; we lived in southern California amidst a diversity of landscapes and physical beauty, I had a very meaningful and responsible job, we both had good friends who depended upon us, and our children had well above average opportunities.

But, once again I considered only Mark and what he thought he wanted. God and my family were not really included in that picture. This was of course unintentional ignorance, for I knew nothing of true contentment—had no knowledge of the attitudes required to form it. I was too busy living three lives—the good, the bad and the ugly.

God's many blessings eluded me—forgetfulness of God is our nature; I considered neither the stability nor the early retirement that the police department offered. I considered not the truly unmatched diversity of the Western landscape. Most destructive was the fact that I considered not the daily and hourly needs of my family, both presently and for the future.

I didn't even know my family! I was just a man who lived from one anxious moment to another. I was truly wallowing in the mire of iniquity. A great light could have shined upon me and I would not have seen it. Yet, how could I not stop and consider what I saw from atop Mt. Whitney? The truth is I saw nothing from up there at that time—I made no connection with God.

I did not see the supernatural through the natural. I missed that profound spiritual light, seeing Whitney only as a great hiking experience. Yet, it appears that I wasn't even thinking about that! I was a fool, and in my foolishness, Jenny's decision to move to California and have a good family life was about to be thwarted. It was late March of 1971 and I was about to shatter *all* of her plans, hopes and dreams. Her tenderly constructed, delicately woven California dream would be torn asunder—plowed over and buried by my own bulldozer attitude.

I later felt that God should have killed me right then and there—should have struck me by lightning at the foot of my driveway, and just for good measure, allowed me to fall headlong into the street and get run over by the mail truck. I would have been express-mailed to where I belonged—in hell. Should that have happened, Jenny would most certainly still be in California, and my sons surely would have had better opportunity in life. I took those blessings away from them. The Apache Indian story rings true: *a man cannot protect his family from himself.*

I don't know if Jenny entertained thoughts of grabbing my gun and shooting me at that time—when I announced to her my selfish plans, when I spit on her dreams and resigned from the police department, when I put the house up for sale, or for all the horrific, personal anguish I put her through those last few months, causing the putrefaction of her dreams—but she should have. I would have shot me at close range and then dumped me out in the Mojave Desert. I would have told people, "He just wandered off—chasin' that damn hawk."

I broke her heart—pierced it with the arrow of my indifference and then crushed it into powder and ground it underfoot—into the dirt. It's like I murdered her—took away her life through my selfish words and actions. Indeed, I had broken all of God's laws. When I look back and consider how difficult it must have been for her to find healing somewhere in all that mess, I am unable to bear the remorse.

Yet, would you believe that her devotion to me was too strong to allow those events to destroy our marriage? She never fought or argued with me about any of those things during that very difficult period of time for her, in which we made all the preparations involved in moving away from our home. She would just say, plainly and calmly, while struggling to hold back the tears, "I really don't want to go back east, Mark."

During the first few months in Ohio she would encourage on occasion, "Mark, let's go back to California." Why didn't I listen? Why didn't I hear? We were nearly a whole year in Ohio before I even found a job! That's called, among other things, being stubborn—doing things your own way no matter what—traveling that monumental road of pride and ignorance, and lastly, plunging a knife into the heart of your best friend. That I am ashamed of who I was in those days would be quite an understatement.

It has been and is indeed difficult to tell this story, but it needs to be told—that hawk was still flyin'. Besides, all of this might help *you*, dear reader, in getting yourself together. Don't quit now—hang tough —there's much more to learn. It's good to dig up old bones. Through the resurrection of your memories dead and gone it becomes extremely evident that God has been indeed patient—unfathomably patient with you over the years. The skeletons are proof!

I ask you now in the presence of your skeletons, are you seeing perhaps for the first time His generosity—His patience? Think about it. In fact, stand in front of a mirror and think about—there is no way that anyone can actually like what they see, yet God continues His patience with us, waiting for us to admit how much we need Him.

In June of 1971 our little family moved back across the country to the Akron, Ohio area, the place of my youth. Our California friends, especially the Lesniaks, were devastated. Their son, Ken (remember Ken?), moved back to Ohio with us, where his natural mother resided with his stepfather. Ken had also been a member of the police department, joining up about a year after I did. He had married a gal from California (Sheri), and the two of them decided that they wanted to seek a future in Ohio as well.

They chose to leave California at the very same time, and we ended up traveling together. Ironic, isn't it—two high school buddies walking away from the same job and both heading back to their roots at the same time? Trouble is, neither of us had actually realized that high school was over and we had moved on. Things in Ohio would never be the same as they were in the days of our youth.

Jenny didn't say much on the trip back, nor was she rude or vengeful when she did speak. I on the other hand was in good spirits— spirits of deceit, and somewhat arrogant about the whole thing. Like I said earlier, I guess I supposed I would find something back in Ohio that I had been missing in California. Wrong. We *always* look outside to solve the problems on the inside. We always look somewhere other than where we should. We keep on relentlessly pursuing that hawk, never stopping long enough to consider how and why he flies.

A Navajo Indian whom I once shared a campfire with in a remote part of the Arizona desert wisely said to me, *a man whose spirit continues to wander is unsettled in his heart. He does not make himself a happy man.* That trail experience was in the fall of 1999. In 1971 I did not at that time have this yet-to-come enduring wisdom within my heart.

After one difficult year of unemployment in Ohio (my father footing most of the bills) I finally managed to land a job. My father had arranged for me to meet the head of security at the Goodyear Tire and Rubber Company. I was encouraged, but that emotion did not last for very long. They hired me shortly after my interview and I worked a graveyard position, walking a beat in a very large factory complex.

I lasted about three weeks. It was so boring, compared to live police work, that I just couldn't cut it. I had no desire to cut it. But, I couldn't land an Ohio law enforcement job—those tightly knit, good ol' boys were prejudice against (jealous of) California cops, and still are to this day. People from various parts of the country have their own way of looking at anything and everything except themselves, in most all matters. That is indeed sad. Only when one looks to God for wisdom are these typical barriers removed.

On the other hand, it was just not meant to be for me to return to law enforcement at that time. God would instead take away a few blessings (that I from a human standpoint would consider blessings) and allow the consequences of my sins to become my teachers for many years to come. From that point on I worked a variety of laborious jobs and never found personal satisfaction.

I was lost. I seemed to be just existing, with no worthy goals of any kind. Being irresponsible, I didn't think like a family man. I never looked directly into the eye of that particular accountability. I didn't know how. I had no experience—I had been literally on my own from the age of fourteen. You can't paint a portrait without a model, and I didn't even have any paints.

Shortly after we had arrived in Ohio, two different police departments in California had contacted me, asking me to move back there and go to work for them. I declined at that time, in spite of Jenny's encouragement to do otherwise. That's blind pride for you— bypassing the exit to understanding on the road of pride and ignorance —forgetting and ignoring God.

However, my friend, Ken, took a P.D. job offered to him and He and his wife returned to California after just three months in Ohio! They have been there ever since—they're no longer married, but are still in the West where they have raised two fine children, a girl and a boy, who are now both successful adults.

Mark Taylor was not nearly as wise as his buddy, yet we have both reaped as we have sown. We've each run in vain, yet we each bear different burdens. Everyone under the sun bears burdens of one kind or another and we all run in vain. The effect of sin within the human is much like the effect of alcohol or drugs or tobacco in the blood stream.

It takes one captive, so much so that you become incapable of doing right!

The Apostle Paul said it well to the Roman Christians: *No matter which way I turn, I can't make myself do right…when I try not to do wrong, I do it anyway* (Romans 7:18,19 NLT).

We also find ourselves doing things that we do not *understand* (Romans 7:15). That dilemma defines the heart, for *who can know it?* (Jeremiah 17:9) We indeed become prisoners of the sin that is within us. Yet, this is all due to a simple lack of spiritual knowledge on our part—from not knowing who we truly are. Knowing who we are then, from the very days of our youth, becomes the most important endeavor that we could *ever* undertake. If you don't know who you truly are; spiritually, even if you *think* you know, you need to return to chapter 1 and read it again—soak it up.

On the other hand, whatever I did in the physical realm I did well —dotting every 'i' and crossing every 't' so to speak. Through the grace of God I had a variety of skills with an eye for detail, yet had no true understanding regarding my need to develop spiritually. I did not at that time comprehend the depth of my spiritual failures. I had not cultivated up any self-control in the garden of my attitudes. My mind (soul and spirit) and my body were always on the move within the realm of the material world, and so I went nowhere except deeper into sin—toward a total decaying of spirit. I saw no stop signs on my highway. If they were there I blew through them.

By late 1972 I was working as a production line supervisor for American Safety Corporation in the city of Medina. About ninety percent of the people I supervised there were women. My decaying spirit began to succumb to the temptations of my work environment. I flirted, I boasted, and I acted like I was really somebody important. We want to be important in the world, though it's truly not necessary, so we allow pride to lift us up only to be struck down. I was a man about to take a plunge that God labels, 'a fool in his folly' (Proverbs 13:16).

The evil deeds of a wicked man ensnare him; the cords of his sin hold him fast. King Solomon also wrote: *A man who commits adultery lacks judgment; whoever does so destroys himself* (Proverbs 5:22 & 6:32 NIV).

At American Safety I began an affair with a married woman. It was purely the flight of a deceitful imagination—a sexual attraction.

This woman in no way, at that time, could compare in character with my wife. Yet, sin deceived me—it blinded me and therefore it slew me. I fell headlong, down beyond the roots of the mountains, into the great depths of sin, awash in its murky waters (Jonah 2:6).

Within a year, in spite of Jenny's tearful pleas, the result was a divorce. She said something to me at that time that I will *never* forget: "Mark, you need God." She was right—I was oblivious of what I had done to our little family. Have you ever done something terribly wrong and later wondered how and why you ever did it? Was it to the point of being *unbelievable* that you could ever, ever do such a thing?

You have previously witnessed in this chapter that sin can cause you to do unbelievable things. It robs you of natural affection and fills you with unrelenting iniquity. It literally consumes you. If you do not turn and run from it, it will eventually destroy your life. The consequence of sin is death—which can come at any moment. Yet, we run with it, perhaps deceived into thinking that our sin will have some wholesome result.

The only result is that there's not a day that the sins of my youth are not before me. You start out with one shovel full when you break ground in sin, but you end up in a hole that only a bulldozer could excavate. I would continue to have a mouthful of sand for the next fifteen years—the gritty stuff that you just can't get out of your teeth. I was indeed at the roots of the mountains where the earth had imprisoned me like the dead.

Jenny and the boys later moved away, back to her southern Ohio hometown of Marietta. The woman with whom I committed adultery eventually divorced her husband. She had two children by him. We later married and had two children of our own—my son, Marc, and my daughter, Carrie. I eventually found myself in a most difficult situation —trying to support two families. It didn't take long for the eight-legged consequences of my choice of lifestyle to spin their webs.

I had visitation rights with Mike and Mitch, but my second wife was exceedingly jealous of these children from my first marriage. I did the best I could to cope with her attitudes, but there seemed to be an impenetrable wall of resistance there, which eventually drove me into such remorse and bitterness that I decided to get out of that relationship—to live alone. I knew how to run—so I ran and kept on running. Unfortunately we cannot run away from ourselves—from who we are.

Children of divorced parents and the parents themselves know the strife connected with divorce and re-marriage—it fills volumes upon volumes of self-help books. It is no wonder that God's law of marriage is for one man and one woman—until death. Divorce is worse than death. It is a living death, especially where children are involved. Broken marriages are like an empty well that holds no water—like a spring in a parched land that produces only salt water or bitter water.

Yet, we marry and divorce according to our own will—we do what we feel is right in our own eyes, never considering what the will of our Creator is—in any matter (Judges 21:25). Jenny and I almost got back together while I was on my own again, but my continued promiscuity got the best of me. I was still the fool in his folly; who continued to pursue his natural passions.

Within the next several years I lived somewhat unrestrained and married two more times for romance and companionship, but had no children. Both relationships were short-lived. An American Indian said, *'You search in vain for what you cannot find. But, you've found instead a thousand ways of runnin' down your time.'* The Indian didn't scream it, he said it in a song—and he's never been known to be wrong.

During those marriages, from late 1973 through about 1981, things on the work front were rather steady. The B.F. Goodrich Company of Akron, Ohio was my primary employer. I worked in various departments there, which included some time as a dockworker, as an assembly line worker, and eventually was assigned to a security position. However, Goodrich was forced to lay me off in the early 80's, when the U.S. economy and its major industries were experiencing a recession.

During those BFG years I visited my children regularly, no matter where I was or what I was doing—God's undeserved grace upon me. Sometimes I had all four of the kids together, but on many occasions just two at a time from each family, alternating Saturdays and Sundays. The periods of separation between us were indeed difficult times, but each of my children always appreciated his/her time with me, and those were always the *best* of times.

We had many, many adventures together—did a lot of exploring in the wilderness areas of Ohio, Kentucky and West Virginia. A neighbor once remarked to me, "You spend more time with your kids than most full-time fathers do." I thought the man might be an angel (*messenger*), for his words were a great comfort to me and gave birth to tears of thankfulness the day he uttered them.

—Regarding the two marriages during those years, my third wife lived a life of her own, so that didn't last very long—she was into the drug culture. I have been fortunate not to have ever had to personally deal with that particular 'thorn' in the flesh. All humans bear a thorn(s) of one kind or another, which kinds are as variable as fingerprints. These thorns are usually the forces that keep us from doing our best.

They are Satan's ministers—hindrances, weaknesses or oppositions, which war against us (2nd Corinthians 12:7). God sometimes allows them to remain, in order to keep us from exalting ourselves above measure or above others, which compels us to acknowledge that it is only by His grace that His purposes are attained in a fallen world.

My fourth wife was many years younger than I, and she loved all my children, who were growing up fast. She was very close to Marc and Carrie, as they lived nearby and were able to visit more often than Mike and Mitch. I got along with her fine, however, my inability to live beyond my past got the best of me—it always did. Life had not turned out the way I had expected, and it was most difficult to endure the mounting consequences of the fall. Add to that, my proneness to wander—to drift. I was torn asunder at heart all those years and unable to, on my own, repair the damage.

I wanted to go back and make things right with Jenny, but I never did. For one thing, she had remarried, but that really made no difference in the emotions surrounding my heart. My mindset was that I could undo everything that I had done wrong. Yet, even if I could have reunited with her in those days, it probably would have failed because, again, I did not know who I was—a guilty sinner, overthrown by iniquity, wallowing in the mire of his own brokenness.

Yet, one's brokenness can serve to build *humility*—the greatest blessing of brokenness (Dr. Charles Stanley has written a book on the *Blessings of Brokenness*—a great reading). But, I had also broken God's heart, and that's truly what I failed to see. You can't build *true* humility when you fail to comprehend the *depth* of your need for it; our personal choices in life continue to bruise us, but never break us. Only God can break us.

We are wild by nature—each of us a bucking bronco that *only God can break,* and He chooses His own method(s) to break us and does it in His own time—according to *His* schedule. So, when the time comes for your life to take a turn or changes for the better, it has nothing to do with any efforts on your part. Only God can turn us about or change something in our lives for the better.

Only God can break us from sin. Within ourselves we are incapable of change for the better, and unable to stop sinning. If you think you can change/stop sinning, then you truly do not know who you are. You'll never change in this life. You'll always be a sinner—your *nature* does not change. That's why you need a Savior. So don't brag or give yourself any credit for any change that takes place in your life.

Goodness (change for the better) is produced *only* when God is allowed to work through you, and any desire in your heart to make a change originates from Him. Without Him you can do nothing (John 15:5). This is something that God endeavors to teach you throughout your lifetime. However, we push God away, in one way or another, thinking that we know better—assuming that *we* are in control.

The outcome of this thinking results in nothing but hard times because we don't allow Him to do His work. Hard times are therefore most often the result of living without God. Yet, hard times can be times of great spiritual learning. Hard times can be times that cause one to actually make an attempt to seek out *some* type of God.

He allows your hard times for that very purpose. He is the author of your attempts to seek Him. It is during these times that the one, true God can do tiny little things that make you feel like you've found a fresh cup of cold water, right in the middle of that parched desert you've been wandering around in.

So that we *can* find God, He reaches out to us—the worst of sinners—at the strangest of times, drawing us toward His Son (John 6:44). He seeks us, whether we want Him to or not. That's what He does for a living—for our living. He seeks out His wandering sheep and returns them to the fold. He also seeks out new sheep from a variety of pastures, to teach them His ways and bring them toward eternal salvation.

I had worked at various jobs and lived by the seat of my pants during those fifteen years back in Ohio, yet I was able to attend college at night, thanks to the veteran's G.I. Bill. During those years I also began an intense study of the Bible—it was late 1976. A traveling evangelist, who taught me to bring the Scriptures to life, like a play that I was a part of, tutored me for some time. Dan Campbell was quite learned for one who had been a freedom-seeking biker for most of his life, and many of the local churches sought him for his teaching abilities.

Mr. Campbell is currently the Regional Director of Advancement for Harding University, in Searcy Arkansas. As a result of his personal encouragement in my life (we became the closest of friends), I studied the history of the Bible and the cultures of the times represented within, that I might better understand the book by seeing things through becoming, in an analytical manor, a living part of them.

This came rather easy for me, as I always liked being somewhere other than where I was and someone other than who I was. Yet, I began to learn much about *who* I was through the lives of so many Biblical characters, whose failures paralleled and many times exceeded those of my own. I was shocked!

Biblical stories are a hallway of mirrors that reflect who and what we are. It is a book about attitudes, and attitudes never change. That's why the Bible becomes relevant in all generations—that is the way God designed it. Some characters reflect grievously concerning their spiritual condition, which was indeed my own condition:

Oh Lord, do not rebuke me in your anger or discipline me in your wrath. For your arrows have pierced me, and your hand has come down upon me. Because of your wrath there is no health in my body; my bones have no soundness because of my sin. My guilt has overwhelmed me like a burden to heavy to bear. My wounds fester and are loathsome because of my sinful folly.

I am bowed down and brought very low; all day long I go about mourning. My back is filled with searing pain; there is no health in my body. I am feeble and utterly crushed; I groan in anguish of heart ... for troubles without number surround me; my sins have overtaken me, and I cannot see. They are more than the hairs of my head, and my heart fails within me. (Psalm 38:1-8, 40:12 NIV)

My father died in 1980. I hadn't seen him since late 1974. Shortly after Jenny and I were divorced he drifted from me, saying that he had lost respect for me because of my wayward living. I didn't blame him. I visited him a couple times following the divorce, allowing him to spend time with his grandchildren, but he retired from Goodyear after Florence died, then moved to Florida in 1975.

I never heard from him or knew anything about him until his death. He had remarried in Florida and his wife (Lillian) was the one who contacted me about his passing. I was told that his heart failed early one morning as he was rising out of bed. His funeral was held back in a rural area of Akron, Ohio where he was laid to rest.

In 1983 I was allowed an unexpected blessing. My younger children, Marc and Carrie, came to live with me for a time. Their mother was encountering both personal and financial difficulties that year, so she asked me to take care of the children for awhile. I was living in southern Ohio at the time and occupying the lower half of a duplex with a big yard in a small town. Things couldn't be much better for the kids.

I enrolled them in grade school in Marietta, and we had some exceedingly wonderful times together, being involved in both the activities that the school offered, and the recreation programs available through the city. I was able to purchase each of them a new bicycle as well, and so there was adventure galore at all times. They worked hard at their schoolwork too, of which I was very proud.

This special time together along life's trail was indeed an uplifting experience for each of us and we grew quite close. After Christmas that year they reluctantly moved back in with their mother, in northern Ohio. I suppose I could have fought for them in the courts, but that's an old song and dance that just stirs up strife, and everyone involved had already experienced enough hardship.

Their mother was happy that she was able to care for them again, they were happy to see her, and both things were good things. Sure, I didn't want to let go—like hanging onto the edge of a cliff, but, I was indeed fortunate to have had the time with them that I did. God threw me the rope of acceptance, I climbed up and off the cliff's edge, and that was that—I was allowed to hold on to the incredible memories.

Time continued to march on for me, and the winds of change always blew. I found myself working here and there—at this and that and the other—while still attending school. It seemed like night school was a lifetime thing for me. By late 1984 there was literally no work in Ohio. I was 38 years old, four times divorced, with absolutely no prospects.

I had entered the pit of despair, however, I learned to well understand this pit of despair, through researching and examining the despairs of David and Solomon, which they had experienced in the latter part of their own lives. Like many of us, David and Solomon were strange mixtures of both good and evil, though Solomon was much more indulgent in the latter and was influenced by his many foreign wives, who eventually turned his heart away from the Lord.

David had multiple wives—Solomon had 700 wives and 300 concubines. They both dealt with various personal failures, and fatherhood was not one of their better qualities. They encountered numerous problems with their offspring. The writings of David and Solomon (Psalms, Proverbs, Ecclesiastes, Songs) teach us that we are not alone in our actions or our resulting despair—nothing is new under the sun.

Living in sin, which ends in despair, is part of human nature. These writings encourage us and produce hope within us, allowing us to learn to *accept* despair, which in a way conquers it. We all reap what we sow—that's God's law. We just have to deal with our despairs in light of that understanding.

One day I dropped out of school, sold what little I had, put my clothing in a duffle bag, climbed onto the back of a 175 Honda motorcycle (I had no car), and headed out in the month of November for Florida. There was supposed to be all kinds of work down there in the Sunshine State. I had two hundred dollars cash to my name. It was a cold, numbing, one thousand mile, non-stop ride (save for gas and food), and I crossed the border and cruised leisurely on into the city of Orlando during a heavy rain. I slipped once on some sand in the roadway and ended up underneath my motorcycle and duffle bag.

The Lord was however gracious to me, allowing no injuries to befall me, and I found a rooming house in the center of town that very night. I rented a bunk in a large room with five other men, all transients like myself. My share of the rent and kitchen privileges amounted to fifty dollars a week. Everyone pitched in on the cooking. We got along like a pack of coyotes, our den being much safer and more hospitable than the outside world. For six months I lived in that room and worked out of a labor pool. I started at five a.m. and usually worked two shifts at minimum wage, six or seven days a week.

Most of my work consisted of washing dishes in a variety of restaurants at the Walt Disney World. I worked some construction as well. I also spent some time as an apprentice meat cutter in a Winn-Dixie grocery store. There wasn't much else to do but work and I really didn't want to do anything else. I eventually wanted to get out of

Florida—no breathtaking scenery there—but I had to exist for a time and that's exactly what I did. There was a big lake near the house where I resided, and I found time to walk around it daily. I wasn't one to sit around, develop laziness, or feel sorry for myself—thank God.

A man like me makes his own way and has to live with it—there were a lot of folk's like me out there in those days—five others just in my rented room alone. One was a medical doctor, experiencing a love loss. Another was a New York City chef, who could make dirt taste good. The other three were just good ol' boys, on the mend from bad experiences—like most of us, just trying to make our way in a difficult world. Those were indeed some hard times, however, God allowed me to experience them for my own good (Romans 8:28). I certainly owe Him for that—whew!

Near the end of my six months in that part of the country I was notified that I was being called back to work at my last Ohio position. The next day I sold my motorcycle, bought an older car, and said good-bye to those transient fellows with whom I had roomed. Through God allowing me that particular time with them I have learned to truly honor the homeless—to understand why these special people who are in need become some of Christ's best disciples.

They are also among those who are most in need of being discipled. I did my best, considering what I knew at the time, and they did their best with me as well. Our comradeship in itself was great therapy, and thank God that we all knew there *was* a God, who cared for us. It's like God says, "If you missed the dawn I made for you today, it doesn't matter; I will make another tomorrow."

After a tearful round of good-byes I headed north. I had been laid off from Elkem Metals in southern Ohio just prior to my Florida adventure. I had worked as a research technician there and was needed again for a special project. Upon my return I worked there successfully for another year, but was laid off once again due to foreign steel alloy imports, in the first month of 1986. I spent some time in the area looking for new work, but there were just no good jobs to be found, so, I delivered pizza, painted houses, mowed lawns—did whatever came along, know what I mean?

I also began to take pleasure in writing at that time, something my mother had instilled in me as a youth, when she helped me write a little book about the Lone Ranger. She typed it all out for me, as I told her the story, and designed a handsome cover for it. She even took it to her workplace and proudly shared it with her associates.

I no longer have that book and I don't know what ever happened to it. That's one of the many consequences of wayward living—things get left behind and eventually forgotten. I do have some particular writings authored by one of my granddaughters, Hannah, which I am saving for her and will present to her in the future (she was quite young at the time).

Along with working, hiking and sitting in the late evenings along the riverbank, I began writing an adventure tale about an 'Indiana Jones' type of character (indeed adventurous), who is a resident of Ohio. At the beginning of the story he gets a phone call from a friend, who lives out in California. This 'Jones' type character, a former police detective, is invited out West to help solve an intriguing mystery.

As things begin to develop and deepen, the friend eventually becomes his partner. The two of them end up parachuting into the Nevada desert, where they encounter hair-raising adventure in search of a particular lost treasure. The writing project kept my mind active during some difficult times, and my imagination was always out West. *(That book, *A Second Chance*, a daring tale of high adventure, will be available on 1 February, 2010. It's an 'E' ticket—hang on tight!)

In reality, at the time of that writing endeavor, it had been fifteen long years since I had left the state of California. How I missed it! How I missed those brief but truly good years. How I missed Jenny and our original efforts there. I recall speaking into the wind one evening while sitting along the riverbank: "Fifteen years ago—where did all that time go?"

I had worked so many jobs during that period, moved at least ten times (even lived in a tent for six months), and scratched to exist the whole time. I was just about played out—ready for the funny farm. I look back now and wonder how I ever made it. Sin had indeed robbed me of a better life, yet, God had allowed me to continue living as I had chosen, mercifully sparing me from serious illness or death.

From a human standpoint I don't understand how I kept going, unless it was the fact that I carried so many anxieties. I had lost everything and was like a man striving after the wind. In reality that was all that I was doing. I was also child-support-poor. I wanted to climb up from the roots of the mountains where I had descended. I wanted to become somebody worthwhile, but had no idea how to accomplish that monumental task.

I suppose it was because I was still fairly young, desirous for something better and hoping for a happy ending, that I had any motivation left at all. I am indeed fortunate that there has always been a lot of 'little boy' in me. I didn't think about God taking over, providing a way out, but that's what happened. Even though I was guilty of the worst kind of sins—breaking faith with the wife of my youth[1]—God still reached down to help me—to return his lost sheep to the fold.

Prone to wander—that was the story of my life. We do not consider sheep to be too terribly bright, yet we can learn much from them in relation to our wandering ways and our inclinations toward following those whose ways, ideas or philosophies can lead us astray. The Bible is consistent in comparing us with sheep. Animals can teach us a great deal about who we are and how we should be—which way we should go. I will share with you some insights from the animals in chapter 11.

As I look back to 1986, I see a little lamb (maybe an old goat) that had strayed recklessly and ignorantly *far* from the flock, which God searched out, found and then placed upon His shoulder. Actually, He had always been there—He had determined my course in life before I was even born, and used the poor choices that He knew I would make to educate and correct me.

The consequences of my sins became my best teachers. He had also taught me much through my Biblical studies and related research over the years, however, through my own choices in life, I had unknowingly fought against Him. That's what we spend most of our lives doing—saint or sinner. We want to be a 'self-made' man or woman, but God remembers perfectly how He made us.

We say we believe in God and we say to others that we are doing what we think He wants us to do, but at some point in life we are all found out to be liars. Even the greatest among us make the worst of mistakes. We pursue lusts that constantly deceive us. Fortunately, for us, God brings about events that serve to turn us from our vain pursuits and leads us instead in the direction He has planned for us to go.

Our detours only delay our progress—and can be painful to both God and us. Someone has wisely said, "If you what to know what God has to say, read the Bible—it's His best seller." Though at that time I truly didn't know how to pray for help, I prayed anyway. During those quiet times in God's presence the thoughts of my heart continued to drift toward the West—to California.

I decided I wanted to be like the guy I was writing about in my adventure story. It was April of 1986. I picked up the phone and called my old friend, Tim Murray (Butch Cassidy), of the Arcadia Police Department. I asked him what he thought my chances might be of becoming an officer once again. I brought him up to date on my life, and informed him also that he and I were the characters in an adventure story I was writing—fictionally of course—yet with some hope that perhaps part of the fiction would become a reality.

Tim, over the years, had been promoted to lieutenant and was indeed glad to hear from me. Actually, the last time we talked was in '71, just after I had left the department. We discussed my life somewhat in detail during several conversations we had in April and May of '86, and he said that he felt my fifteen years of varied experiences would serve me well on the streets of Arcadia. He felt that I had the knowledge and sensitivity needed for dealing with troubled folk's, family disputes, wayward juveniles, etc. He was a great encouragement to me each time that we talked.

He told me that quality life experience was hard to find among the younger policemen, most of them having had no military training or time in public relations education. Things were just not like the old days, when we had both started out in law enforcement.

"Little quality out there anymore," he said. "Young men comin' in from all over the country. Ain't none of 'em too terribly bright. I pull my hair out sometimes dealin' with some of these rookies—ain't got much hair left, but you get a good one now and then—one who rides lonesome—know what I mean?"

He suggested that without hesitation, if he were me, he would pack up his belongings and make the trip. Pardon me, but his exact words were as follows: "Hell, a man what don't come West, don't wipe his ass."—Tim was always quoting lines from the Westerns—that's what made him very special among his peers. Hang around him long enough and you start talkin' like that yourself. He assured me that he could put me up at his place while I was going through the application process with the P.D. He felt that I would have little trouble being reinstated, even at my age—approaching 40.

By the way, Tim passed away in August of 2006. He was living in Arizona at the time, a good place for him to be. The man fought cancer for three years. I've got some cherished letters from him that he wrote during the height of his illness. His movin' on was a great loss to many, especially yours truly. Yet, I know that he won't be ridin' lonesome in heaven. I 'spect however he will be doing just that when God gives him his own herd of horses on the new earth. He'll be ready to run with them when I see him again. Perhaps we can ride together— no more lonesome rides for either of us.

Wouldn't that be a dream come true? When you learn to know more about who God is, you start leaning toward those types of thoughts and dreams—dreams of your dreams coming true. There's a lot of mystery to life, but God's deep love is *not* a mystery, and one day all things will be revealed. One day all of us who believe in Him will be changed—made incorruptible and immortal in the blink of an eye. I am certainly looking forward to that—and surely there will be horses there in that new world. So far I've never been able to afford one in this earthly life. Thank God I won't need any money in the next.

For Tim to consider, in 1986, that I had some *useful* (quality) experience was indeed a new way for me to look back at nearly two decades of *miserable* failure. He also told me that he believed a professional police officer should be humbled by life, and use it accordingly in his many dealings with the human race—on both sides of the law. His kind and intelligent encouragement determined my course.

Close friends can do that for you. It turned out to be one of the best choices I had made in a long, long time. A great, non-fictional adventure was about to begin...

Chapter Seven...My Pursuit of the Hawk, Part 4
California or Bust

In the early summer of 1986 I loaded up everything I owned, which 'warn't much,' into an old Ford station wagon. I was fortunate in that my son, Mitchell, who had just graduated from high school, chose to ride along with me to the Golden State—he was missing me already.

Mitch and I have always been rather close, despite a broken home. I'm close to my other children as well, all things considered, but Mitch and I had lived in the same town for the last few years and were use to one another's company. He said that he would like to visit his birthplace once again, and of course, he wanted to keep me company on the trip. He suggested that he could fly back home from California at his leisure.

I was indeed excited about both his desire and choice to come along. It would be wonderful to share with him at his age some of the great scenery of the American West. I don't recall on what day we left, but it was quite early on a warm morning in June, just before sunrise. We camped along the road (literally) the first night, just past St. Louis. From there we mapped out a route to Williams, Arizona, for a look at the Grand Canyon. Neither one of us had ever seen the Canyon before.

113

The thought of visiting this popular expanse was exhilarating. That most impressive area turned out to be a very wise choice for both of us.

We headed southwest from St. Louis, through Oklahoma and Texas, then on to New Mexico and into the heart of Indian country. We took turns driving, talked about a variety of things, remarking often about the unequaled scenery, and deeply enjoyed one another's company. Sightseeing with one's child or children is a great honor, a time to thank God for such an experience. I had always thanked Him for the little journeys over the years, but this Grand Canyon journey was going to be worthy of a big 'thanks'—indeed an unequalled time of discovery.

Though I did not foresee it, ten years later I would be allowed to make a similar journey of discovery with my only daughter, Carrie. That would turn out to be another quality adventure as well. Anyway, after spending the night at a motel in Williams, we headed up to the Canyon very early the next morning. Our first stop was the popular viewpoint known as *Desert View*. We parked the car and wandered up to the viewpoint's edge together. There weren't but a few folk's there at that time. The sun was just rising above the distant mountains and it was already comfortably warm.

If you've never been to the Grand Canyon you are in for more than a thrill when you arrive there. Your first view across and down into its massiveness will literally take your breath away. Several minutes passed by before my son or I could utter a word. At the time I wasn't sure what caused our delay in speech, but I now believe it was the reality of seeing the aftermath of the Great Flood of Noah before our very eyes—so much impressive carving by water in one place.

It is truly unfathomable until you've seen it first hand. When you do see it, there can be no mistake. The television's History and Discovery channels recently advocated that archeologists can find no evidence of a global flood? This particular area certainly unveils their ignorance. The Grand Canyon was carved in a very short period of time by a tremendous force of water, both conclusions vindicated by the fossil record.

This history is still obvious (we'll take an up-close look at the Great Flood in chapter 9). Mitch and I were indeed fortunate to have shared the Canyon, each of us for the first time and most importantly, together. I have been allowed a few more trips into this area over the last several years, and these times of discovery have been a great inspiration in the creation of the *Hiking the Trail of Truth* video series and website. However, from the time of this very first visit until this present writing I would have much to learn.

A few days later we arrived at Tim Murray's residence in the city of Monrovia, which borders Arcadia in southern California. His coal black hair had turned gray in the fifteen years we had been apart, but he was still ol' Butch, the best friend I had ever known in my early days with the APD.

It was a grand reunion. Tim had a young wife and two daughters who treated us with great respect and concern during our stay. Mitch and I also spent about a week visiting some scenic places in the area, which included a visit to his birthplace and our old home on Loma Avenue in Temple City. We took in as much as we could during his short stay, and I believe our adventure from Ohio to California turned out to be one of our best 'quality' times together.

I was sad the day that I had to take him to the airport. I think my whole life flashed before me. I wanted to be closer to my children than my father was to me, but it turned out that I was a lot like him—I wasn't very family oriented. Nevertheless, I got lucky over the years— my children have been closer to me than one might expect, under the circumstances. That's God's *unmerited* grace at work. Neither Mitch nor I knew it at the time of his departure, but he would himself move to California about six months afterward and spend over five years there.

Shortly after he departed I began the application process at the Arcadia Police Department. They didn't want to consider me at first, due to my age; forty years young at the time, but some old friends there (Tim being at the top of the list) convinced Chief Johnson that he would not be disappointed.

It turned out that they were right. About four months later I was elected class president at the Rio Hondo Police Academy, for class #81. At the end of a 16-week training period I came out among the top ten of recruits and had the honor of giving the opening speech at our graduation. Chief Johnson attended that event, and christened me *The Old Man, who conquered*.

After that early 1987 graduation I joined the rank and file at APD, where I received congratulations from my peers on being the oldest person at that time to graduate from a police academy. Others did follow. One fellow who later graduated at Pasadena was 56. The men and women of the APD continued to refer to me as the Old Man. Very seldom did anyone ever call me "Mark" or "Taylor." It was always, "Hey, Old Man." Some went as far as, "Old Buzzard" or "Ancient Warrior," and to them that was who I was. I didn't mind. I was just glad to feel like a somebody once again. In the next eight years I was destined to become a legend among my fellow officers.

A few weeks after the academy graduation Mitch arrived in southern California, with his girlfriend. We lived next door to one another for some time, and later lived under the very same roof. It was so wonderful to have my son around! We did go on several adventures during his nearly six-year stay in California, but after he left in '92 it dawned on me that we just hadn't spent *enough* time together. I was caught up in work and also had a few relationships with women that kept me away from the closeness that should have increased between us. I was still pursuing the hawk, in spite of the lessons learned during those fifteen difficult years in Ohio.

That's the ol' sin nature at work—we always strive to live like there's no tomorrow. When things get better for us we tend to forget about the difficult times and in particular what attitudes and actions brought them about. We commit the same sins over and over. We should all wear two names—Pete and Repeat.

I guess I was like Sampson: In my profession I was a bold defender of what was right, but a moral failure who lived life his own way, weakened through the lustful pleasures of sexual indulgence (Judges 13 thru 16). Or, perhaps somewhat of a Solomon—quite knowledgeable in the things of the Lord, and wise in the matters of His counsel, but obsessed with many women (1st Kings 3:12-13 & 11:1,2).

A close friend recently asked me, "Why are you writing so boldly in your book about such personal matters—don't you think people are going to be offended?" I answered him, "King David said in his prayers to God, '*Behold, You desire truth in the inward parts—the sacrifices of God are a broken spirit, a broken and contrite heart—these, O God, You will not despise.*'

"These confessions helped to confirm David as a man after God's own heart (Psalm 51:6, 17 & Acts 13:22). God expects *truth*. How can others be helped in their own struggles if the truth is not told—not shared? We're all sick; a plague resides within our hearts. Why not confess our faults to one another, pray for one another, and be healed?" (James 5:16)

I actually had a second chance at life when I returned to California. I had a great paying job—with lots of benefits—including full dental and medical, paid sick leave, training officer pay, educational incentive pay, and far above average retirement pay. I worked in all areas of my profession—the patrol division, the traffic division and the detective bureau. A patrol captain once told one of my peers, when I turned in a fellow officer for physically abusing a man at a traffic stop, "Taylor's a good officer, a man of integrity, and we need more like him around here."

I continued and completed my college education, became both a patrol and traffic enforcement training officer, coordinated the city's reserve officer training program, lectured on law enforcement at the local high school, and counseled young people in the junior high and grade schools.

By 1994 I had received in excess of fifty commendations and honors from the police department, which included commendation letters from citizens and business professionals. Most everyone in town who had any dealings with the P.D. knew and respected Officer Taylor, and that was quite an honor to live with. I also worked enjoyable and profitable overtime at the Santa Anita Race Track, at local high school football games, at local parades, and for the movie industry.

I also attended a local church, where I was allowed to teach many informative classes, thanks to such a wide variety of life experience and Biblical study. I was able also to continue my research into Biblical geology and archeology, which was most exciting. I took some great desert and mountain exploration trips with my son and my friends, and hiked whenever and wherever I wanted, encompassed by both the most beautiful and rugged terrain in the country.

My sister came out West to visit me during those years. We spent a great vacation together, exploring scenic areas in both California and Nevada. Marc and Carrie (my third son and only daughter) flew out from Ohio and spent a few weeks with me as well. We had many adventures in a short period of time, and they helped me to produce a special video related to the police department.

Marc played a transient character in a comedy segment of the video that we labeled *Trash Pickin' Blues*, and he did an outstanding job. He was quite excited about having some real-life police officers as his buddies. Carrie worked as my production coordinator, helping to set up the various scenes. Both children are uniquely creative.

I had taken up video photography late in 1987, and by the time Marc and Carrie arrived I was turning out some great videos, which allowed us to relive the many adventures that my friends and I had encountered throughout the wilderness areas of southern California. I enjoyed especially the technical side of making videos—adding music and editing scenes, which in a way is a form of art that weaves a production together and gives it life. My friends and co-workers were always looking forward to watching the finished product. We had special get-togethers for that very purpose.

All things considered, I had a great opportunity in this second chance at life. It probably all sounds really good to you—all of the job security, the personal reward and adventure of being a lawman, the honor of being respectably popular, the opportunity to live in continuous sunshine, and the off-duty time to explore, discover and play in the wilderness areas of California and other areas of the American southwest. Things could not get much better—it was the American Dream come true—again—right?

Wrong! If you don't have the priorities right on the inside—within your heart and spirit—then it doesn't matter who you are, where you are, what you're doing or what you have. Sin will rear its head—because it *is* who you are. Satan will still be there to accuse you and entice you at the same time, robbing you of total peace.

God on the other hand will continue to encourage and discipline you, working to conform you to the image of His Son. These two forces war against one another, making it difficult for you to do the things that you truly should. If you don't stand still and look into the eyes of God, the sin nature takes control of your life—again and again (Galatians 5:17).

Back when Mitch came to California to reside I did not consider, in depth, the reason God had allowed him to be there. Bear with me now, as I never understood at that time what I am now teaching or passing on to you: God had allowed me that time that I might strengthen my relationship with my son—that I might live life in a way as to be a good example to him—to be helpful to him as a father and to nurture him in wisdom and in truth. But, because of continued moral failure, God's way was not my first priority—*I* was still my priority. Yet, I *believed* that God was my priority—deceitfulness of the heart.

Most of us who believe in God believe that we believe in him, yet, we do *not* give him the very first place in our hearts—in our lives. We hold back a little and tend to rule our own hearts. However, we never come full circle and admit to ourselves that we're doing that—we just go on and allow our deceitful hearts to play games with us (we talked about this on the Whitney climb in chapter 5). I was not at this time ready to confront in battle certain strongholds within my nature—I couldn't say 'no' to certain passions—just didn't think about it—didn't want to think about it. I mentioned this to you earlier—my continued pursuit of the hawk.

I had both casual and intimate (sexual) relationships with a few different women during those years—lived through some wild beer-drinkin' times with my P.D. buddies as well. The success of my 'second' life in California served to place the needed remembrance of old failures, related to these particular activities, on the back burner. This is so typical of our nature, but the Scriptures warn us not to forget that we have been *purged* from our old sins, and that we should keep them in mind so as *not to repeat* them (Pete and Repeat) or continue to live in them (Romans 6:21).

These personal activities, which actually ignored God, kept me from spending more quality time with my son and his girlfriend. They needed me more than anybody else did, and hanging around with them more often would have allowed me to pursue something worthwhile. Some adults don't feel that way when their children are grown. These adults (like me in those days) attempt to live their own lives and don't concern themselves so much with the activities of their adult children. That might work for families that have not been torn asunder by divorce—I honestly don't know.

All I know is that not ever having a normal in-home-parent relationship with my children—not having been close to them day by day until they had matured and left the nest—becomes a very difficult emptiness to deal with. How does a sinner ever escape the arrows of guilt and the wounds of shame in this situation? Is it through the forgiveness of God? His word assures us many times over that He *does* remove our sins. But I never read about anyone in the Bible who did not live with the *consequences* of their sins—loss, heartache, guilt and shame. We'll look more into that subject in a later chapter.

119

Though I was basically a loner and not prone to settling down, there was one woman during those years with whom I developed a strong and I believe meaningful relationship. Her name was Sharon Anderson. She was a jailer for another (I won't name) police department (she's still there and due to retire soon). Our courtship was indeed romantic and we eventually lived together for a while, sharing many adventures—I could write more than several chapters on them—and she loved Mitch like he was her own son. He came to live with us in '91, just after he and his girlfriend had split up.

The three of us enjoyed many outings together. But, the bottom line was that I didn't want to get married again—I was afraid of marriage—my record in that regard was living proof, but I never really knew what I was doing anyway. Sharon never pushed me for it, but one day I just moved away—not sure why—just chasin' that hawk I suspect, and Mitch went with me. I probably broke Sharon's heart and did some more damage to my own, but I guess it just wasn't meant to be at the time. Do we ever truly understand why we do anything?—the heart is deceitful above all things; who can know it?

I believe that God's patience finally wore thin with me for not giving Him my full attention. I was still living life on the edge and had fallen back into most all of the bad habits developed in my very first California adventure (Pete and Repeat). I continued to act impulsively, allowing most any type of natural warnings and feelings to rule my life —shortsighted living—a little bit of no-consideration-of-the-consequences type living as well.

As a dog returns to his own vomit, so a fool repeats his folly (Proverbs 26:11). I just never seemed to be able to get a firm grip on my personal life. I believe God then once again took some action to wake me up—to break that buckin' bronco of a man. I guess it was time for Him to take things seriously regarding this ol, cowboy (I say that from a human perspective, for He is 'serious' about us from our very conception—even before that).

God deeply loves us—His chastisement is living proof. In early 1992 He stepped back for a moment and allowed Satan to strike me with a severe attack of pancreatitis. Some might argue here with this concept of 'God stepping back' and allowing pain to be inflicted on His children. I won't argue with them, but it did happen time and time again to Biblical characters.

God does work in mysterious ways, allowing pain and hardship, but promises us that *all things* work together for good (Romans 8:28). We are in nearly constant need of discipline, so we should not then be at all surprised when it comes to roost. We'll look at this concept when we hike the Wilderness Trail (chapter 12).

The pancreas disorder literally knocked me off my feet. I was visiting my good friend, a dentist, who was at the time working part time at the Huntington Memorial Hospital in Pasadena. I was having a conversation with him when I suddenly doubled over with severe stomach pain. I fell to the floor, nearly unconscious.

My dentist and another friend, Vaughn Whalen, literally carried me into the emergency room of the hospital. I faded in and out during their transport and later found myself lying on a gurney. A male doctor who was quite short in stature was leaning over me. When he saw that I had awakened, he took a step back.

"Good morning," he announced.

I was a little groggy. "Am I going to live?" I muttered.

Having been informed I was a police officer and knowing that he could be up front with me, he glanced at my friends then moved closer again and replied, "I'm Dr. Glenn Littenberg, a gastroenterologist— I'm chief surgeon here at the hospital. You've got pancreatitis. You've got about a fifty-fifty chance."

That's just the way he put it; up front, no frills. After that I passed out again and was carted off to a private room. I slept most of the time, being sedated on morphine for pain. I wasn't allowed to eat or drink anything. Two weeks later I began to stay awake more often. They even gave me a roommate, but he didn't talk much.

There were three movies that were displayed on an overhead screen for an entire month; Quigley Down Under, Doc Hollywood, and The Natural. When I was awake, that was my entertainment. They of course remain among my favorites. Dr. Littenberg visited me twice a day. Mitch and Sharon, along with many friends from the P.D., also visited me regularly. After a little more than thirty days in the hospital, and having been observed doing 'push-ups' in the hallway just outside my room, Dr. Littenberg decided to send me home.

A nurse came to the home and taught me how to feed myself intravenously, and I did that for 18 hours a day for the next two-plus months, still unable to eat or drink anything—not even water. The nurse came every three days to check on my welfare and to deliver more liquid for my intravenous feedings. During the third month I was permitted to drink water, eat soft foods—like jello and pudding—and I could also drink milkshakes; mmm' mmm,' good!

By early May I was doing much better, though I had lost some thirty pounds through the ordeal. The doctor told me that as long as I watched my diet, things might get better. On the financial side, I had run out of sick leave pay back in March. At that time my comrades-in-arms at the APD had begun working extra hours each week and donated their earnings to a fund that allowed me to receive a bi-weekly paycheck—a full paycheck—until I returned to work. Their proven loyalty to me as friends was indeed a humbling experience, once again the unmerited grace of God. Even if you are a scumbag like me, God will take care of you.

I returned to work in late May, but was limited as to my duties at the police department. I had to run to the restroom a lot, and worked the report desk so that I could do just that (the report desk handles 'walk-in' cases). The work went well, but it was difficult for a man with my anxieties to remain indoors and work a full shift.

Each day I took my breaks outdoors and would spend my lunchtimes out there as well, where I had an impressive view of the San Gabriel Mountains. I spent my days off hiking in them, which renewed my strength and allowed me to appreciate those particularly fine things in life (mountain trails, sunshine and fresh air). I returned to patrol a few months later, but was not doing well, often having to be relieved from the scene of an investigation so that I could go and relieve myself—if you know what I mean.

Just prior to returning to patrol my son dropped a bomb on me. He had taken a short vacation back east to visit his mother, Jenny, and had found a new girlfriend while he was there in Ohio. He said he was going to move back to Marietta. He had returned from that vacation in late May and was packed and gone a few weeks later. In fact, Jenny flew out and drove back across the country with him. What a great act of kindness on her part!

I was crushed that he was leaving. But, I had always told Mitch that a man has to do what a man has to do. He took my advice. I can't blame him for that. However, I felt his decision to move was due partly to my irresponsibility—not having been the best example for him while he was in California. He married that sweet Ohio girl, Kelly, in July of 1996. They were married in Niagara Falls, New York.

They returned to Ohio and held a wedding reception later that year, and it turned out that I would be there at that time to both attend and film the festivities.

In January of '93, nearly a year after my pancreatic attack, I was forced to go back into the hospital for an emergency operation related to the healing of the pancreas. During the surgery to drain a natural pseudo-cyst that had developed, they also removed my gallbladder. It was producing what they called 'sludge,' which they believed was directly responsible for the original malfunction of the pancreas. I was in the hospital for a week that time, but in less than a month was well enough to return to police patrol.

I had gained some weight back, and actually wasn't doing too bad —except for the fact that I became somewhat depressed. It was a bad time—for the first time in my life I was not physically strong, and I missed my son. The doctor had told me that he wasn't sure at the time how long my condition would allow me to live. Some folk's develop cancer from it, others continue to have acute attacks of the pancreas, which can eventually kill them. Diabetes is also in a matter of time a guaranteed result (it finally hit me in 2000).

I did have some problems with stomach pains and bowel movements, but as long as I could get to a toilet, I survived. I dirtied my underwear from time to time, but was able to keep the other guys at work from knowing about this embarrassing disability. Sometimes I dirtied my uniform while on active duty in the middle of town, and was forced to run into any nearby business and request the use of their restroom. That was not fun. I loved patrol work, but it was hard to keep up with it—to stay alert. Wearing a badge and a gun requires the utmost of awareness.

I was later given a position in the detective bureau, as court officer. This allowed me easier access to the facilities I needed. But, as time went on, I became bored in this work and went back to patrol. I wasn't feeling a whole lot better by 1994, and began to ponder what type of work I might do instead. I also thought about what the doctor had told me in regard to my life expectancy. Since he wasn't real sure about things, I entertained thoughts that I might be going to die—perhaps sooner than later.

I had much physical discomfort then, but didn't tell anyone about it. Having a pancreas disorder would not qualify me for a medical retirement anyway. It was just something I had to live with. I told the

Chief of Police that I was planning on leaving the department to do something else. Naturally, he tried to persuade me not to give it up. I only had one more year and I would have been eligible for about a 20 percent pension. He said if I stuck around 11 more years I could receive a 75-80 percent pension.

The Chief offered me a full-time job in the detective bureau if I would choose to stay for the full-term retirement. That was indeed kind of him, but I declined. Mark Taylor was still doing things his own way. At least I was Mark Taylor at that time—not the Lone Ranger, Zorro, Robin Hood or the Sundance Kid. I eventually decided that I wanted to go back to Ohio and be around my children, in case anything *did* happen. Three of my children were there—all working. My oldest, Michael, was in Boston and doing well for himself at that time. He had graduated from Boston College and was attending dental school.

In May of 1994 there was much fanfare at Mark Taylor's going away (semi-retirement) party, followed by a sad farewell to and from my many friends. I drove away from California that same week, once again bound for Ohio. My friends and associates from the P.D. environment were the best of the best.

I could probably write another book—just on our unique relationships and profound experiences in the West—which would no doubt be a best seller in the category of 'high adventure' or 'real stories of real cops.' I honored some of these folk's in the *Acknowledgments* at the forward of this writing, but that barely opens the library of impressively important memories within my heart concerning them.

I had cashed out my own retirement contributions when I departed, some 36,000 dollars, and reckoned that I would be just fine. It was difficult however when I crossed the State line. I stopped for a while, taking in the scenery—thinking about the last eight years of my life— eight exceedingly good years. I was fortunate however in that I did not have to make that journey back east on my own.

An old railroader from Ohio, who had become my close friend during the lean years of the early '80's, had flown to Los Angeles to ride along with me on my return to that State. He is known in his neck of the woods as Railroad Ron Friend, a dedicated railroad worker and family man with a great heart. His last name truly fits him. He has always been a helpful friend, and his accompanying me on my journey was no small act of kindness.

I filmed much of the western scenery on the way back—figured I might never see it again. Ron and I were able to do much exploring and captured most all of it on film. Ron is a hiker like me, and we filmed a 'mountain man' skit in Colorado while exploring a portion of the Rocky Mountains. It remains to this day a classic in my collection of home videos.

Combined on the film are some adventures that Ron and I shared in the Grand Canyon, Monument Valley, Arches National Park, the Agate Fossil Beds of Nebraska, the Devils Tower in Wyoming, and the Black Hills of South Dakota, including the memorial at Wounded Knee. It was a great trip and lifted my spirits during a difficult time. I will always be beholden to Ron for the unequaled pleasure of his company.

When I got to Ohio I bought an old house (built in the late 1800's) along the river in Marietta, for 25,000 dollars. I made a project out of restoring it and spent the remaining 11,000 dollars retirement money on that venture, part of which was my living expenses. I did most all of the work myself, which kept me quite busy and also kept my mind off my pancreas problems.

I was not working a 'real job' at the time. I actually began feeling a little better. I was hiking in the mornings, working on the house during the days into the evenings, and sleeping well each night. One afternoon while I was resting from my labors, sitting in an old front porch swing that I'd just restored, Jenny stopped by to visit me. I was about to doze off when I heard her walk up onto the deck

It was a most pleasant surprise—an exceedingly special event. We talked about the restoration project for a while, sipped on some iced tea and talked a little about the old days, and then I invited her into the house. A few days before her visit I had completed another video project—a story of my life, from a photo album, complete with a live audio narration.

She was kind enough that afternoon to sit and view it with me, as our time together was no small part of it. Naturally we both wept as we watched the video. When it had ended, I told Jenny that I carried around with me great remorse for who I was and what I was in those former days, and that I had great regret that I had been unable to 'stay the course' in our marriage.

125

She smiled at me and said, "How could you have known what you were doing—you were so young." The evident depth of her forgiveness caused me to weep once again. She held me close before she left that day. It felt more than good to embrace her as well. I still remember her words—to this day I recall much of her wisdom from the years of our marriage. The thoughts of her encouragement have always been like a green shoot on parched ground—like the rush of adrenalin that surges through a hiker as he/she reaches a difficult summit.

The hope she has instilled in me is no small part of the force behind my success in reaching many summits throughout my lifetime, which have allowed me to gain the knowledge that serves you in this writing. This book would have otherwise not been possible. I was like Forrest Gump *in a way*; my 'Jenny' has always been a part of my heart and mind as his 'Jenny' was for him. She was my strength in times when there was no strength, my hope when there was no hope. Jenny has always walked with God. She is fortunate. By now, having journeyed through much of my life, I am sure you can understand why I wish I could have been like her.

Another very special event took place on June 28th of 1995; a fiftieth birthday party for yours truly. This event was organized and hosted by my dear friend, Patricia Palitto, a former high school classmate. She was able to encourage my sister and all of my children to participate in the activities. As of this writing, it was the last time my adult children were all together at one time. Mitch was living in Marietta, not far from me, but Mike had come all the way from Boston. Marc and Carrie had made the trip from northern Ohio, as did my sister, an aunt on my mother's side, and my host.

It was a great time, and I will always appreciate the considerable work involved, which allowed that event to take place. I've remained in contact with Patti and with a few other old classmates as well, but you know how that is—we all go our separate ways and live our different lives. High school seems like a long time ago now, but a few of those friendships do endure. Sadly, there are a number of my former classmates who are no longer physically with us. That time is perhaps now drawing close for me as well—who knows?

I could write a few more chapters on my adventures in Ohio, but I'll briefly tell you about two of the more important ones, because we'll be heading back to California again in chapter 8, and that is where the very best part of this whole story, from a spiritual standpoint, unfolds. With respect to one of these Ohio events, the house restoration was nearly finished in a year, but before it was completed I took a position teaching law enforcement at a local vocational high school (juniors and seniors) for a semester. It was in September of '95 when I began that adventure.

In teaching law enforcement, one has to teach some concepts from the word of God. No law enforcement officer can properly perform his/her duties if they do not understand the depravity of man. With this understanding, the officer can learn to properly enforce the spirit of the law—not necessarily the letter. However, the State Faculty did not accept the teaching of God's attributes, and they were the ones who supervised the curriculum of the school. With this grave hindrance, it became impossible for me to balance my teaching and give the students true and accurate enlightenment. This 'conflict of interest' eventually forced me to walk away from the teaching position.

If you can't teach others about God then life's not worth much. I was however able to stress the importance of physical training and problem solving, and shared many interesting and active field problems with my students during that semester. The faculty eventually hired some boring, retired Ohio State Patrolman to finish out the year in my stead, and this caused several of my former students to randomly drop by my house to let me know just how much they missed my insight and leadership (which was in reality God working through me—I had nothing to do with it).

"We sure wish you were still there, Mr. Taylor," they would say. In spite of the difficulties encountered, I believe the semester I taught there turned out to be an informative and rewarding experience in relationships—both for my students and myself. When we are allowed to have God work through us (and He can work through anyone at anytime He chooses) good things are accomplished. This is something we need to recognize and to honor. When you understand that 'good' comes only from Him, you are more apt to appreciate His presence and to seek His attributes.

By January of 1996 my health was still good—I was actually feeling a hundred percent better than I did when I arrived in Ohio, just over a year and a half earlier. I longed for the West once again. It was such a part of me and I wasn't dead yet, so I figured I would take my chances and head back. I had enough of Ohio by that time, so I put the house up for sale.

I finished the restoration on the place and it turned out very well, however, it took over eight months to sell it. Times were hard there and the house wasn't in the best of locations. But, it finally sold in late August of '96, and I had about 15,000 dollars in profit to my name when all was said and done. I then began to make definite plans to return to California.

The second important event, in another respect the most important while I was back there, took place in early July of that year. My son, Mitch, and his sweetheart, Kelly, were united in marriage at Niagara Falls, New York. They had been together about four years by that time, so I figured they knew each other pretty well.

They asked me to make a movie of their reception, which was to take place upon their return to Marietta, and I was quite honored to do so. It turned out well, and remains a great treasure to the family. Mitch and Kelly are very close in their marriage to this day—I am so relieved that like-father-like-son does not apply here. Mitch is quite responsible —thanks to his mother.

I asked them to move back to California with me, but they didn't think it in their best interest at the time. Nowadays they speak of it often—moving out West—but they can't afford it. They have a daughter in school (my granddaughter, Hannah), have an average income with job security, and moving out West in these current times is an expensive adventure—for them just a dream—yet they *are* happy where they are. They have like a little farm on the property of a big farm. Mitch puts on his ball cap and rides his tractor all over the place, doing his chores—I love it! His family is his life, which attitude is esteemed high in the sight of God.

Escrow finally closed on the house in the very early part of September. I loaded personal items into my Bronco II and a small U-haul trailer to the max. My daughter, Carrie, had some vacation time and decided to join me on my return trip. She was single at the time and wanted to share some of those 'sights of the West' with me. I was to drive to northern Ohio to pick her up and greatly looked forward to it. Mitch came to the old house to see me off shortly before I departed on that journey.

He was indeed sad to see me leave, but he hoped that perhaps I could go back to work for the police department—maybe buy back into my retirement. He told me that if I could get that buy-back, it would make acceptable his loss. I was honored of course by his unselfishness, and hugged him for a long time.

I had spoken on the phone just prior to that with my oldest son, Mike, who was back in Boston and doing well. He was then and always has been an encouragement. He would later be married, in 2001, and begin to raise a family in Massachusetts. He is also quite responsible, again thanks to his mother. He currently owns a home there in Littleton, and fathers three of my grandchildren.

My youngest son, Marc, was in those days much like I had been—he had a difficult time searching out his feelings. Not having a Dad around is a hard road, paved with insecurities—but he was doing well in northern Ohio and continues to do so. He now fathers three more of my grandchildren. He lives reasonably close to Carrie, in the town of Wooster. He runs his own business there and devotes much time to his family. We had some adventures together during my stay in Ohio, but I was unable to see him or speak with him before Carrie and I left, due to the fact that he was working out of town at that time.

On the morning that I left Mitch and I stood outside the old house of sweat and good memories, where we shared some morning coffee. The exterior of the house at that time looked like it belonged on the cover of Home and Garden—a vast improvement from the way I had found it. Yet, I wouldn't miss the place—too much work associated with it. But I was definitely going to miss that old porch swing—for more than one reason.

The furniture I bought for the inside; three bedrooms, living room, dining room, kitchen, basement and attic, remained with the house as well. Personal belongings? As I mentioned, the trailer *was* loaded—and heavy. Mitch just shook his head when he heard the strain on the Bronco's trailer hitch as I pulled it out onto the street. I saw his gesture and laughed out loud.

"Don't worry," I uttered out the window, "I'll make it."

"You're skinnin' out, you ol' sodbuster," he yelled back. "Have a good ride, Dad—don't let them wolves get'cha—and watch out for Injuns."

He was frequent with those Western movie lines—leaned that from me, I guess. I watched him for a while in the rear-view mirror—until I could no longer see him. I then turned my head and eyes north and headed for Carrie's place. I thought much about my two years in Ohio on that little trip—about 120 miles worth of thinking.

I glanced into the side mirrors once in a while—the trailer wasn't hauling too badly—wasn't slowing me down any. It took about three hours to reach her apartment in Wooster, not too far from the rolling fields of the Amish country that she loves. I enjoy passing through that country as well. It's a different world there, but I believe it's a good one. They're peaceful folk, and honor the God who formed them.

 **Chapter Eight...Hiking the Trail of Truth**

My daughter and I headed out early on a September morning in '96, enroute to Denver and points west. I have now traveled back and forth across the USA several times in my lifetime. One thing is sure—nothing you've seen beforehand reaches into the greater depths of inspiration until you get to Denver and beyond.

You hit the Rockies first and from there you begin to soar like an eagle, seeing a diversity of sky and terrain that helps you to somewhat understand why the eagle soars. When the awesomeness of it all hits the center of your brain, you might begin to ask yourself, "What part of 'Thou shalt not' don't I understand?" Surely the wonder of God is more satisfying than any carnal desire or pleasure.

It was at this time and on this particular journey that the summation of my life's experiences began to weave themselves together with the creation and the teachings of God's word. Long journeys are good for us—they give us plenty of time to think about things. The hawk was actually beginning to land and my pursuit of him was nearing its end.

My eyes were opening to how and why he flies: *He flies by God's direction to make known the wisdom of God.* This should be the endeavor of every human as well—to walk in god's way and share His attributes with others. I began to understand why one should not attempt detours along the road of life that God has granted him/her. We are definitely not our own.

You have to just live life the way it happens, accepting the good times and working through the bad times. God must have His way if you are to succeed. Anxiety should not play a part in this drama—don't run—toward anything that's harmful or away from anything that's good. And, as I mentioned in another chapter, you have to live life forward, but it can only be understood backward. I was at this time allowed the insight that would eventually help me to understand the absolute necessity of walking with God 24 hours a day—moment by moment.

Some of the more self-righteous folk's might say here: "What do you mean, *eventually*? You either walk with God all the time or you don't!"

To them I say, though we boast often of loyalty and sincerity, we do not give our lives completely to God. If we could do that we wouldn't need a Savior. We can only walk in God's way by means of a lifetime, in-depth learning process, allowing the Spirit of God to teach us and the grace of God to carry us through. We will always fail at one thing or another or in one way or another *many times* while attempting this walk. Don't be deceived—we are by nature rebellious and prone to wander. Only when Christ returns will we be made perfect (1st Corinthians 15:52).

After passing over the great Rocky Mountains, my daughter and I visited three more very scenic areas—Arches National Park, Monument Valley and the Grand Canyon. I was able to relate to her many of God's attributes while in these particular areas. Walking among the telltale evidences of Noah's Flood provided a living backdrop for this type of conversation. I had studied in depth the relationship of these sites to Biblical archeology, geology and history by this time in my life, and had no trouble relating and reasoning the teachings of Scripture regarding these wonders to those along the way whom I was fortunate enough to have been allowed to teach.

These things were quite interesting to my daughter, and her presence among the red rock wonders was no small help to her own understanding. We drew closer together on that adventure, and my daughter was just a few years later (1999) baptized into Christ in my presence, near here home in rural Ohio. I had previously baptized my oldest sons; Mike, in 1977, and, Mitch, in 1983, in southern Ohio, when I was a younger student of the Bible. They have remained true to their beliefs and God is honored as a result. My youngest son, Marc, has not approached me about becoming a Christian, but I am hopeful —he's a wise young man.

After my daughter and I left the Grand Canyon we crossed the mountains into Nevada. Along that route I began to lose the gearing in my old Bronco's transmission. This was the third time in the ten years I owned the vehicle that the tranny gave out. The other two times were during adventures out in the middle of the Mojave Desert. Anyway, we limped off the freeway at Las Vegas, pulling up in front of the first unpainted curb in town, in front of a rather large building, and came to a stop. The truck was over-heated from pulling that heavy U-haul behind it and wouldn't budge an inch further.

We climbed out of the truck, looked it over, then walked up the street about a block and ate lunch at the first available restaurant. After lunch, as we walked back toward the truck, we observed that men dressed in suits, who were looking into the truck's windows, had surrounded both it and the U-haul trailer. There were several of them and they appeared quite anxious in their activities.

As soon as I said, "Hey that's my truck—what are you doing?" the group of men suddenly drew out handguns, flashed badges, and ordered my daughter and I to face the wall of the Federal Building, which we had unknowingly parked in front of.

"Hands in the air!" they shouted, and began a pat-down search on each of us while inquiring as to the contents of the trailer. It turned out that they were FBI agents, and thought that we had a U-haul full of fertilizer—a bomb! It hadn't been too long since the Oklahoma City bombing had occurred, and folk's in Federal Buildings all over the country were more than a little bit nervous.

Once they established who we were, and after looking as best they could into that stuffed trailer (only being able to pry the door up about two feet), they let us go. I was parked legally, but they wanted that trailer out of there in a hurry. Fortunately the Bronco had cooled down enough for me to get it started. We limped to a motel where a transmission service later arrived and towed the truck away for its needed repair.

That Federal Building incident has remained a good source of humor unto this day. Unfortunately the Bronco's transmission bill was

133

2500 dollars, which knocked a big hole into my 're-establishment in California fund.' Pulling that heavy U-haul also shortened the life of my trusty old Bronco, and I was forced to get rid of it not too long after that.

We spent a couple of days in Las Vegas waiting on the truck before we could begin the drive to the Los Angeles area. That day however did arrive and we pushed on—or should I say 'pulled on'—across the Mojave Desert. I was a little anxious about the tranny for over 250 miles—right up until we reached our California destination.

In spite of that slight bit of anxiety, crossing that section of the Mojave felt good. The landscape was more a part of me than I realized. Add to that the scent of the air and the caress of the wind—indeed inspiring. The unique inspiration of the wilderness has always been the Creator's way of teaching me its important relationship to my purpose in life.

I cannot believe the wonders He has allowed me to behold through the years. It had not all come together at that time, but it would not be long until it did. I wasn't thinking about who I was at the time or what my purpose might be—I just wanted to get back to California and land a job. Perhaps the P.D. *would* consider rehiring me.

Let me say this at this particular time: I believe that God uses the creation in drawing many of us to Himself. We were made from the dust of the earth and our human spirit, when we allow God to speak to us through it, knows this. We catch a glimpse of this truth whenever we are allowed to visit or vacation in the wilderness.

Do you not feel strangely attracted to nature? Do you exercise or jog in a local park, or do you go there perhaps for medicinal quiet time? There's no mystery in these attractions, for you are indeed a part of nature—made from the very dust of the earth (Genesis 2:7). Only God's Spirit can make you aware of this profound relationship. If He has done that, if He has indeed revealed that to your inner being, you should consider yourself blessed.

Being drawn toward Him in this manner is a great honor—should you respond properly, it's perhaps the beginning of an enlightenment that can ultimately lead to your eternal salvation. God does great things past finding out, yes, wonders without number (Job 9:10). He does these things entirely for our benefit. His generosity is quite evident. He has made all things from nothing and has allowed you to become a witness of them, should you choose to continue to believe in Him.

I found an apartment in the city of Sierra Madre the very day we arrived. The elderly landlady was a sweetheart and allowed me to move in immediately, without having to go through the application process. Her considerations were that I had been a police officer in her neighboring city and that I had my "charming" daughter with me, along with a trailer full of things that needed to be unloaded. She was indeed kind—very helpful during my entire stay in that apartment building. Carrie helped me to unload, unpack, and we got things organized inside the apartment within a couple of days.

Why do we haul so much junk around with us when we move? Clothes and toiletries would have been enough, but I was dragging things around that I really had no need for. Actually, the entire U-haul was full of junk. I suppose certain things remain familiar to us over the years, even though we only use them once in a blue moon, and so we become pack rats.

Then, when we die, someone else sorts through it all and throws half or more of it away—perhaps all of it. Bottom line is that none of it will fit into your casket. We wouldn't be able to take it along with us on the next journey anyway. If you have any questions about your focus in life, one can certainly learn where his/her focus is by considering the things they accumulate.

Carrie and I spent a little time touring southern Cal until the day I had to put her on a plane back to Ohio. That was a difficult day—for both of us. It was much like the day Mitch left California. Your whole life flashes by, you deal with the remorse of losing your children all over again, and then you nurse a broken heart for a long time afterward. You curse yourself for your choices in life, but do you learn from your mistakes, do you glean something from the profound lessons they can offer, or do you just shove them into the suicide box?

The suicide box is that place in your heart that you open up when loneliness and despair come upon you. Some who open this box at that time feel unduly overwhelmed and choose to end their life. Others, who come to understand the love of God and learn of their importance to Him as one of His children, realize that the dreadful contents of this box have actually drawn them to God.

It is in fact God Himself who allows your misguided choices and mistakes so that He can draw you toward Him. We are not alone when

135

we have Him. "Trust in Me," He says, for He wants the best gift for us. "Put yourself in My hands and watch," He says. Would it not be wonderful to confront one contemplating suicide and gently coax them into accepting these truths and save a soul from hell?

The first place I went to look for work was the APD. A new chief was in charge at that time, who did not come up through the ranks and did not know Mark Taylor from Adam. Nevertheless, he was the one I first had to interview with if I was to have any hope of returning to work there.

Actually, the interview went quite well, but he did not fight for me like former Chief Johnson would have. I had to take a written test again, pass an oral review board again, run the physical agility course again, and wait on a background check, again. This process took over ten weeks. During that time I kept myself busy at two other jobs.

I worked part-time as a bodyguard for a team of roving nurses, through a private security agency run by an LAPD sergeant. I also worked full-time, for a short time, as an Animal Control Officer in the city of Pasadena. That job eventually fell through. The males in charge there were homosexual.

Accepting their lifestyle was obviously a conflict of interest in my being a believer in God. No true believer in God has survived long in an environment of that type—consider Abraham's nephew, Lot, who lived in the depraved city of Sodom, the entire population of which was morally and sexually perverted (Genesis 19:4).

Unfortunately the entire world is accepting this behavior once again, yet, it's only a matter of time until it will be judged. Hang in there until that time; the tares won't remain among the wheat forever. Though I never got into an actual conflict with them about their sexual appetites, they eventually fired me, accusing me of allowing some vagrant to trespass on Animal Control property.

It was just about that same time that I was contacted by APD, who advised me that they could not rehire me. It had been the City Attorney's decision that in considering my past illness, even though the doctors had, in writing, released me, I was a risk the city could not afford to take.

I realized that the City Attorney had acted in the only way he could have, but my hopes of buying back into my retirement faded into the sunset. I later learned that my former captain, Rick Sandona, along with other P.D. members who were my close friends, had fought hard for my return. Rick told me there would have been no fight at all had I re-applied in May instead of September. The reason was that I would have been covered under a two year 'leave of absence clause' in the police contract.

I had missed that deadline by just a little more than three months. Within my heart I blamed this loss on the fact that it took over eight months to sell my house back in Ohio. I was upset for a while, but later I would look back and see God's hand at work in the matter. I would see this rejection, not as a punishment for the foolishness in my life, but to protect me from continuing in that foolishness. God would instead take me down a trail of enlightenment, upon which, as a result of many hiking experiences, I would come to know Him through His creation.

Knowing myself as I do now, through the grace of understanding, God was indeed just in not allowing me to return to the P.D. I know that the good pay, benefits and stability of the police department would have allowed me to, by nature, ignore the cost of past foolishness in my life and would not allow me to experience some further consequences that needed to be lived out.

I would also have more than likely continued in the same old fashion—wasting money on toys, perhaps chasing women, and holding to a form of Christianity that so many do, but actually denying, through continued indulgence in carnal behavior, its true power (2nd Timothy 3:15).

I would point out here, for one to be successful at Christian living, there needs to be daily self-examination and communication with God. In fact, it is most wise to communicate with God moment by moment. This begins when we actually see Him in His creation, and when we begin reading a portion of His written word (the Bible) on a daily basis.

We have to stop and look into His eyes. I have mentioned this before. How do we 'look into the eyes of God?' Naturally we do not know what He looks like. We have artist's who have presented varying concepts of Jesus, but we cannot be sure they are accurate. Yet, we do know, according to Scripture, that His eyes are gentle and that He watches over us constantly as a compassionate friend would. Do you look into the eyes of your friend when you converse? You should.

Believe it or not, most folk's do not look directly into your eyes when they are speaking to you. They look at the sky, look from left to

137

right and even at the ground. This is very distracting. They do the same thing when you are speaking to them, which may indicate that they are not listening to everything that you are saying.

We're all at times guilty of this. We need to make eye contact. This adds much value to the words we speak. It is the honorable thing to do, so when you are conversing with God, imagine that you are looking into His eyes. Always consider His eyes to be compassionate, for they indeed are. Unlike the days of old, we are not to be fearful in approaching Him.

We may be ashamed for one reason or another, and lower our heads or prostrate ourselves on the ground, and that's okay. But once you have confessed to Him what you need to confess, then get up and talk to Him as a friend. With your confession you are forgiven, and He expects you to stand up, look into His eyes, and speak to Him as a friend. If you don't do this, you *will* wander away from His presence. You *will* in this process encounter forgetfulness.

We are so prone to wander away from God and *not realize* that we *are* wandering away from Him. The Scriptures teach that we could witness a great miracle, such as the Red Sea parting, right before our very eyes, and forget about it in just three days by wandering into a carnal mindset and finding something to complain about (Exodus 15:22-24).

In fact, three days or less is the 'average' period of time throughout the Scriptures that anyone remembers any blessings or miracles of God. That's hard to accept, yet our hearts are prone to wander at all times. That's because Satan works against us moment by moment to deceive and to corrupt us. You have to guard your heart at *all* times— against both what goes into it and what comes out from it—moment by moment.

The heart is deceitful above all things, and each of us are more prone to certain temptations than others. We each have significant or special weaknesses—'thorns' in the flesh (2nd Corinthians 12:7). I spoke of this earlier in chapter 6. We therefore need to take time in attempting to understand our weaknesses and the individual spiritual failures that we face as a result of them, that we might be victorious through some of our struggles.

Knowing who you are (chapter 1) will help you to grow spiritually. I presently know that these things I am informing you of are true, but when the P.D. rejected me I was not fully aware of these things and was forgetful of other (good) things, consequently embracing a 'down and out' attitude for some time. I was most forgetful of God's many blessings—wandering in the wilderness. We all spend time in the wilderness.

The Bible is full of 'wilderness wanderings,' and the list of characters that did the wandering is indeed a long one. Wilderness wanderings are the times in our life when God brings about circumstances or events to discipline us for better things, namely, to accomplish His earthly purpose for us.

These wanderings usually encompass the difficult times of our lives, which may or may not come about by our own choice. They include, among others, the wilderness of failure, the wilderness of doubt, the wilderness of affliction, the wilderness of fear, the wilderness of despair, the wilderness of loneliness and the wilderness of anxiety. We will explore each of these seven areas in chapter 12.

Shortly after my rejection by APD I went to work as a chauffeur for a fellow who owned an air conditioning business in Pasadena. It was a non-demanding job mentally, which allowed me time to consider more in-depth the things that were taking place and had taken place in my life. What did I think about the most?

I thought about my first marriage—about Jenny and Mike—when we first came to California in 1967. It was a very special time in my life—but I had blown it. I thought about Mitch's birth, our little home in Temple City, and I drove by it many times, stopping in front of it on one occasion just to sit and think.

Instead of trying to conquer the world back then, why wasn't I just a simple sort of guy who could have been satisfied with a job like this? If I had been a chauffeur, perhaps I would have not fallen into the grip of the world. Perhaps I would not have been blinded by selfish ambition. I could have just been a regular ol' guy who went home to his family every night and loved them—just a happy-go-lucky guy, content with the little things that mean everything. I envy those folk's who have always lived this way—there are some out there.

Maybe we could have had a couple dogs and some horses instead of me trying to be the macho cop, who lived life on the edge, and then came home to worship all those insignificant material possessions. What the heck happened to me? Well, I knew what had happened to me—those years were destroyed by the locusts—eaten away by the locusts of pride and arrogance, of selfishness and greed, of blindness and ignorance. But I had also learned and kept in mind that God could restore those years that the locusts had eaten (Joel 2:25).

In early 1997, prior to my chauffeur duties, I had submitted an application to the U.S. Forest Service. In May of that year they got in touch with me. They informed me that, out of many qualified applicants, I had been the only *veteran* who had applied for a technician's position in the Angeles National Forest. The job was to 'assist in the operation and preservation of the off highway vehicle area' (OHV), in the San Gabriel Canyon. When they asked me to report out there "right away" for an interview, I was elated—to say the least! I was to meet with a man named, John Seals.

The day I drove eleven miles out that winding canyon road was like no other. I just couldn't believe it was happening. The scenery that I hoped to become a part of was breathtaking! I prayed in earnest for that job, through each bend of that road, all the way up that road. I eventually located the well-marked OHV area and parked my jeep. I exited the vehicle, smelled the air and took courage from the scenery, then walked up to the field office where Mr. Seals welcomed me with a warm handshake.

Lush vegetation on granite mountains strewn with tall, cone-bearing pine trees surrounded the office. The San Gabriel River moved powerfully, yet with much grace over a picturesque, boulder-strewn wash nearby. The sound of this rushing water over rock was the atmosphere that I was to be interviewed in. John Seals, looking over my application, asked me a few questions regarding my background and then, with what they called "veterans preference," he hired me on the spot.

In a couple of days I was issued uniforms, including the traditional forest green jacket with the Forest Service emblem embroidered on each of its upper sleeves. I didn't know what to think or how to act—like a little boy with a new toy, or like the tin man with a new heart, or somewhere in between! All I know is that I went out among the rocks, fell to the ground, and there gave thanks to the Lord for granting me the unearned privilege of earning a living in such a manner. I thanked Him over and over, day after day, for the honor of that job.

I went at the forestry experience hard and learned well. I figured I was as happy as a squirrel in a walnut tree in those days. As for the pancreatic problems, well, if you carry a shovel in your truck, the outdoors is one giant toilet—I was free! I took to hiking most of my days off. I hiked a lot during my work routine as well. You know, dear reader, that I have hiked most all of my life—but here, in this pure environment of mountain scenery and trails that never ended, I turned into one hiking son-of-a-gun. This had an *increasing* medicinal effect on the spirit within me.

How truly boring it would have been had God created the world in black and white. I am indeed glad that He chose the colors that He did. He surely doesn't need to put out an ad in the local newspaper to remind us to witness His attributes in the wondrous displays before us. Hiking among his exhibitions is the ultimate 'rush' that each of us seeks.

I hiked the highest mountain in southern California—San Gorgonio, 'old grayback,' and many others of the San Bernardino range. I hiked all the mountains in the San Gabriel range as well, the highest being Mt. Baldy, which crowns the escarpments of that range. My hiking partner, when I had one, was a dentist—Dr. Michael J Mucci, of Glendora California (he currently has an office in Ft. Collins, Colorado). I had trained Mike as a reserve officer while on the P.D., back in the late '80's. He became my dentist after that, and if any of you readers live in the Ft. Collins area, he's the best—go see him.

He is also the dentist who helped carry me into the hospital emergency room the day that the pancreatitis hit. When we learned that we shared a common interest in hiking, we hiked—Mt. Wilson, Strawberry Peak, North Baldy, Mt. Baldy, and many other notable peaks in both the San Gabriel and San Bernardino ranges. We climbed Mt. Whitney in the High Sierras together in August of '98, but that part of the story comes later.

A good hiking partner is a hard find. Some do nothing but complain—about the terrain, the weather, the political problems within our society—but a good partner speaks about the wonder of the hike itself and is always inspired in one way or another by the scenery. God doesn't really want us to talk about ourselves anyway—He wants us to hike out there together and talk about Him.

Naturally, along with enjoying the scenery when out hiking, one spends much time in thought. I spent a good amount of that time looking back over my life and thinking deeply about God. I hiked in some very desolate areas of the wilderness. I hiked the high places also, where there are few humans about—only the most dedicated to hiking.

When on a solo trek in the high country, it is always a pleasure if you encounter someone along the trail. Most stop to converse, and I would always try to comment in some way about God's grace upon us. People seem the most encouraged about God in their conversation when they're out on the trail. I believe that's because it's how we're meant to be as well as where we're meant to be. God never wanted us to build towering cities and hang around the metropolis in the first place (Genesis 11:6).

Hiking has taught me that one can feel God's presence most vividly amidst His wonders—through the deserts and the back country, and most strongly in the high country. One reason I see things this way is because these are the easiest places to concentrate on God. I mean, it's quiet out there—why wouldn't God be there? He doesn't like continuous noise.

The high country is one place He can get through to you—where it's scenic and silent—where He can open up your eyes, that you might truly see—and your ears, that you might stop in your tracks and actually listen. He can even walk along with you there and you can talk to Him as a friend—and oh, how we so desperately need His counsel!

King David loved to meditate on God during his years in the wilderness, as did so many of the patriarchs before his time. They did more than their share of hiking about in those days. The psalmist wrote: *I have more insight than all my teachers, for Thy testimonies are my meditation* (Psalm 119.99 NASB).

When you think deeply about (meditate upon) God and His wonders, you learn about Him. His counsel comes so vividly alive amidst his wonders. He gives you insight into His creation and into His word, and both of these testimonies (*declarations*) give you insight into Him—more insight than your human teachers.

In addition to a Bible I always carried my video camera along when hiking into remote and scenic areas. While thinking about God on these journeys I started talking about His creation on video. I would pick a remote spot and set up the camera—and I would talk—as a teacher, instructing his students. I would sometimes talk into the camera while I was actually hiking, holding it out at arm's length. One day, as I was engaged in that very pleasure, I determined that I would create a video series and name it *Hiking the Trail of Truth*—discovering God through the things He has made.

It all started on a Sunday morning in early September of '97. I normally worked in the canyon three Sundays a month, but was scheduled to be off that particular day. I was up early in the morning, hiking in a wash on the north side of the San Gabriel's near a rock formation called the Devil's Punchbowl. Ironic, isn't it? I don't know what idiot named it, but the Devil's Punchbowl is merely a multi-colored rock composition, bowl shaped, with its unique mineral coloring clearly visible from the higher trails.

In fact, I was hiking on North Baldy (Mt. Baden-Powell) with an old P.D. friend, Ed Ostashay, when we first saw the Punchbowl, some 5000 feet below us. It was indeed an eye-catcher from up there, a beautiful formation, and I told Ed that I was going to seek it out within the next few days. I later found it to be a somewhat remote area, but accessible from a sand wash just to its east. The three-mile trek to its rim took just over an hour. Like I said, it was on a weekend, in beautiful weather, yet I saw no one else in the Punchbowl or along the trail.

I asked myself that day, 'Where is everybody? Were are their minds? Doesn't anyone want to be out in this place—to walk in the beauty of its silence and contemplate God, its creator?' That became the theme of my first video. I wanted to share with others what life was so graciously teaching me. I wanted them to understand the truth about life and the truth about God's existence—through His creation.

And oh, how we need the *truth* in this generation that is so polluted by false religions and inaccurate Christian teachings. We need a strong voice from the wilderness and I wanted to be that voice. No, I am not John the baptist, but I am certainly of similar spirit—thank God! I must say that I was moved to tears just thinking about that endeavor.

Emotions such as these develop rather easily when you have seemingly made a wreck of your life and then God suddenly gives you thoughts of hope or a nudge of one kind or another; to let you know that He is still there. Actually, He does this often; usually when you least expect it. Sometimes you're not even aware if it—unless you are in a place where He can more easily communicate with you—where there's little or no external activity to dominate your thinking. *Hiking the Trail of Truth* was born in such a place.

From that time on I hiked and camped in a variety of places, putting together a series of twelve videos. The first one was completed in January of 1998, and there would be eight more by the end of that year. I was living in the Forest Service barracks at Crystal Lake at that time, located in the high, white granite, several miles above the OHV area where I worked.

I was one of two full time occupants in the barracks, which stood in a grove of pines amid the granite boulders, just above the 6000-foot level. It was indeed a wonderful place for inspiration, yet it was just the beginning of many illuminating adventures that God would allow me to become a part of. The other occupant in the Forest Service barracks was a man named Hal Deckhert. Hal worked for L&L Campground Management, a private group who operated the large campground at Crystal Lake. Hal also assisted me in making some of the HTTOT films. We had been graciously allowed equal enthusiasm for the Lord and for the high country.

He and I were able to talk (howl back and forth) to the many coyotes in the area—that's on film too. We spent time among the bears, the big-horned sheep, the hawks, the owls and the eagles. We conversed often with campers about these wonders of the Lord. Hal was indeed a great inspiration and a faithful brother in the outreach of the truth. He currently resides in Needles, California. I hope to look him up, Lord willing, next time I'm through there.

The first video I produced from shots taken at the Devil's Punchbowl, Crystal Lake, and the Mt. Whitney region was copied fifty times over and mailed out to friends and relatives, along with a newsletter that described the contents of the 30-minute film. I also wrote short articles of inspiration in the newsletter, and mailed out this package with its contents free of charge.

I always figured, freely you have received; freely you should give (Matthew 10:8). In other words, nobody had to mail in fifteen dollars to view God's scenery and hear a sermon. Here it is, folk's. Enjoy and learn—free! What a feeling of satisfaction *that* can generate! I didn't have a lot of money and still don't—but it didn't matter at the time. I had enough to fund what I was doing and was truly happy in what I was doing.

I continued that year to film and mail out new editions of the HTTOT series of videos and newsletters, on just about a monthly basis, and the list of recipients continued to grow! There were nine films in all by the time of the December '98 edition, which included video of the Taylor/Mucci, August, '98, Mt. Whitney expedition (more about that in chapter 9).

I eventually took over management of the campground at Crystal Lake, and would manage other campgrounds in California over the next few years. I worked with two other mountain men during that time; Thom Hutchinson and Raymond Laird, with whom I became great friends, strengthening our relationship through gleaning much from our mountain experiences together.

In good time I would also do some additional traveling, which would allow me to camp for extended periods of time, several times, in the areas of Arches National Park, Monument Valley and the Grand Canyon. I would work spring, summer and early fall during each campground season, then be free to travel and explore during the winter months.

I also spent much time at Lone Pine and Mt. Whitney, some time in Death Valley, and was also allowed to venture into the deserts of southern Arizona; including the Saguaro National Park and the Organ Pipe Cactus National Monument. It was through all of these adventures of exploration that I came to know much more about God through His creation.

I was able, if you will, to walk with Him as He taught me. I would eventually call these most privileged and enlightening encounters *my time among The Monuments*.

Chapter Nine...Hiking into the Monuments

During the last year that I had worked for the P.D. (1994), I was renting a room from one, Sandie Eisenhower. Sandie, during that year, was experiencing some hard financial times, having been laid off from a major California employer, which is why she had the room for rent in the first place.

By the time I went to work for the Forest Service, some three years later, Sandie was still scratching at a living through several part-time jobs. I was able to get her some additional weekend work at the campground, even though it was nearly fifty miles from her home. Sandie became one of my very best friends and continues to be at the top of the list. More importantly, she is an artist. I often tell her she's missed her calling—and her means of self-support.

I think her time up in the campground inspired her, as she started painting more often after she spent some needed time in the mountains. Sandie was as taken with the wilderness as were Hal and I. During her first winter up there I was doing some particular writing on the Great Flood and needed some special artwork done, which Sandie proceeded to create in the finest of style.

I was planning a trip into the *Monuments* that spring, my third for filming HTTOT videos, so I encouraged Sandie to come along. I knew it would be good for her spiritually, and hopefully would inspire her to take up painting on a full time basis. Talent of any kind is a gift from

God, and oh, what a substantial gift to be able to recreate His wonders on canvas—with such precision! Sandie's artistic eye is able to penetrate discerningly into the wonders of created things. She is truly gifted. She first traveled with me to the Lone Pine and Mt. Whitney region in early April of '98.

There's an area just west of town and east of the mountain, known as the *Alabama Hills*. Many Western movies have been created here, the formations visited by just about every Western movie star you can name and then some. The rocks and boulders in the Alabama Hills are distinctly unique—a most remarkable display of the diversity in God's artwork.

But then again, every rock formation in every part of the world has a uniqueness of its own. Hills and mountains are distinctly different. Forests and deserts are distinctly different. Every rock and tree or grain of sand is also distinctly different. These characteristic differences are what make them *individual wonders*—from the greatest to even the smallest.

Among the larger wonders, their individual uniqueness is the main reason that millions of people are drawn to them. What makes them so unique—as variable as the entire world population's fingerprints? This uniqueness may have something to do with millions of people, but has absolutely *nothing* to do with millions of years.

Actually, most scientific dating techniques today indicate that the earth and solar system are very young—possibly less than 10,000 years old. My own calculations are somewhere between 6000 to 7000 years old, and a host of well-known scientists agree with me. One primary indication in support of this, among many others, is *excess fluid pressure*.

Abnormally high oil, gas and water pressures exist within relatively permeable rock all over the globe. If these fluids had been trapped more than 10,000 to as much as 100,000 years ago, leakage would have dropped these pressures *far below* what they are today. Therefore, this oil, gas, and water must have been trapped quite suddenly and recently.[1] Personally I hold to the Biblical age of the earth, which is now just a little over 6000 years, and, as I mentioned earlier, many scientists are in agreement.

Approximately 1,656 years after the creation of the first man, God brought a catastrophic global flood of waters upon the earth. At that time mankind's wickedness upon the earth was exceedingly great.

147

Every imagination from the thoughts of men's hearts was only evil continually (Genesis 6:5). The population of the earth at that time is estimated to be 900,000,000 (nine hundred million), and that is a conservative estimate.[2]

I spoke of these things briefly in chapter 2. In keeping with His promise to bring a Savior into the world, God determined to save just one family from the worldwide flood, who found grace in His eyes. That particular family had just eight members. The family was that of Noah (*rest*), a man of integrity. Noah was not chosen for his personal integrity, but through God's grace as a type of Christ.

Noah represented his own family as Christ represents His. Noah's descendants would eventually bring the Savior into the world. The population that currently exists has descended from Noah (that means you and I also). The effects of the Great Flood are important to us today because it helps us to better understand the geography and geology of our present earth. It also helps us, through recorded population studies after the Great Flood, to more accurately trace our ancestry back to Noah.

However, most importantly, knowledge of what the Great Flood has produced allows us to see God in His creation—His attributes— with indeed much clarity. By continuing your journey through this writing—your hike along the *trail of truth*—your eyes will be opened to the unfathomable love of God, if they haven't been already. This love, which passes understanding, can convince the most rebellious in heart of their need to learn to love Him in return. It can break the most stubborn will or serve to heal the loneliest among the brokenhearted, downtrodden or afflicted.

What person would not want eternal life, if all things in this present world could be made new—if he/she could start life all over in a perfect world? How would you like all of your dreams to come true? I hope you'll continue this hike and see for yourself what is possible. What you can discover through the creation can help motivate you to learn more about God from the pages of the Bible, His *only written revelation* to us.

Most people are familiar with the story of Noah and the Flood. Unfortunately most are unaware of how to actually *see* the story in the earth, due to the shortsightedness in a host of modern scientists and the 'educational' philosophies of the times. However, though the story is nearly 5000 years old, its evidence remains all around us (Romans

1:20). The earth tells us this profound story without wavering—without question.

You do not now see the earth that existed at the time of the Garden of Eden. It was much different in those times before the flood. The earth was perfect and complete in every detail. There were no desolate lands, no barren hills nor polar icecaps, and no scorching desert heat—no desert at all. But that perfection gradually changed after the Fall in Eden, and then changed dramatically through a series of cataclysmic convulsions associated with the Great Flood.

The fossils have accelerated the imaginations of men since the time of the early Egyptians. Many later cultures have had some very unusual ideas about them as well, but in today's times of advanced archeological and true scientific discovery the evidence becomes much clearer. The fossils offer conclusive proof that the physical conditions of the world before the flood of Noah—the climate, animals, plant life and living space—were vastly different from that of our world today. Fossils do not lie and have certainly been preserved by God for a purpose.

With respect to climate, the fossils show that there was a consistently mild climate in high and low altitudes of both the northern and southern hemispheres. That is; there was a perfectly uniform, non-zonal, mild and spring like climate in every part of the globe.

There were a far greater variety of birds and animals in the pre-flood world. As to size they ranged from the stature of a wolf to that of immense creatures over one hundred feet in length. In the Canadian province of Alberta alone twenty-six different species of the pre-flood world have been identified. Thousands of marine specimens have been found in several of our own western states, which indicate that a sea on the pre-flood earth may have covered these areas.

The pre-flood earth contained more living space for the human race than this present world offers. The world of Adam and his immediate descendants contained proportionately more habitable land. There were no enormous waste areas, such as the great deserts of Africa, Asia, America and Australia, nor were the landmasses separated by such a vast expanse of ocean water, which today constitutes over three quarters of the earth's surface. Because of such vast oceans, ice-covered continents and other barren land areas, only about one half of the land that now exists on the earth is habitable.

The earth after the flood was not only reduced considerably in land area, but the fertility of the soil and the natural resources necessary for human existence are now unequally apportioned. Because of this unbalanced distribution of land conditions the people in some areas live in plenty, while others eke out a miserable existence. This difference gives rise to envy, strife, opposition and brutal wars between the nations.

Each area of land however is not without its particular beauty and specific contribution to the whole. If all humans in all parts of the globe could focus on these more important aspects, our cultures might better relate to and cooperate with one another.

The pre-flood earth probably had only one very large super continent, covered substantially with lush vegetation (Genesis 1:9). There were seas and major rivers (Genesis 1:10 & 2:11-14). The mountains were smaller than today's, but perhaps 9000 feet high. This is established by the fact that marine deposits of great thickness, formed in deep water, have been and are continuing to be found at elevations from 10,000 to 16,000 or more feet above the current sea level.

The fossils show also that thousands of land animals died suddenly in all parts of the world, the majority buried alive under tons of sediments. Large deposits of animal bones are found in all parts of the world. It is said that the vast arctic plain of Siberia contains so many animal bones that it is assumed that the frozen ground matter consists *entirely* of them.

Masses of fish fossils have also been preserved, caught by sediments and instantly fossilized in swimming positions—uninjured, eyes bulging and fins extended in terror. The world's dense vegetation (thick forests, plants and all other growth) was also compressed rapidly and under extreme and even unimaginable force. The great coal beds found in every continent of the earth today are the proofs concerning the density of vegetation that once existed before the flood.

Coal is simply compressed vegetable matter. It has been estimated that it requires from 10 to 14 feet of vegetable matter to produce a seam of coal just 1 foot in thickness. There are many seams of coal throughout the world ranging from 40 to 50 feet in thickness. One particular Antarctic expedition found an entire mountain of coal at the South Pole. A coal seam measuring from 60 to 90 feet in thickness was discovered in a strip mine in Wyoming. This particular large seam of coal represents a solid mass of vegetation, trees and other plants from 500 to 1000 feet in thickness.

Oil is also found in fossiliferous strata and is therefore not an original creation, but a product of organic matter. Some scientists conclude, with convincing proof, that myriads of fishes destroyed in the cataclysmic cycles of the Great Flood are the source of practically the entire supply of crude petroleum. It is also believed that animal fats are a portion of the supply as well.

A German scientist placed animal fats in a sealed container and exposed them to extreme heat and pressure. The end result of his experiment was petroleum. There are many books in print authored by a variety of scientists that can give you much more detail regarding the profound fossil evidence of the Great Flood.[3]

It becomes obvious why God, with exceeding grief, would not allow some of his larger living creatures to resume life after the flood. They were predominately vegetarians who would no longer have the great abundance of lush vegetation available to them on the post-flood earth. The post-flood earth is what you and I see on the landscape. If you go into the areas where there has been little human influence (no large cities, highways, or works of men) you can see the results of the flood. Though the evidence is about 5000 years old, it is still quite distinct in the mountains, valleys and canyons of the world.

In the Alabama Hills of Lone Pine, California, I began talking much about the flood on video, demonstrating the uniqueness of its aftermath. Great water-carved formations abound here, and from atop Mt. Whitney you can get a most revealing aerial view of the formations that were constructed by the cataclysm, as well as the distinct floodplain that was later formed by the receding waters of the flood.

The Great Flood formed even Mt. Whitney itself and the entire range of the Sierra Nevada. Do you think the earth is beautiful now? Indeed it is, yet it is entirely the aftermath of the Great Flood—you've actually been looking at *flood damage* all of your life. I don't like to think of it as *damage*, but, considering the supremacy of the pre-flood earth, it *is* damage—yet, one can see God's hand in the entire work.

We see beautiful mountains, deserts, canyons, trees and plants and flowers of the field—myriads of varieties of beautiful things—unsurpassed in our time! But, before the process of nature allowed these things to bloom to such perfection once again, the world was

151

indeed a barren place. The Great Flood reshaped the entire earth; moving its mountains, carving its canyons, laying down its deserts, forming its vast oceans, and cleansing it as well—of all life.

Only eight people stepped out of an ark onto a bleak earth, an earth washed clean of wickedness. They had all the animals and birds that would populate this bleakness aboard their ship! *Note*: There are those who do not believe that the Ark could have contained all the pairs of animals and birds that God chose to bring aboard it. There's evidently some misunderstanding here; the Ark had a capacity of nearly 3,600,000 cubic feet. In reality, nearly 1000 railroad boxcars could fit into a ship of this size—more than enough room for the chosen species and ample room to spare for food.

Can you focus your mind and imagine yourself to be in their place when the family of Noah first stepped out onto dry land, after residing over a year in the ark? Can you fathom yourself as one of the eight people in the entire world whom God had chosen to save? Think about this. There are places in the wilderness where you can hike and find yourself completely alone—far from the civilized world. There's no man-made noise—nothing but scenery and silence. You can actually hear an eagle in flight a long way off. You may hear a bee buzzing about a flower. Such silence is glorious. It is breathtaking!

I'm going to give you a brief overview of the physical flood itself —how it came about—before we hike into some of the *Monuments* it left behind. However, before I go into that there is some additional information that has been gleaned from the fossils—information that you probably won't find in your modern day science journals. Fossils teach us that mankind before the flood had not only multiplied and become a great people, but had also taken possession of the earth and had reached perhaps a higher stage of civilization and culture than we know today.

Pre-flood mankind was, in spite of their eventual fall into depravity, a much greater and more intelligent species than previously thought. They were not strictly cave dwellers who were physically deformed and didn't know how to speak, as commonly taught by modern educational institutions. Actually, it would only stand to reason that the generations before the flood had extremely more mental capacity than men of today.

Consider Adam, who named all of the birds and animals. There is no one living today who could commit that much knowledge to memory. Adam was extremely intelligent as were his immediate descendants. The Bible teaches that Adam's descendants had a considerable knowledge of mathematics, the creation and use of tools, and an advanced understanding in the art of building.

They were master metal craftsmen as well, and had an unequaled appreciation for gold and precious stones. They engaged in farming, industry, arts and inventions, music and poetry, and those things of life that are only found in an advanced civilization. The fossils tell us that it was actually the golden age in the history of man, of which the various mythologies of later ages are but a faint and indistinct echo.

But, there is another side to this picture, for parallel with these great material and cultural achievements there runs a steady course of moral decay and spiritual degeneracy (Genesis 6:5). Their thoughts were bent only upon doing evil continually. However, depraved as they were, they might not necessarily have been a pagan or idolatrous race.

Archeology of graves found beneath the flood sediments have produced no figure of a god, or any symbol or ornament that strikes one as being of a religious nature.[4] If they were not a religious people by nature then deductive reasoning tells me that they were intelligent enough to know that there was only one God, and that they chose to rebel against Him, which reasoning the Bible verifies as accurate.

Religious practices are a product of a lesser intelligence—of not knowing that there is only one true God, who made all things. Religious beliefs and superstition are what is produced when people choose to worship man-made gods—creations of their imaginations or handmade idols, which they foolishly consider to be sacred. If these pre-flood people made no physical idols, then they were an idol to themselves, which explains their practice of only evil continually. They separated themselves from their Creator by choice; they did not honor God nor were they thankful, as Romans 1:21 suggests.

The great worldwide flood of Noah took place somewhere around 2460 BC. There are some who disagree with this date, but a careful study will reveal it to be quite accurate. Also, a detailed and scientific reconstruction of this event can at present be made independently of the Scriptures. You can see on our planet seventeen or more very strange features, which can now be systematically explained as the result of a cataclysmic, global flood, whose waters erupted from subterranean chambers, with an energy release exceeding the explosion of 10 billion hydrogen bombs.

Take your time on this—concentrate on each paragraph and develop a mental picture here. This explanation will come alive for you. This explanation shows us just how rapidly major mountains formed. It explains the widespread coal and oil deposits and the rapid continental drift. It explains why, on the ocean floor, there are huge trenches and hundreds of canyons and volcanoes. It explains the formation of the layered strata (layers of soil and rock) and most of the fossils. It explains the frozen mammoths, the 'so-called' ice ages, and major canyons, especially the Grand Canyon.

The Bible speaks of subterranean waters below the earth's surface (Genesis 2:6). This water conceivably amounted to about half of what is now in our oceans. This water was contained in interconnected chambers, forming a thin, spherical shell about a half a mile thick, perhaps 10 miles below the earth's surface. In keeping with His promise to judge the old world and bring forth a Savior, the Spirit of God, on a chosen day, allowed the pressure in these subterranean water chambers to increase. His method of course remains unknown.

Increasing pressure stretched the crust of the earth, much like a balloon stretches when the pressure inside increases. Failure in the crust began with a microscopic crack, which grew in both directions at about 3 miles per second. The crack, following the path of least resistance, encircled the globe in about 2 hours. As the crack raced around the earth the overlying rock crust opened up—like a rip in a tightly stretched cloth. The subterranean water was under extreme pressure because of the weight of the 10 miles of rock pressing down on it.

As the crust opened up the water then exploded violently out of the rupture. Along this globe encircling rupture fountains of water jetted upward supersonically, reaching almost 20 miles into the atmosphere. The spray from these enormous fountains produced torrential rains, such as the earth has never experienced before or after the flood. The Bible says that, in one day, all the fountains of the great deep were broken up and the windows of heaven were opened (Genesis 7:11).

The water jetting up from the rupture into the cold atmosphere froze into super cooled ice crystals, producing some massive ice dumps; burying, suffocating, and instantly freezing many animals, including the frozen mammoths of Siberia and Alaska. These high-pressure fountains eroded the rock on both sides of the crack, producing huge volumes of sediments that settled out of this muddy water all over the earth. The sediments trapped and buried plants and animals, both large and small, all over the earth, forming the fossil record.

The erosion continued to widen the rupture. Eventually the width was so great that the compressed rock beneath the subterranean chamber sprung upward, giving birth to the *mid-oceanic ridge* that wraps around the earth like the seam of a baseball. The continental plates—the hydroplates—still with lubricating water beneath them, slid down hill away from the rising mid-oceanic ridge. After the massive, slowly accelerating continental plates reached speeds of about 45 miles per hour, they ran into resistances, compressed, and then buckled.

The portions of the hydroplates that buckled downward formed ocean trenches, while those that buckled upward formed mountain ranges. This is why the major mountain chains are parallel to the oceanic ridges from which they slid. The hydroplates, in sliding away from the oceanic ridges, opened up very deep ocean basins into which the floodwaters eventually retreated. On the continents, each bowl shaped depression or basin was naturally left brim full of water, forming many post-flood lakes.[5]

The Great Flood and its receding waters formed the most beautiful hiking country in the world. Within this continent alone; Grand Canyon, Monument Valley, and many other National Parks such as Death Valley, Yellowstone, Yosemite, Grand Teton, Saguaro, Joshua Tree, Sequoia, Bryce Canyon, Shenandoah, the Great Smokey Mountains, Kings Canyon, and many, many other unique formations all over the continent. Very special artwork comprises each of these formations. Design is also evident in the myriad of formations, both small and great, throughout the entire world.

It is important to note here, so that you might understand the scope of the Great Flood and therefore be better able to comprehend its results, that the waters of the flood were *extremely high* upon the earth. The waters prevailed at over 22 feet *above the highest mountain* for several months (Genesis 7:20). The effect of this enormous amount of water pressure on the earth's surface, which brought about such radical changes in the landscape and formed the fossil record, would, under the *normal* operation of the laws of nature, require *millions of years* to accomplish.

The water was so high when recession began that it took over five months for the newly formed mountains to become visible. During this recession, water moved with *incalculable force* over the recently deposited sediments of the flood. The rock, sand and debris in these powerful waters fine-tuned the mountains, re-shaped the landscape, opened valleys, carved immense canyons, scattered rocks and huge boulders over hundreds of miles of territory, leaving us thousands of diverse formations—formations that we see nowadays and seem to take for granted.

We are currently taught to believe that they evolved 'somehow' over millions of years and have always been here.[6] Nothing could be further from the truth. When one stands in the presence of these formations there is no 'somehow.' The mysteries of the ages unfold by merely opening your eyes to the incredibly creative power of a loving God.

You can see His strength and His gentleness. You can see His passion and His sense of humor. And what did He use to form it all? He used water, the most powerful force in nature, to cleanse the earth and give it new birth. Water is significantly essential to new birth—to salvation—to life. Nothing lives without water—that's just the Designer's way. Water is a great witness to His work, which undisputable witness you will examine more closely in chapter 14.

Water saved Noah in bringing the ark to safety during the Great Flood. Water saved Moses and the Israelite Nation when the pursuing Egyptians were drowned in the Red Sea. Under the New Covenant, water also represents the cleansing of one's past sins by the word of God through the blood of Christ in baptism (Acts 2:38, 22:16, Romans 6:3-10, Galatians 3:27, 1st Peter 3:20,21, etc.).

Again, that's the Designer's way. It is also a 'scientific' fact that nothing can come into being without water. It is scientifically true that nothing can live without water. It is an ingredient in the makeup of every living species of plant and creature on the face of the earth. Water is both a creator and sustainer of life. Water was a primary force in the initial formation of the earth, long before the Great Flood.

God used inconceivable amounts of water in the creation of things —a myriad of things.[7] We are going to look throughout the remainder of this book at some of the wonders He formed through the waters of the flood. You can learn much about the character of God from these formations. We're actually going to hike among them, together. The Bible warns us that we are without excuse—we *can* know that He exists and come to understand Him through the things He has made (Romans 1:20). God strengthens us, increasing our faith in Him through this readily discernable knowledge.

When Sandie and I visited Lone Pine that April, in addition to filming and picture taking, we did no small amount of exploring. When you examine boulders and rocks up close there is much you can learn about God, the Artist. Unique displays of colors abound in rocks of all sizes and shapes. From the tiny pebbles under my hiking boots to the large boulders, slabs, and huge granite mountains upon which I have trod, I have found unfathomable diversity in both color and design in stone. I have seen a *quality* of love that motivates within me a compelling desire to appreciate—to love in return.

The Lord shapes these many-sided rocks, then dips His brush into a palette of multiple colors and strokes a distinct personality into each formation. When you pick up a handful of pebbles along the trail you will find no two alike. This is why hiking is such an honor. Even the sound of these pebbles rubbing together under your hiking boots is distinct, allowing you to realize the security and presence of God in His creation. This distinct sound echoes through one's soul, radiating wonder and joy, while at the same time creating a yearning to know more about the Creator.

All this comes through the simple (yet profound) senses of sight, touch and hearing that God has so graciously allowed you. Reaching out and touching a large boulder, or a slab of red rock, can produce an excitement that literally burns within you—that makes you want to radiate the truth of God to the world.

These rocks and the various granite mountains, with their impressive, lofty crags, are the rocks upon which our faith becomes tangible. They are the truths that can form the *rock of knowledge* within our hearts—a firm foundation that we can build upon, ever increasing our appreciation, our understanding, and our faith in our Creator and Friend. This is indeed a love worth finding.

Consider the patriarch Jacob: While journeying in the desert he came to a certain place and stayed the night because the sun had set. He took one of the stones at that place and put it under his head as one would a pillow. During his sleep that night he dreamed about God—an awesome dream. When he awoke from his sleep, he said, "Surely the Lord is in this place, and I did not know it." He rose up and took the stone that he had put under his head, set it up as a pillar (*witness and monument*), and poured oil (*anointing*) on top of it. Jacob's faith sprang to life through a mere stone, which he humbly learned to honor (Genesis 28:10-19).

*

In August of 1998 I made my second successful hike to the summit of Mt. Whitney, just west of Lone Pine's Alabama Hills. My partner was Dr. Michael J. Mucci, long time friend and hiking enthusiast—a man of kindred spirit. We arrived in Lone Pine with much anticipation on August 18, spending the first night at low elevation. Early the next morning we left the Portal (8000 feet) and climbed to Mirror Lake at 10,600 feet.

After a brief rest we continued on to a position above the lake, where we had our first view of the Owens Valley far below us. That view is available for you to experience; at the beginning of the previous chapter (page 131). After soaking in that view for some time we began the arduous journey up to Trail Camp, at 12,039 feet, where we chose to chow down and spend the night.

As darkness fell the temperature at that elevation dropped to about 20 degrees. You're a little closer to the stars up there, and they were out in full that night. After enjoying a trail meal there's nothing like crawling into a warm sleeping bag and looking up at the stars— especially when you're on Whitney without a tent. Some go 'tentless' up there for that very purpose—stargazing.

What is a star—actually? Well, the sun is an average star, so it might be a good place to start for an idea. The sun in all of its grandeur is nearly unimaginable. It is an enormous ball of simmering and explosive gases, believed to be about 864,000 miles in diameter. Its distance, as best as men can tell with their limited knowledge, is in theory about 93 million miles away from the earth. It is indeed a huge star, but scientists tell us that they believe there are stars out there over five hundred times bigger than the sun.

In dealing more with what we can see and almost imagine; if the sun could be hollowed out, it is believed that a million planet earths could easily fit inside. But the sun does not appear to be hollow. It instead appears to be an enormous, fiery furnace, where internal gas temperatures are estimated to be in the *millions* of degrees. I for one can't even begin to fathom such intense heat. Scientists too are not really sure where all this extreme high energy comes from. There are theories and presumptions, but no one is absolutely certain what makes the sun shine.

It is believed that each square inch of the sun's surface illuminates with the intensity of about three hundred thousand candles. This incredible energy production goes on 24 hours a day, 365 days a year. Yet, it is estimated that only about one billionth of the sun's energy output is radiated to the earth! In just *one second* the sun releases more energy than mankind has produced since his origin, including all power plants, all types and sizes of engines, and any type of explosives (including bombs) ever constructed.

This dramatic energy output of the sun illustrates what is also happening at this moment on an innumerable number of stars throughout the entire universe. Due to this massive energy output, God has placed the stars in positions that allow our planet to be protected. God is precise. For instance, the 93 million miles that separate us from the sun serves to insulate us from great catastrophe. If the distance were any less, the raging solar inferno would vaporize the entire earth in an instant. If the distance were any greater, we would literally be an ice planet.

If the expanse of space between the sun and the earth were not a vacuum, the explosive sounds on its raging surface would destroy our eardrums. There are also molecules high in the earth's atmosphere that protect us from harmful radiations. The ozone protects us from ultra-violet radiations. The earth's magnetic field protects us from the solar wind, deflecting its atomic fragments to the Polar Regions. These securities provided by our Creator results in our privileges to both use and enjoy the many benefits that sunlight affords us.

The sun of course is only *one* star. It is believed that there are over one hundred billion stars in our Milky Way galaxy alone. Beyond the Milky Way there are other galaxies of various configuration. About one hundred billion such galaxies are currently known to exist. If we should take the Milky Way as an average of these galaxies, the approximate number of stars within the *known* universe is then ten to the twenty-second power, or 10^{22}, or 10,000,000,000,000,000,000,000. That is an unfathomable number of stars!

New instruments continue to probe deeper into space, unable to find where the stars come to an end.[8] The actual number of stars is indeed infinite. It's like trying to count the grains of sand on the seashores. However, the Bible teaches us that God determines (created and knows) not only the number of stars, which scientists have been unable to number, but calls each *individual* star by name (Psalm 147:4, Isaiah 40:26).

Do you recall that Adam called every species of animal and bird on the earth by name? He himself named them, remember? He was not as smart as God, but he was a lot smarter than you or I, or anyone else living today. Think about it...

When I consider Your heavens, the work of Your fingers, the moon and the stars, which You have ordained, what is man that You are mindful of him, and the son of man that You care for him? For You have made him a little lower than the angels, and You have crowned him with glory and honor. You have made him to have dominion over the works of Your hands; You have put all things under his feet, all sheep and oxen, even the beasts of the field, the birds of the air, and the fish of the seas. Oh LORD, our Lord, how excellent is Your name in all the earth. (Psalm 8:3-9 NKJV)

We started for the summit at 0600 hours the next morning. The temperature was still hovering around 20 degrees. The 96 switchbacks to Trail Crest were iced over, so we inched our way up over 1700 feet of rocks and boulders until we reached the Crest. Once there we took a little nourishment break—munched on some dried prunes and drank a little water.

I had a little trouble getting the liquid from my water pack to my mouth. Every time I sucked on the water tube the incoming liquid would freeze inside of it. I finally had to remove the tube and drink out of the insulated water pack. Mooch got a laugh out of that one.

"It's mighty cold up here," he said. "It's so cold, you probably won't be able to hear what I'm saying until it warms up a bit and my words thaw out," he added.

"It should be a little warmer on top," I replied. "Looks like we're going to make it—not far to go now. That climb over the switchbacks was brutal—piece of cake now, though. You ready?"

"I've got my mind right," he answered.

With that we started down the backside of the mountain on the John Muir Trail and reached the Summit Trail cut-off in just a short time. We took a pull on our water and headed back up again, passing the summit Needles around 9 a.m. They sure look different from the backside. The westward view down into Sequoia from that elevation is also breathtaking. Talk about a rugged expanse of unending wilderness —wow!

We climbed onto the 'great block' of Whitney, just up a few bends in the trail from the Needles, and then climbed boldly to the actual summit, reaching it just after 10 am. We stood over the same geologic benchmark that we had each stood over once before; myself, in 1970, Mike, in 1991; 14,496.811 feet.

For 360 degrees around the summit we viewed the distant peaks, valleys and deserts just below and far below us. The weather was incredibly warm in the sun at that elevation, and the sky was a deep blue—it's real, real blue up there. There were no clouds. Visibility was 100 miles plus in all directions. You could see the high pinnacles beyond Bishop to the north and the entirety of Death Valley to the east.

Death Valley is some 125 miles or so in length from north to south, but from atop Whitney it looks to be the length of a football field. Sequoia National Forest dominates on the west, and the southern Sierra stretches out majestically to the south. The view along the High Sierra from atop Whitney is like no other I have experienced. It appears to be some of God's finest sculpturing.

There's no noise, except an occasional hawk squealing overhead, or a heartening wind mounting up and caressing hundreds of surrounding peaks. If a man/woman wants to talk to God, this is the place to do it—Oh Grand Father, how majestic are the wonders You have made! What a great place to chant like an Indian and celebrate (I did exactly that on the way back down—'the dance').

We humbly acknowledged the compassionate God of the universe, who made all things. We took the time to thank Him for creating that magnificent, lofty view. We thanked Him for the life and for the health and for the motivation and for the many peaks we had ascended together in training, that we might experience such an awe-inspiring wonder.

We pondered also the many sacred, exhilarating steps upon His granite rock that we had been allowed to experience in climbing up there. We were encouraged that He had brought us further along on life's trail, both once again to the very top of that immensely bold pinnacle of white granite. We ended up spending quite a bit of time at the summit. We took some pictures and of course I had the movie camera along, filming some takes for video number 9 in the HTTOT series, the final film for 1998; *The Legendary Mt. Whitney*. It was a good day for photography of any kind. It was 50 degrees on the plateau and there was no wind—a much more pleasant experience than the windy conditions and the 7 degree temperature I had confronted up there in early September of 1970.

We had packed a small bottle of campaign, so I drew it out, popped it open, and we toasted our adventure while standing atop the highest point. The photographs of that celebration came out well. There were a couple other climbers on top, with whose help we were able to get pictures of Mike and I standing together, over-top the benchmark. Our hike was, to say the least, *monumental*.

It was indeed a great climb! We talked about it all the way down the mountain and for months afterward and still talk about it whenever we converse. It was eleven years ago this year, yet the emotions from the good fortune associated with that endeavor are felt to this very day, and its anniversary date is celebrated each year—August 18th through the 20th.

In Mike's dental office in Colorado, and above my writing desk in California, currently hang identical 16 by 20 inch framed photos of he and I on the Whitney summit (a representation is presented as the very first photo in this book; see 'For the Reader,' on page 4). Mt. Whitney is of course my primary physical inspiration for *Hiking the Trail of Truth*. My spirit soars whenever I stand upon the landscape that surrounds it.

The Mt. Whitney region is one of the most ruggedly beautiful expanses of spiritually motivating wilderness that I have been allowed to experience. I visit the area often, and will most likely move to that area and live there on more or less a full time basis, Lord willing, in the late spring of 2010. I hope I have the good fortune of meeting the Lord from that area when He returns—no finer place to rise from when one ascends up into the air.

I don't know if I will still be alive when He returns, or my bones just lying somewhere up in the rocks when that event transpires, but either way, that's where I'd like to be, as long as the earth remains. I figure it's kind of fitting for me to be in that area—don't you?

Chapter Ten...The Desert Trail

Sandie and I were fortunate to have visited the American southwest several times from 1998 to 2002. I lived in and worked from a Prowler trailer at that time, a cozy 17 footer, which I hauled around from place to place with a sturdy and dependable, slightly old Ford pick-up truck. The trailer had a most comfortable and convenient layout inside, warmly decorated with a variety of inspiring souvenirs that I had both collected and created from the wilderness areas I had been allowed to both visit and work in.

Now, it's your turn. You are about to embark on a unique journey into the deserts of the American southwest. Within these vast, spiritually captivating, rugged areas of sand, rocks, ravines and exquisite formations, you will have an opportunity to draw privileged nourishment from the things that God has so wonderfully made. This particular nourishment can serve to greatly increase your understanding of God, as well as that of yourself. It can teach you how to love the One who loves you.

Each of us are given certain abilities and special purpose in life that we might, as individuals and together, accomplish God's will for us. The quality time you're about to spend on the Desert Trail may indeed serve to enlighten you in the relevant knowledge and comprehension of these things. All you will need on this journey is an adequate supply of drinking water, a few snacks in you backpack, a Bible, and a good hiking stick. You will need your mental camera as well. Ready? Let's do it…

God and Arches

He does great things past finding out, yes, wonders without number (Job 9:10 NKJV).

Arches National Park is quite a distinguished monument of our Creator, a garden of sculpture and one that definitely leaves you in awe over the creative power of water. God has indeed left some real images of art for us to view here. Some of them are actually humorous. Don't think for one minute that God doesn't have a sense of humor. Consider Uluru (Ayers Rock) in central Australia.

Here is one solid rock, hundreds of miles from anywhere in the middle of a flatland nowhere, some 986 feet high and over 5 miles in circumference. It's been called, "a remarkable pebble." Everyone in the world wonders how the heck this big 'pebble' ever got out there in the middle of nowhere? Don't think for one minute that God did not laugh when he planned its placement there during the convulsions of the Great Flood.

Geologists from all parts of the world speculate on this wonder, hiking all over it and offering many suggestions as to the origin of its formation. God laughs, not at them, but at their foolishness of heart. They look at it, scratching their heads in wonder, while He sits in heaven and grins, hoping that they will get a grip on reality, acknowledge His creative work, and thank Him for His kindness in allowing anyone the pleasure of hiking upon it.

Our hike through Arches National Park will also confirm God's unprecedented artwork and sense of humor in a most remarkable way. The initial flood deposits in this area (about 2460 BC) consisted of a vast number of hills and mounds of good quality clay, which were, just a brief time later, reformed and finely sculptured by the divinely guided movement (operation) of receding waters.

God indeed left some profound shapes here. I call it the *check this out, folk's* display of God's handiwork. The artwork here is most impressively representative of the human race and of the present animal inhabitants of the earth. There are some Biblical students who believe that this area is the remains of an ancient city; that the sculpturing is actually the work of men. That's a possibility but not a probability.

The secular opinion of course is that Arches was eroded into these shapes by wind and water over millions of years. We know that idea is absurd; an absolute impossibility in the mind of the true Christian or the true scientist, since the earth itself, as we know it, is just over 6000 years old. The young earth explains many things that the unbelieving wrestle with and are ignorant of. Deceitfulness of the heart and the inability to reason are the culprits. Having your eyes open yet closed play a prominent role as well.

My personal opinion is that God challenges mankind here at Arches, but in a kind and humorous way. Knowing that we *should* be able to see His mind in these works here (Romans 1:18-20), knowing that He is going to have the so-called experts come up with all kinds of explanations here, and knowing thirdly that He is going to *delight* those who have true understanding (His *own* children), He allowed that this area, later named by men as *Arches National Park*, would be a monument to the creativity of God and perhaps a preview of the eventual history of mankind in the United States of America.

Take a close look. There are a myriad of shapes here. Of the animals there are elephants, horses, cattle, sheep and rams, lions, coyotes, and birds such as the eagle. Of men there are the images of George Washington, Thomas Jefferson and other figures of the Revolution. There are infants in the arms of women, patriots marching and casualties of war.

Abraham Lincoln is giving an oratory at a podium. There are civil war soldiers lurking about and slaves huddled in fear. There are statues of American Indians, while on a considerably larger scale are the scar-faced profiles of Indian warriors and chiefs. There are also groups here and there which appears to be a diversity of people engaged in prayer. Then there's Park Avenue; walls of rock that resemble downtown New York City.

There is indeed much more to be found here, and it doesn't take *any* stretch of the imagination to do so. The famous *Delicate Arch*, the location of which is indeed an inspiring hike over red rock, looks like the torso and legs of a bowlegged cowboy wearing a pair of chaps. He may have been whole at one time, as there is a lot of broken rock in the valley directly below him.

In a canyon just behind this arch is a group of women standing around a well. There are huge bowls that resemble pottery here and at other locations throughout the park as well. There are rocks that resemble pueblos and still others that resemble castles. Depending on the time of day, the shadows created by the sun making its way through the park serve to highlight this grand display of artwork in a diversity of ways. Towering spires, pinnacles and balanced rocks perched atop seemingly inadequate bases are among these scenic spectacles.

Then there are the many and varied arches themselves. There are more than 2,000 arches within the park, ranging in size from a three foot opening (the minimum considered to be an arch) to the longest one, *Landscape Arch*, which measures 306 feet from base to base. Some of the arches are extremely tall, with huge spans, and you will seasonally find an occasional rock climber atop them.

I myself enjoy viewing the clouds through the archways as they pass behind, providing an excellent backdrop and continuously changing their exquisite formations. There are great photo opportunities here. I once photographed the moon during daylight hours through the span of a lengthy arch. It was indeed an impressive photo for an amateur—postcard material for sure.

After sunset many arches throughout the park provide unique views of the evening stars through their open archways. *Why* so many arches? God likes arches. He is not unlike us in having favorites; the first thing He gave us after the Great Flood was an arch. Remember the *rainbow*? It is still around—a tribute to the flood and a sign from God, confirming His promise to never again destroy the earth with water.[1]

Again, there's much to see in this unique area of land where most of this particular composition of clay, over the last 5000 years or so, has hardened to stone. All of the clay formations in the area look as if they were baked in an oven. Indeed, the sun's heat over a period of time is surely responsible for this work. Perhaps it only took a few years after the formations were born to accomplish this. Geologists have numerous theories on this particular aging process, but only God knows.

Modern geology does not take into consideration that God made all things and a variety of them full grown; therefore their conclusions on any matter regarding the aging process require a great deal of scrutiny.

In other words, no disrespect intended, their intelligence is more foolishness than it is anything else.[2] All I know for sure is that the entire area of Arches National Park is a most remarkable display of His handiwork. (Psalm 95:5 & 104:8 Isaiah 40:28, Acts 7:50 & 17:24).

There's a particular arch within the park that is called Delicate Arch. I mentioned it earlier. It's about a 3 mile round trip hike over the most beautiful expanse of red rock that one can imagine. It is a well known monument, frequently pictured in travel journals. I've been allowed to hike to it several times over the years. The first time that Sandie went to the Arches with me she chose to make the hike to the Delicate Arch. She has always had trouble with her ankles and I questioned her, surprised that she wanted to make the effort.

Well, she did it, living with the ankle discomfort along the way. When she finally reached the Arch she burst into tears. I asked her if she was in pain. She just shrugged her shoulders and said, "It is so beautiful—I am really glad that you let me come along." To me, her hike was a monumental accomplishment. I am sure it was to her as well. I took a photograph of her standing in front of the arch, and later decoupaged it onto wood. It is currently on display in her home office. When she on occasion allows herself to get down in the dumps with life, I just tell her to gaze in wonder and awe at that picture.

Thanks for taking the time out of your day to hike here with me through this outstanding red rock country. I hope you too were inspired! It is certainly a great place to wander through, to allow your mind to take the time to ponder the wonder of God in His unequalled creativity. It is a place to meditate deeply on all His works and to consider, within our finite minds, the infinite height and breadth of His wisdom.

All things were made through Him, and without Him nothing was made that was made (John 1:3 NKJV).

Monument Valley

Remember His marvelous works, which He has done, His wonders... (Psalm 105:5 NKJV).

If you've never hiked *Monument Valley*, well, it's time you did. These impressive wonders, sacred to the Navajo nation, are located in an area of about ninety-two thousand acres, which is just a small part

167

of the nearly 16 million acre Navajo Indian Reservation of the great American southwest.

The monuments themselves are scattered across the landscape from northern Arizona into southern Utah. The elevation here is high desert country, from about 5000 to just over 6000 feet or more above sea level. The first thing you may want to take note of on your trek through this land, if and when the wondrous awe generated inside you ever settles down long enough for you to do so, is to note the *height* of the various monuments.

For the most part they are all very close to the same height above ground. The floor of the valley presently consists of small, rolling hills and flatland, mostly hardened clay and sandstone (similar to the terrain of Arches National Park). The monuments themselves are composed of a tightly compressed mixture of the terrain found at ground level.

The point is that during the Great Flood, about 5000 years ago, when the soft and hard rocks, clay and other materials were first deposited into the area at the height of the flood, this 92,000 acre land mass was laid out as fairly level terrain, equal to the now existing height of the monuments themselves.

Since the area is so large and the monuments are some distance from one another, a view of the region from Muley Point in Utah, about 15 miles west of Mexican Hat, may help you to better understand what actually took place here. If you've never been there, just concentrate on what I am about to describe to you—hopefully you'll get the picture:

The receding floodwaters, as they were passing through this recent deposit with great force, washed, to a *considerable* depth, all of the loose sediments away, while the more rigid deposits held their ground. Tremendous masses of sediments as high as the current monuments were moved from this area as they were in all areas of the world during a five month period of water recession from the unimaginably high crest of the flood.

Though the more rigid deposits remained immovable, they were however shaped dramatically by the commanding persistence of retreating waters—the profound strokes of the Artist's brush. *All* of the monuments within this vast area have shale, pebble and sand deposits at their base. The bases themselves are gradually contoured outward.

When the high volume of receding waters significantly decreased, which according to the Biblical record took a minimum of five months, the bases of the newly formed monuments continued to remain under water for a period of time, which accounts for the watermarked contour visible on the base of each monument. The entire valley was a seemingly endless lake, while the newly formed monuments, at varying distances from one another, protruded up out of the shallow waters over several miles.

What an *overwhelmingly awesome sight* it must have been! A smaller version of this 'picture in time' exists still to this day, about 300 hundred miles to the west in the Lake Mead area, where separate red rock monuments protrude out of the waters there. Similar monuments are found in the water at various areas along the Colorado River, however, with the recession, the remaining floodwater in Monument Valley, which stands at a considerably higher elevation, was draining out—slowly *decreasing*. Over a period of time the earth eventually dried up in this higher area (Genesis 8:14), and Monument Valley was born.

It is indeed an inspiration to hike among the monuments of Monument Valley. When I do this I try to contemplate what actually took place here during its formation. The thought of it overturns the imagination. It is, of course, sacred ground. I couldn't look at it in any other way, nor can the local Indians.

Then again, all of the planet earth is sacred ground to the Christian, or at least it *should* be. But it is here, in this obviously immense moving and shaping of land, in this place where widespread, diversely yet harmoniously sculptured sentinels give glory to the One who formed them, where I fall on my face with exceedingly great thanksgiving in *awe* of the untold *wonder* of God, our Creator.

The first time Sandie and I went into the monuments we parked the trailer in a campsite that overlooked what the locals call, the *Mittens*. There are two formations. If you could see them you would understand why they were named as such. Across from them is another formation called *Merric Butte*. The three formations are pictured on postcards available from the Navajo Tribal Park, and are usually the scenery used for advertising the area in a variety of travel magazines.

While we stayed there, Sandie painted the exquisite desert scenery, which included all three of these formations, across the front awning (rock guard) of my trailer. The entire painting was about 6 feet wide and 2 feet in height. Her well-stroked work allowed me to take

Monument Valley around with me, wherever I went. The Navajo's say that Monument Valley inspires us to 'walk in beauty.' I was allowed to '*live* in beauty' from that day on, thanks to Sandie's most fine reproduction of God's artwork.

Oh, the depth of the riches both of the wisdom and knowledge of God! How unserchable are His judgments and His ways past finding out! (Romans 11:35 NKJV)

Into Death Valley

And they did not thirst when He led them through the deserts. He caused the waters to flow from the rock for them. He also split the rock, and the waters gushed out (Isaiah 48:21 NKJV).

Death Valley in California, perhaps at the bottom of a sea in the pre-flood world, is a notably vast formation of hills and buttes—an extremely picturesque mixture of multicolored sand, mud, clay and rocks. Water-carved arroyos and boulder strewn washes abound throughout this region and hiking among them and through them is quite impressive, to say the least.

About 60 miles wide and over 125 miles in length, Death Valley is still another true monument to God's creativity in the power of receding waters during the Great Flood of Noah. It is now however a very dry, still (quiet), restful place. It is a medicinal location to set up camp under the stars or to leisurely dwell in during the day. I have been fortunate enough to have spent many rewardingly quiet times within its tranquil borders.

Quietness is indeed a good thing. The Bible teaches us; *in quietness and trust is your strength* (Isaiah 30:15 NKJV). Unfortunately, unending noise, most of it man made, pollutes life on our planet. Mankind rushes on not knowing their end, but when death comes there is truly nothing we can take with us save silence. The noise and futility of this life are left behind. Why not choose then to learn the value of living life here and now amidst quietness? Not externally of course, for that would be nearly impossible—unless you lived in a remote section of this desert.

I am talking here about *inner* quietness. Inner peace is developed through a learning process of trusting in God. It's something you just can't accomplish on your own. It is a reserved quietness, not tuned in to the world's noise. It is a result of knowing that God is in control—

170

of accepting that life-giving fact within your heart and within your mind and within your spirit. He made all things, including you. There's great peace in that, for if He *formed* you, He will indeed *care* for you.

Lord, my heart is not proud. My eyes are not haughty. I do not concern myself with matters too great or awesome for me. But I have stilled and quieted myself, just as a small child is quiet with its mother. Yes, like a small child is my soul within me (Psalm 131 NKJV).

Inner peace, like all sound Biblical teachings regarding the principles of understanding, is developed through a timely learning process. It is the utopia in mind and body control. No man-made meditation practice can ever achieve it. You don't need to stand on your head in thought, nor contort your body through some man-inspired ritual, nor do you need to be an expert in Kung fu to obtain it. Inner peace comes only from a focus on God and a trust in God.

If you will, notice that the psalmist wrote that *he* had stilled and quieted *himself*. He had learned through experience not to be proud or self satisfied. His eyes were not haughty or arrogant or self-magnifying. He had become as a small child within his thinking, and he emphasized that. His focus and trust was in God (Psalm 131:3). Yes, he certainly had to find a resting place for the turmoil and cares of this life, both past and present, as well as find a refuge for the natural frustration of spirit encountered in achieving that particular quietness.

His trust then could have *only* been in God and not in himself, nor in human wisdom or philosophy. Only unwavering faith and trust *in God*, with patience, will develop that type of peace and quietness within. Contrary to the theories of modern psychology, there is, in pure reality, just no other way to go about it. The Bible teaches that the peace of God passes human understanding. We can obtain it if we are willing. Trust in God is the only attitude that can permanently conquer life's problems and difficulties. A God-centered attitude has power over all things.

You may have never been to Death Valley. There are many other similarly remote and quiet places all over the earth. Yet, if you have developed the quietness within which the psalmist speaks of, you could probably sit down in the median of a freeway during rush hour and be at peace. I wouldn't recommend that, but it is possible. Personally, I still prefer the external silence of the desert, the mountains, within a forest or down beside a quiet stream. These particular areas of God's creation 'speak' of His peace.

You might first take notice as to the silence of the rocks or the trees or the plants nearby as you wander about in these remote places. Believe me, if they could speak out in your language, they could teach you many things about God and inner quietness (Job 12:7-10). Death Valley is indeed one of those places where nature becomes your teacher. The quietness there is unique and may have something to do with the area's relation to sea level. It is the lowest point of land in the United States.

The Biblical book of Job teaches us in numerous passages that the *creation itself* trusts in God. That is why it is so quiet and peaceful within—following the natural order of life on the earth, remaining in subjection to its Creator. The creation itself knows that God is in control and will one day restore all things—including external peace (Romans 8:18-24). Learning more about the things that God has made, as well as the distinct peace He has endowed them with, can help you to trust in Him and to become at peace within yourself. You can become 'one with the earth' so to speak.

Again, you cannot rely on the teachings of men to still your soul, unless they are founded upon the Word of God. Allow me to share with you a 'tutoring' on inner peace from Death Valley, an area created for our inspiration by God during the Great Flood:

The terrain in Death Valley is indeed *rough*; much like the turmoil and frustration that goes with living in this world and much like who we are inside, yet the area itself we find to be still and peaceful. It has been quieted by time since the upheaval of the Great Flood, some 5000 years ago. An ancient waterbed, Death Valley is full of collectable rocks of all sizes, shapes and colors—indeed a rock hunter's paradise. Nowadays you're not supposed to remove them; just permitted to look at them.

There are hundreds of impressive water-laid canyons and arroyos here. Due to the natural environment of the area nearly 1000 species of plants flourish within its borders. To date there are at least twenty-one or more different species of plants that are found nowhere else in the world.[3] The valley is also home to many varieties of marsh grass. There are spectacular spring wildflower displays. There are numerous species of reptiles, birds and animals.

Once while journeying there, being occupied in a leisurely ascent of a multicolored rock butte, I was allowed the sudden honor of observing a most handsome and interesting desert specimen—a coyote. As I rounded an outcropping of rock, I spotted him on the narrow ridge just ahead of me. The rarely hiked and washed out trail that I was on bore a weathered posting at its trailhead—'Hike or Die.' I had made the right choice—I kept on moving forward in the desert heat.

He saw me immediately and stopped in his track to investigate my intrusion into his domain. I felt 'at one' with him for a moment—we were both alone in a remote area of exceptional inspiration. He took a few steps away from me, then stopped and turned his head back to observe me once again. He then gracefully moved his body around, facing me head-on. He was indeed very healthy looking for a desert coyote. His hair was coarse and colorful and his size well above average. He stood so majestically there, an air of gentle boldness about him. I was of course quite thrilled by his presence—actually, beyond measure.

I instinctively said, "Hello," to him. He perked up his ears and continued to watch me. I wasn't sure that he'd ever had the English language spoken at him before. I then climbed on around toward the ridge approaching him, just below his perch, and continued on my journey, stepping down on a somewhat lower outcrop of red rock and passing by just underneath him. I could have reached up and nearly touched him. He kept watch on me for a short period as I did on him, then he turned and moved on, crossing a sloped expanse of red rock, bound in another direction from me.

He came to a dead stop once on his journey and looked back, as if to say, "Farewell—watch yourself out here, man—snakes about." He continued on after that and I soon lost sight of him among the rocks. I called out to him, but he did not come into my view again. He had appeared the whole time that I was allowed the honor of His presence to be very untroubled, not at all apprehensive like most coyotes I have come in contact with in the wilderness. Perhaps it is Death Valley itself that inspired the behavior of this particular coyote.

The valley is indeed quite captivating in nature, breathtakingly still, full of some of God's finest artwork; beyond any shadow of doubt a most adequate tutor on spiritual nourishment. You can actually take a deep breath and smell the strength of the *enriching quietness* in

173

this place. Realms of quietness have distinct scents of their own—did you know that? The Apache Indians teach us that stillness is an *unequaled* pleasure. This is of course all God's doing.

You can develop the very same quietness and stillness within yourself; an inner peace that passes understanding (Philippians 4:6,7). It is a process of training your attitudes and your senses in learning to rightly appreciate God's wonders—a process of giving 'thanks' as you learn to trust Him in and for your daily walk, carrying those wonders along with you in your heart and mind. The psalmist well understood this concept.

Within Death Valley there is a road named *Artist Drive*, where oxidation has produced a rainbow of colors in the eroded clay deposits of ancient ocean or lake bed sediments. The colors are most intense during late afternoon. *Artists Palette*, about halfway along the drive, is a particularly unusual mosaic of red, yellow, orange, green, violet, brown and black hues. Being an artist, Sandie was most inspired in this area. To me, it looks like the place where God may have mixed his paints for the entire valley. Whether it is or not, it is encouraging to think of it in that way.

The Lord is my shepherd; I shall not be in want. He makes me to lie down in green pastures; He leads me beside quiet waters. He restores my soul... (Psalm 23:1-3 NKJV).

Listening to the Wind

Who can this be, that even the wind and the sea obey Him? (Mark 4:41 NKJV)

Hello, from the vast and beautiful Arizona desert. I've been allowed to travel around the West for several years now, working at various campgrounds, doing some writing, teaching and hiking amidst breathtaking, God-sculptured scenery, while at the same time experiencing many extremely valuable lessons that God has so graciously taught me along the way. However, there have been some times when I wasn't quite sure where I was going spiritually.

You know how we are sometimes not sure about things in our mind, traveling that road of human uncertainty? I was once told by an American Indian (Sioux) that when I am walking with uncertainty, I need to stop and "listen to the wind." There was a time when I would have thought that he meant that I should just blow on out and away from wherever I was and whatever I was thinking and forget about uncertainty.

But we do fear change, unfamiliar circumstances, new beginnings, don't we? And, most of us are not use to listening to the trees or talking to the sand to get answers. There are indeed many who think that this particular type of advice is strange—to listen to the wind. Yet, true Christians are supposed to be born of the Spirit (John 3:5). Jesus himself describes one born of the Spirit in John 3, verse 8:

Just as you can hear the wind but can't tell where it comes from or where it is going, so it is with those who are born of the Spirit (NKJV).

It is true; we cannot physically pinpoint the Spirit of God. We cannot tell where it comes from, nor can we determine where it goes. But, we can hear it. Like the wind, His spirit moves over the deserts and plains, over the fields, the mountains and the waters. We can see its affect in nature and on the environment. It can also speak to us within our hearts, within our inner man (or woman), in unserchable ways (1st Corinthians 2:10-16). If we are listening with our hearts and become obedient to His Spirit, we can see its affect on our lives as well.

This particular Arizona desert region we are hiking along the Colorado River is surrounded by lofty, pointed buttes. It is full of numerous canyons and colorful hills. There are sandy, rock-strewn washes containing many varieties of desert brush. It is obviously an area blessed with a medley of winds. Winds carry the seeds from existing plants to produce even more plants, allowing the desert to become a lush wilderness. These winds can be soft and gentle, gusty and strong, relentless in nature, and are always unpredictable with their sudden changes in direction. They also speak.

They speak of the ancient Flood and of its diverse marks on the land. They encircle the mountains among these craggy peaks, boastfully threatening them with their demonstration of immeasurable, usurping power. They reshape the hills, seed the ground and carve the dunes. They whisper the dramatic stories of ancient patriarchs who dwelled in similar topography. They tell of warriors and shepherds, of kings and queens, of princes and nomads, of explorers and pioneers, and serve to encourage the weary, lonely desert wanderer.

The winds forever speak of God's presence. They build the foundations for the clouds, moving them into gorgeous sunrises and sunsets. Yes, this desert is indeed a remarkably inspiriting area for *listening to the wind*. If you are like me and love the caress of God against your face, then this is the place to be. God can reach out and touch you in a marvelous way through His elements of snow, wind and rain. What encouragement and inspiration His wonders can bestow upon you!

Winds do not speak of cities, of high-rise buildings nor other man-made structures. They don't talk of dams or power plants. They don't whisper of trains or of airplanes or of automobiles, or of modern technology in any form. Their conversation is not of this world. Being spiritual in nature, winds could care less about those particularly earthly things. They do, as I mentioned before, speak to the waters and could overthrow the land and destroy its structures and its inhabitants, at any time, in any number of ways.

Yet, winds are prone to God's mercy and do not overrule His established boundaries (Psalm135:7). They were created by Him and therefore operate by His authority (Psalm 147:18). The winds have understanding as well as might; they are *lovingly obedient* in all ways to the Lord their creator. They know their place in God's natural order of things and speak in accordance with His will. They do His will, but beware; they are permitted, with limitations imposed by God, to also do the will of Satan (Job 1:19).

And so, being as diverse and influential as they are, they can be truly uplifting in spirit and uniquely instructive to one whose desire is to listen to them. As the wind can be a reminder to us of God's presence, it is also a reminder for us that God is in control. My daughter recently spoke to me of her experience in viewing the results of a tornado in a rural Ohio town. Profoundly, she was more concerned about identifying the purpose of God's work, if it was indeed God's work, than in contemplating the value of material losses among her relatives and neighbors.

Incidentally, that tornado struck with great devastation on all sides of her home, but did not so much as lift a shingle on her house. Even if it would have struck her house, I am confident, through an understanding of her mindset regarding this event, that she is one who listens to and has understanding regarding the wind. Her obvious respect and growing love toward her Creator and His sovereignty have allowed her great insight—she is aware of who is in control and confident in His judgments.

Listening to the wind is not really strange advice after all; *Who but God goes up to heaven and comes back down? Who holds the wind in His fists? Who wraps up the oceans in His cloak? Who has created the whole wide world? What is His name—and His Son's name? Tell me if you know!* (Proverbs 30:4 NLT)

Desert Prayer

Charge Joshua and encourage him and strengthen him, for he shall go across at the head of his people (Deuteronomy 3:28 NASB).

We're camping in the great eastern Mojave Desert region of southern California. It's morning and last night's campfire is just simmering coals now, but adequate for brewing trail coffee. It is easy here in this wilderness, with that cup of trail coffee in hand, to hike a short distance from the trailer and find myself within the shield of a deep ravine, with no man made objects in sight.

One might think that it would be mighty lonely out here, and I do sincerely miss various friends and family, yet, I am *encouraged* nonetheless. What I have is the *encouragement* of rugged desert topography, all around me, and the vast, open sky above me. It is indeed beautiful here and extremely quiet as well.

Though it should be first and foremost, encouragement is not something you always find among people out there in the world. It is indeed like pure gold—a hard find. But with God, encouragement is available on a daily basis—even out here in the desert. When and if you seek encouragement, honoring its heavenly source, you will surely find it.

A variety of brush grows here in the desert, which is now in gorgeous bloom. Sand washes and multicolored rocks abound. Rolling hills and pointed buttes are indeed impressive as well. Most importantly, I am alone with God amidst these wonders—a fine place to be in the morning. His creation is the very first thing I face, and the awesomeness, as well as the stillness, is an extreme pleasure. My thoughts are drawn toward Him immediately; I give thanks for the air that I breathe and the desert scents that I smell.

I thank Him for my sight; that He has allowed me to behold yet another glorious morning among His wonders. I look down at my hiking boots on the desert terrain and give thanks that I have been allowed to walk on His sacred earth. The worries of the day have not crept in as of yet, and the warmth of His mercy, which is new every morning (Lamentations 3:23), now surrounds me. I am therefore encouraged beyond understanding (Philippians 4:7).

I descend to my knees and ask for His strength so that I might endure this day among the human inhabitants of the earth, with the majority of their minds so far from Him. I ask that I might be allowed to continue to think of Him, so that I myself can survive the day. I have learned to understand that the world was formed by Him, that I was formed by Him, and as I walk out of this protective ravine I am encouraged that, no matter what I am about to face this day, I can endure because He is with me; guarding me, guiding me, all the day, all the way; something I didn't realize at all in my youth.

I cannot turn back the hands of time, but I am indeed thankful for this present knowledge of Him. He does not hold yesterday against me. If I am willing, He will walk with me each day of my life. The gift of this knowledge and the faith it can generate is the *absolute elite* in encouragement. Among what friends or relations will you find this extreme height of encouragement?

On the earth it is impossible, yet, with God, all things are possible (Mark 10:27). You can draw from this higher level by allowing the Spirit of God to work through you, and you can give the gift of such encouragement to friends or relations—to anyone with whom you come in contact. No matter where you live, no matter where or what you have been, no matter who you are, no matter what your circumstance and no matter how deep your scars or how repulsive the stains of your sins, you *can be* an encourager. You can create encouragement.

You were designed to create! You can also encourage and inspire the creative abilities within others. Those who criticize can create nothing. There are those who believe in 'constructive criticism'. To the contrary, *all* criticism is *destructive*. We therefore need to turn our negative criticism into positive encouragement. We have each been given the *opportunity* to create. We were each created in God's image, thereby giving us the *ability* to create. As our talents vary, so our creativity varies. We, each and every one of us, have something unique to offer—something 'different' to add to encouragement.

The earthly Webster defined encouragement as follows: To inspire with courage, hope or resolution. To help or to foster (promote) growth or development. In other words it means to *build up*. As God encourages us (*builds us up*), we need also to encourage (*build up*) others. We need to ask His help when speaking to others. We need to ask Him to guard our thoughts and our intentions.

We need carefully then to *season* our words and/or actions toward others. We need the right 'flavor' in speaking or acting. The Bible describes the 'right words spoken' as *spiritual weapons* with the ability to *knock down* the devil's strongholds, to *capture rebels and bring them back to God* (2nd Corinthians 10:2-5, italicized for emphasis).

Properly seasoned, words can be indeed powerful! It is vitally important then to take the time to commune with God before or even while you're interacting and/or conversing with others. Also, when you are alone at night, go over the day's events with Him. Confess your faults and ask Him to help you in applying His counsel toward others and to guard your tongue in this process.

No one of course can tame the tongue (James 3:8), but, by increasing this practice of communing with God, it is through Him that you can gain the wisdom and understanding needed to *control* your tongue. You can indeed be developed into a productive tool of creative encouragement.

You can also help through sharing your life, your worldly goods, your active talents and seasoned speech; to inspire and to motivate the creativity in others. This sharing of your life, of your goods and of your talents, is an element of *love*, something we all need so desperately to do. Keep in mind that everything you have has been given you from above (John 19:11). You are the steward of each of the things you have been given.

There are a lot of folk's out there who have no homes, no daily bread, and many who have never even heard a kind word spoken. This should not be. These folk's don't need the world nor what it offers—they need you. Try then not to lose patience in your continued endeavors to make the world a better place for those along your path.

Go often to your favorite retreat, or to any place where you can engage in quiet prayer and seek the Lord's help. His encouragement toward you, *freely given to you*, is your greatest power for the influence of goodness toward others. Encouragement can make all the difference in the world in one's life. Pray that He will strengthen you in your efforts to *encourage* others…

And after He had sent the multitudes away, He went up to the mountain by himself to pray (Matthew 14:23 NASB).

Looks like our early morning campfire is close to burning out. Perhaps we had just better let it be and build a new one tonight. Coffee's lukewarm, but you're welcome to a little. We'll be headin' out shortly to view some of the desert's finest creatures. That's coming up in chapter 11. Thanks so much for hiking with me along the *Desert Trail.* I trust your trek was well worthwhile. Come back anytime and we'll do it again. Bring some friends along. Anyone is welcome here.

Chapter Eleven...Ask the Animals

Ask the animals and they will teach you, or the birds of the air, and they will tell you; or speak to the earth, and it will teach you, or let the fish of the sea inform you. Which of all these does not know that the hand of the Lord has done this? In His hand is the life of every creature and the breath of all mankind (Job 12:7-10 NIV).

There's a *little* dog (pictured above) that happens to be a *big* part of my life. He's a Chihuahua, the cutest little guy you've ever seen. His name is *Digger*, and he has taught me more about the *character* of God's love than any other creature on the face of the earth. I am indeed indebted to him.

He has taught me of faithfulness and loyalty, of kindness and gentleness, of patience and forgiveness, and most importantly, he has taught me the deep meaning of friendship and love, which is actually a combination of all of the above. The question is, who taught him these things? No mistake about it—the opening Scripture for this chapter definitely answers that question.

Digger's character had a designer. In order for Digger to be who he is, it only stands to reason that his designer would himself have to possess an abundance of these very qualities. And, the designer would award Digger with these qualities, that I might better comprehend, in accordance with the Scripture, the attributes of the designer—through Digger.

This animal would serve to teach me something very special about the Lord, who made all things. How much more then should I embrace the desire to teach my fellow man/woman these things? Get the picture? By the way, *altruism* (unselfish concern for others) contradicts evolution. I might add that *spontaneous generation* (the emergence of life from nonliving matter) has *never* been observed.

Life comes only from life, not through natural processes as evolution claims. Forget that theory—it is a product of the imaginations of ignorant men and one of Satan's greatest tools used to cloud your mind. Don't be deceived—Digger's existence and character prove the theory of organic evolution to be absolutely false.[1] He is just about the most unselfish character I have ever known, indeed a reflection of his Creator.

Digger is *faithful*. By his own free will he comes to me at all times, no matter what I am doing, no matter what my mood, and lays at my feet in a position of both submissiveness and contentment. He seems to relish being around me at all times, especially when lying upon my lap.

He is *loyal*. If I get up and move somewhere, he follows, no matter where I may go—upstairs, downstairs, you name it, he's on my heals at all times. If I am coming in from outside, he always waits with excitement at the door when he hears me approach. If a stranger approaches, he is quick to warn me with a loud bark.

He is *kind*. He licks my fingers in affection when I reach down to touch him, or licks my face when I hold him in my arms. He warms up to strangers when he senses that they are not a threat. He shares his water with other dogs, wagging his tail as he watches them lap it from his dish.

He is *gentle*. When he jumps upon my bed and climbs onto my chest, he relaxes, then raises one leg in an act of submissiveness. He submits completely whenever I stoke his back or simply touch him anywhere. When playfully chewing on my fingers with his sharp teeth, he never resorts to a pressure that would injure my flesh.

He is *patient*. He watches me when I eat, sometimes motionless and without wavering, waiting for some morsel that I might grant him.

When his need is to go outside, he sits at the door and patiently waits for me to respond. He relaxes in complete comfort while being bathed or having his claws trimmed.

He is *forgiving*. If I should speak harshly at him, which I no longer even consider, he immediately cowers and lowers his head for a moment, but then approaches me and wags his tail, ready to display his love once again. If I accidentally step on his foot (he is small and you don't always realize he is there), he will give a yelp, but immediately draws near to me again, as if to say, "That's okay, I'm okay."

Naturally Digger is a little mischievous and even ornery at times—he's a victim of the Fall, as all animals are. Yet, God has allowed His unfathomable love to work through Digger on my behalf, restraining him from many of his natural traits. Let me take that concept a little deeper:

God knows all things from beginning to end. Every moment of our individual lives are in His hands and have been from our very conception within the mother's womb that he chose for us. Our lives are then of course lived out within the framework of our parent's choices and eventually our own choices.

These choices sometime wrestle against God's purpose and result in us wandering in the wilderness (coming up in chapter 12) for a time, but God is not at all thwarted in bringing about His purpose for us. Though we are rebellious, He continues His work for us—and works relentlessly.

He uses any means available in accomplishing His will, *always* having His best interest for us at heart. For me, I believe *one* of those means happens to be a member of His animal kingdom, which concept is certainly upheld in the opening Scripture of this chapter; *ask the animals and they shall teach you...*

Digger has taught me how important it is to spend time with him and he respects and values every moment of that time. He has caused me to consider my failures in this realm with my human children many years ago. By that I mean that he has taught me the importance of each *moment* in life. He has taught me how much I have missed by not making use of significant moments in that former relationship.

Had I been like Digger in character in my youth, my family would still be intact. The children would of course be grown up and long gone by now, pursuing their own destinies, but my life with them could have been much different—precious moments spent with them would have made a world of difference—in their lives as well as mine. They could have known an unmatched closeness with both their mother and their father. I could have taught them what love is, as Digger has taught me.

I would have known how to truly *listen* to each word that came out of the mouth of every member of my family. I would have known how to reply to them with tenderness and understanding. I would have been the rock that they could have depended upon, no matter what life dealt. I would have been the shepherd that they could have looked up to for encouragement, for hope, and for protection. And, unless I died, they would have *known* that 'daddy' was never going anywhere—their counselor and friend for life.

Digger is a creature that lives moment by moment. Everything seems important to him; touching him, talking to him, playing with him, walking with him and allowing him to run through the grass and among the flowers of the field, sniffing everything in sight in total awareness of his surroundings—for each of these things he is extremely grateful.

He knows how to make the most of every moment. To top it all off, he trusts in me moment to moment—he knows that God gave me authority over him. That particular trust is indeed humbling, allowing me insight into the deeper intrinsic values of responsibility.

He doesn't even consider running away from me under any circumstance. If a big ol' dog growls at him, he just stands erect like Rin Tin Tin and faces the oppressor head on—size matters not. If the oppressor moves toward him, he is quick to retreat and stand between my legs. He knows I'm the guy who will protect him. His trust makes me aware of the great responsibility we as humans have toward the animal kingdom, yet, how much more then should we consider our relationship to others of the human race?

Moments are significant in any relationship. A moment by moment awareness of *words* we are about to speak, of *affections* we choose to bestow, of *behavior* we are about to display, and the *encouragement* that we need to give are the most important considerations in human relationships that we can *ever* contemplate.

Dear reader, life *does* need to be lived moment by moment—with faithfulness, loyalty, kindness, gentleness, patience and forgiveness. These are the qualities that can make your family members your best friends. These qualities serve also to make you a best friend to others.

These qualities display integrity, yet are but a mere shadow of God's qualities, which indeed serve to make Him the very best of your friends. He is a friend who sticks closer than a brother (Proverbs 18:24). He is the One upon whose lap we are permitted to rest—where our trust in Him becomes our greatest security.

Behold all of the wonders this *friend* has created for you! Behold the sky, the sun, the moon, the stars, the mountains, the deserts, the canyons, the plants and flowers! Can His character—His attributes become any clearer to you? Only the insensitively ignorant would not want to imitate Him.

We would be wise to desire the mind of Christ—to imitate Him through our words and actions (Philippians 2:5, Matthew 11:29) on a daily, moment by moment basis. We can learn to love in spite of our proneness to sin, for love covers (*holds at bay*) a multitude of sins (1st Peter 4:8).

Consider all that God has put into the heart of little Digger, who is just a grain of sand among all the animals! You can see that, when the Spirit of God moves in the heart, goodness is indeed produced. God teaches us what love is using a myriad of sources available to Him; and through Him, if we do not quench His Spirit within us, we can radiate this love that He so graciously bestows upon us.

The animals know, the birds know, the fish of the sea know, even the *stones* cry out! (Luke 19:40) The earth is also aware—it can teach you that the hand of the Lord has made all of these things—including you! And you are the *crown* of His creation—you are the love of His life (Psalm 8:5). Why not learn to love Him in return?

There have been times at particular moments during the writing of this book that I have encountered depression. When I consider the world that I live in and the earthly attitudes that are prevalent in society, I wonder if my efforts are actually worth the effort? Is this writing from a sinner, whose eyes have been opened, really going to make a difference—is it going to help someone else? Will the attributes of our Creator become more visible to one who reads this book? Will certain truths catch hold of a reader and allow him/her to gain the understanding needed to motivate them for the betterment of themselves and others?

The last time these thoughts overwhelmed me I sat at my desk in silence for some time. I had been working on this very chapter. I also

185

took notice that Digger was at my feet the whole time, lying in a position of contentment, his big, beautiful eyes fixed gently upon me.

When I reached down to acknowledge him, I realized that his presence was an encouragement—what he taught me about his Creator was expected to be shared with the human race—my entire life's experience of learning in all areas of living was to be bestowed upon others for a reason. Digger's humble presence reminded me that I needed to 'stay the course' in my endeavor and not lose heart. I realized also that this animal had truly become a part of my personal connection with God.

We're still out here in the middle of the desert right now—still listening to the wind. There are no schedules, no meetings, no pressures out here—just raw time. Time to watch. Time to listen in depth. Time to think about God, and time to talk with the animals— and ask them. After all, they were made from the earth as well (Genesis 1:24).

Let us consider what the Biblical book of Job has offered us for our instruction and encouragement. Let us hike around out here and observe just a few of the desert's more popular inhabitants[2] and learn something from them, shall we? Perhaps you are one of those folk's who may connect with God in this way…

Coyotes

The first desert creature I want you to observe today is the Coyote. Lots of 'em out here in the desert. One of the most adaptable animals in the world, the Coyote can change its breeding habits, diet and social dynamics to survive a wide variety of habitats. It is an opportunistic, persistent and extremely elusive predator, skilled in a variety of hunting techniques. It travels over its range and hunts both day and night, running swiftly and catching its prey easily. The Coyote is extremely intelligent in that it honors all attributes given it by the Creator.

Here in the desert its principle diet is composed of mice, rabbits, ground squirrels and other small rodents, insects, reptiles, and fruits and berries of wild plants. While hunting for food the Coyote's hearing is very acute and is used for detecting prey and avoiding danger. With an excellent sense of smell the Coyote tracks its prey, then usually stalks it for 20-30 minutes before pouncing. A Coyote can run at nearly 40 miles per hour. It has the stamina to chase its prey over long distances and then can strike when the quarry is exhausted. They are however truly much more than just great hunters.

Of all the wild animals on our planet they are an outstanding example of devotion to family. They are ideal parents, sharing with their spouse the responsibility of feeding and raising their young ones. In their dens they are loving, loyal, and most willing to work together for the common good. I'm not a family man at this time, but if I were I would take lessons from the mature domestic qualities of the Coyote.

How I wish I would have wandered the deserts in my earlier years and learned both the value and application of these meaningful qualities! I'm sure it would have produced in me the wisdom to be a much better communicator, provider, and leader to and for the family God gave me.

Coyotes use a variety of calls to defend their territory, as well as for strengthening social bonds and general communication. I have heard them 'calling' in great numbers. If you go into their territory and call out in a similar fashion, the Coyotes will indeed call out to you in return. I experienced this most unique communication many times while working high in the Angeles Forest with Hal Deckhert, one of my campground work associates. We were fortunate to get our 'talking to the coyotes' experiences on videotape—I believe I mentioned this to you in an earlier chapter.

A lot of folk's think of Coyotes only as savages and scavengers. When these folk's hear the call of the Coyote, the hair usually stands up on the back of their necks. But, to the seasoned outdoorsman or the Native American, the howl of the Coyote is truly a song of the West. The animal's finer qualities go virtually untold, one of them being that Coyotes are quite necessary in preserving the balance of nature. We are indeed fortunate that the night song of the 'Little Wolf' may still be heard throughout the desert southwest. There is much one can glean from the observation and study of these incredible animals.

Jack Rabbits

The black-tailed Jack Rabbit, a desert dweller, is found in all four southwestern American deserts. Its diet is strictly vegetation, such as shrubs, creosote bushes, mesquite trees, snake weeds, junipers, big sagebrushes and cacti. The Jack Rabbit eats constantly and doesn't require much water, as it obtains nearly all the water it needs from the plant material it eats—they're great harvesters, and preserve the balance of nature in the desert by spreading seed.

Jack Rabbits are born bright eyed, active soon after birth and ready to fend for themselves in just 30 days. They reach adult size in seven to eight months. They are more active in the evening as their eyes focus well at night. They are always aware of their surroundings, and in addition to this keen eyesight, rely on acute hearing and swift zigzag running to insure their safety and survival. They can leap as far as fifteen feet, reaching speeds up to 50 miles per hour in their escape. They are nearly twice as elusive as the cottontail rabbit.

Also unlike the cottontail rabbit they are not found in the more easy to menace social groups. Jack Rabbits are solitary creatures. This tends to make them quite good at survival. Unfortunately they are sometimes the victim of predators, such as bobcats, foxes, horned owls, eagles, hawks, snakes and coyotes. The victimization of this gentle creature reminds me of John the baptist, who was a cousin of Jesus of Nazareth.

John spent his life in the desert. He was a solitary individual whose diet was locusts and wild honey. He went about dressed in camel hair clothing—a lowly man honorably called to prepare the way for the coming of Jesus and the kingdom of God. Many of the common people loved him, but he was indeed hated by the religious leaders of his day. He was eventually caged in prison at a young age and beheaded through the vindictiveness of an evil predator, the wife of a king.

Though John would have been despised in today's world—dressed in camel hair and living like a transient in the remoteness of the desert —Jesus declared him to be the greatest man ever born (Matthew 11:8-11). He was indeed a wise harvester, winning many souls back to God, yet he was a man of simple means. To have any of his qualities today, including his love for the wilderness and his ability to adapt to it, would be indeed a great honor.

Locusts

Locusts, who frequent the desert, are mentioned far more times than all the other insects of the Bible *combined*. There's much to learn from these small but enlightened creatures. Allow me to give you just a few insights into their characteristics. The average swarm of Locusts is made up of 40 billion individuals, who eat 40 million pounds of food a day.

The largest recorded swarm to date was two thousand miles long, and had an estimated population of 250 billion Locusts. That particular swarm could have eaten 250 million pounds of food a day. They are considered mostly to be destroyers. They are unbelievably devastating when in such unity. Their food is vegetation, most of which is for human consumption.

Surprisingly, Locusts do not have any leaders—no king—yet they march like an army in ranks (Proverbs 30:27). The Proverbs also teach us that Locusts are one of four things on earth that are small, but unusually wise (Proverbs 30:24). When Locusts swarm they go in the same direction and do the same thing, accomplishing a common goal without any leadership. Unity in the *right* direction is indeed wise. Much can be accomplished by working together.

God gives us this proverbial picture of unity through the activity of the Locusts. We don't need a human king to accomplish what we were created for (1st Samuel 8:6,7). If we would all have as our purpose to love and to serve God rather than ourselves, we could accomplish many things that we are at present unable to accomplish (John 15:5).

God also makes a wonderful promise to us using Locusts in a spiritual application: *I will restore to you the years that the swarming locusts have eaten, the crawling locust, the consuming locust, and the chewing locust* (Joel 2:25 NKJV). God is ready to forgive you of your many failures and to restore (bring healing to) the years lost in the hardships that life has dealt, if you are but willing.

Owls

Great Horned Owls, whose feather tufts above the ears appear as 'horns,' often spend their winters protected by the rocks and crags of desert canyons. The Owls are birds of prey, hunting rodents and other small animals. These great birds can reach as much as 22 inches in length. Their "hoot" is a classic sound of the wild, and like the coyote, can be heard a long way off. It is still another 'song of the West.'

They are also great parents, both male and female fiercely defending their nest site against intruders. If young Owls fall out of their nest prematurely, the adults will both feed and protect the birds on the ground. When Owls awaken, they use their hearing and eyesight to alert them of danger or possible prey.

189

Great horned Owl's eyes, which are almost as large as humans, allow an abundant amount of light to pass through the pupil so that the Owl can see well in dark conditions. If one of these Owls were as big as a human in bodily stature, each of its eyes would be the size of a small grapefruit! However, their eyes are fixed in the sockets and cannot be moved up or down or from side to side. They are able to rotate their head 270 degrees to compensate for this fixed condition of their eyes.

They also have an incredible sense of hearing. They use triangulation to pinpoint the source of a sound when their prey cannot be seen. By tilting or moving their head until the sound is of equal volume in each ear, the Owl can pinpoint the direction and distance of the sound quite accurately.

The Owl's facial disk is shaped like a shallow bowl. This shape acts like a satellite dish, to help funnel sound into the ear openings. The Owl is indeed unique in its appearance. Throughout history and across many cultures people have regarded Owls with fascination and awe. Among the different American Indian tribes there are various beliefs regarding the Owl.

According to Navajo legend, the Creator told the Owl that men would listen to its voice to learn what would be their future. To the Apache warriors, dreaming of an Owl signified approaching death. The Ogallala Sioux allowed warriors who had excelled in battle to wear a cap of Owl feathers to signify their bravery.

They also believed that the forces of nature would favor those who wore Owl feathers, and that their vision (both physical and spiritual) would be increased. But the Sioux medicine men warned that to actually see an Owl meant that someone, other than the observer, was about to die. The Cheyenne of the Great Plains believe that the Owl represents the north wind.

In England, it's supposedly good luck to see an Owl. That Owls are like gods, with knowledge and wisdom, is a legend of Greek origin. The Romans wrote that the Owl could only foretell evil and are to be dreaded more than all other birds. Each of these legends, as well as hundreds of others, portrays the Owl as a creature that apparently possesses special powers not found in other animals.

It is truly one of the most honored of birds. Being a creation of God, the Owl is of course even wiser than we have come to think.

Legends aside, there is much we can learn from a study of the Owl regarding its unique features, habits and abilities.

Sheep

Sheep receive more attention in the Bible than any other animal. They were important in the domestic, civic, and religious life of the Israelites. The earliest mention of Sheep is in Genesis 4:2, where it is said that "Abel was a keeper of Sheep." This was quite early in the creation, as Abel was one of Adam's children, who continued to honor God's love through caring for His creatures.

The shepherd's integral care is beautifully portrayed in the 23rd Psalm. This continuous care of the Sheep eventually led the early shepherds to know each one in their flock by name. Sheep were always led and never driven; they relied completely upon their shepherd for guidance.

Occasionally shepherdesses cared for Sheep as in the case of the seven daughters of the priest of Midian, whom Moses assisted at a well. Water wells were important meeting places for tribesmen (and women) and their flocks in those days. Both good and poor shepherds are mentioned in the Bible, and during the latter parts of Israel's history their leaders were denounced as being *bad* shepherds.

Figures of speech concerning Sheep and shepherding were used repeatedly as God warned His people of their shortcomings. Through this guidance God became known as the *Shepherd of His people*. Jesus Christ came to earth as the Good Shepherd and His arrival was announced, not in broad daylight to the government of Rome or to the Jewish religious leaders, but to humble shepherds who were watching their flocks by night in the fields. God sees not as man sees nor pays attention to the ranking order of men, but in righteousness (*doing things right*) respects the humble and lowly.

Sheep were kept for their milk more than for their flesh. The common breed could store a vast amount of fat in the tail and this was used as food. They also provided wool for clothing and blankets, and horns; used either for carrying oil or wine, or as trumpets for summoning the people together. Horns were also used in religious rites. The skins of rams were used in making the covering of the tabernacle. Of course, Sheep were also used in sacrifice. Offerings consisted not only of lambs but also of ewes and rams.

The ultimate sacrifice was the Lamb of God, who in many respects was foreshadowed by the ways in which lambs had served as sacrifices throughout the centuries before Christ. Jesus was the Lamb of God, who took away the sins of the world, sacrificed according to God's plan that would allow us to be saved through Him. He was led like a Sheep to the slaughter, and as a lamb before the shearer is silent, so He did not open His mouth (Acts 8:32).

There was a time in my life when I didn't pay much attention to Sheep. Now, I am deeply inspired by them. God in His kindness has given me that inspiration. Each time I observe a flock in the desert or its adjacent fields, I search out the young lambs and watch them play. I want to pick them up and cuddle them in my arms. I thank God for giving me this warm desire to care for each of His creatures. I always consider and long to imitate the gentleness of the Lamb—the One who cared enough to give His life for me.

Ravens

There are many Ravens out here in the desert. These scavengers go most everywhere and will eat just about anything; dead and decaying meat, rodents, insects and rotten garbage left by inconsiderate hikers and campers. They are what we would consider 'nasty birds,' as they store their food in animal dung, in order to prevent it from freezing during the winter. They also sift through various kinds of animal dung in search of tasteful dung beetles. We humans have for centuries considered them a disgusting bird, associating them with filth, evil and horror.

It is interesting to note however that Ravens are considered to be the most *intelligent* of all birds. A Raven will drop a walnut in front of an oncoming car, allowing it to be crushed in order to devour its meat. They are indeed problem solvers. God honored the Ravens when He allowed them to bring food to His servant, Elijah, who was hiding in a barren desert from the wrath of a vicious King Ahab (1st Kings 17:6).

The Ravens brought Elijah bread and meat in the morning and bread and meat in the evening. We are not told how long Elijah stayed in the desert, but he didn't leave until a brook he was drinking from there had dried up. The Ravens fed him until the very day he left. When I see the Ravens I think of this enduring story, of the so-called 'disgusting birds' that kept one of God's greatest servants alive.

It also serves to remind me of how much God has cared for me over the years. The Scriptures teach us to consider the Ravens; they do not plant or harvest, they don't have storehouses or barns to put food in, yet our heavenly Father feeds them. This teaching concludes by saying that we humans are of far more value to Him than many birds (Luke 12:24).

Though these creatures appear to have some strange habits, they are due our respect and admiration, as are all of God's creatures. There is a dire warning in the Scriptures concerning Ravens: *The eye that mocks his father, and scorns obedience to his mother, the ravens of the valley will pluck it out* (Proverbs 30:17 NKJV).

As a Boy my mother use to tell me that if I were disobedient, the birds would pluck out my eyes. Now I know where she got that idea— it did keep me on my toes, and I am thankful to this day for that wise admonition.

Snakes

One of the first things I ever saw out here in the desert was a Snake. A big ol' buck rattler. I remember at that very moment recalling what Jesus had said, 'be as wise as the serpent' (Matthew 10:16). When God made the creatures of the earth He made the Snake more subtle than any of the other creatures (Genesis 3:1).

During the whole of its life the Snake never closes its eyes. It cannot because God designed it without eyelids. A Snake keeps watch 24 hours a day, every day, 365 days of the year. The Snake sleeps, but its eyes continue to see objects that might affect its safety and survival. For example, if a Snake were napping on a rock and a leaf fell from a nearby tree within the Snake's field of vision, the Snake would remain asleep.

But, if the Snake were to see the shape of a hawk, a coyote, an eagle or some other predator, it would awaken and crawl to safety. That's the ultimate in observation. It is something we humans need to learn to do with regard to the cunning deceitfulness of Satan, that serpent of old, who can be lying around while we're unaware, in a watchful endeavor to destroy us (Psalm 37:32). But snakes are not only observant; they're also very sensitive—feeling oriented.

The viper has a labial pit on each side of its face, inside of which is a heat-sensitive nerve. There are many times when a viper crawls through high grass and cannot see its prey. Yet, the Snake can *feel*

193

better than it can see. The viper turns its head from side to side until each heat-sensitive nerve detects the same temperature.

It can sense a quarter-degree of temperature difference five feet away. If it strikes at a heat source while its nerves are experiencing the same temperature, it will hit the source with deadly accuracy. Missile guidance systems were designed after the heat-sensing capability of the viper. These systems were first used to guide the so-called *Sidewinder* missiles.

The Snake has a unique way of finding food. As it crawls it licks the air with its narrow, forked tongue. The tongue has a sticky substance that attracts molecules in the air. When the Snake withdraws its tongue and rubs it across a sensing organ within its mouth, it is able to classify particular molecules. If adequate quantities exist, the Snake knows he's got something. He then curls up and waits for the chance to snatch his prey. Snakes have remarkable patience and endurance. They can remain motionless without eating or drinking for months.

Snakes are at their best after they have been exposed to light for a time. They are cold blooded by nature, but can and do adapt to the surrounding temperatures. The colder they are the slower they move and the less likely they are to catch food. If you encounter a rattlesnake napping in the shade, the chances are he won't move when you walk by him, unless you approach him directly. However, they warm up when they are in the light, and that makes them agile enough to do what they have to do. Many animals are physically strengthened by light. I believe we humans are as well.

Again, the Bible teaches that the serpent is subtler than any creature God has made. By observing the way of Snakes in their natural habitat we can learn *much* about our spiritual adversary. The Devil has been labeled as a serpent since the very beginning (Revelation 12:9).

You should recall that he appeared in the form of a serpent to Adam and Eve in the Garden of Eden. He may take on any form he desires, which is something we should be constantly aware of. He is an angel of light (2nd Corinthians 11:14), who many times makes it difficult for us to discern good from evil. Do not underestimate his subtlety.

Wild Donkeys

Ever encounter a wild Donkey or wild Burro? There are a few out here in the wilderness, but a lot more wander the desert terrain in and around Death Valley. If you're camping out there you can usually hear one braying off in the distance. Sometimes they'll wander right into your camp, but for the most part they're skittish. They move quickly too. You most likely won't get a rope on one of them.

However, if your rope toss is successful, you had better be prepared to get dragged through the desert brush. It's best to leave them alone—best to just watch them, perhaps toss them a carrot or two, and enjoy their company. They'll usually hang around awhile and investigate you, then wander off peacefully.

Donkeys have never been considered among the elite animals. They don't carry great warriors into battle. They never pulled fancy chariots in the days of the Pharaohs. Yet, they are quite dependable and almost tireless beasts, capable of carrying heavier packs than horses quite a bit further than horses.

Pack stations frequently use them nowadays to carry visitors' gear into recreational wilderness areas. Trail crews nationwide use them to haul trail-building materials and equipment. At Grand Canyon they carry hundreds of annual visitors along steep, hair-raising trails into its breathtaking depths on a daily basis.

In the early days of our American West, around 1873, a fellow by the name of W.T. Coleman built the first Borax works in Death Valley. He developed the famous system of 20 mule-team wagons that hauled the processed mineral 165 miles across that arid desert to the railroad at Mojave.

The place where he originally mined is just a ghost town now. I might add here that there are a few ghost town remnants in Death Valley. It's a very interesting place to explore if you are a ghost town enthusiast. The point is, the folk's who moved away from there left *everything* behind, including the mules—mostly Donkeys and Burros. Over the last 130 years or so those animals have roamed wild and have continued to breed. I find it exciting to see these wild and beautiful creatures wandering among the desert plants.

I especially love to hear them bray. Burros are peaceful animals. Like I mentioned before, in ancient times no great warriors climbed aboard Donkeys. Most warriors were all accomplished horsemen. But in the ancient Near East, both kings and princes rode on Donkeys. The difference between the two (horseman and Donkey rider) was related to the prevalent events in the land they occupied.

A horse-riding king was a *warrior*, while a Donkey-riding *ruler* surveyed a peaceful land from his saddle. A warrior would meet out justice with a sword. A ruler pronounced justice with his words. What I am getting at is that Jesus, the King of Kings, announced his authority from the back of a young Donkey (Matthew 21:1-11). He was indeed a *ruler*. Great multitudes of people came to honor this Ruler of Rulers as He rode into Jerusalem on the back of a common Donkey.

He was not a warrior who came to fight our physical battles. He came in peace as a servant King. He came to display a servant's heart and to set an example for us, so that we might learn to depend upon Him and allow Him to express this attitude through our own hearts. He performed many miracles, which proved who He was and where He was from. The thrust of His teaching was that all would come to know Him and His Father as being humble and lowly in heart.

Yet, no one knew Him, even though He had been spoken of in many ways and identified repeatedly as the Messiah (*anointed one of God*) throughout the ancient Scriptures, which teachings the religious leaders of those days were supposedly knowledgeable of. When He finally entered Jerusalem aboard that lowly Donkey, with multitudes of supporters in His train, the religious leaders along with the whole of the city, whom he had ministered to time and again for more than three years, were stirred, and asked, "Who is this?"

Many still ask that question. All *should have known* who He was. A few did, but lacked the courage to stand with Him to the end. Personally, I continue to learn to know Him. Much of my learning comes through a study of the things He has made. So, when I see a wild Donkey out here, that most glorious beast of burden, it brings these things I've just talked to you about into my remembrance.

The teacher is no better than the pupil. It's always good to be re-reminded and made *aware* of the things that truly pertain to this life. After all, we live in a world that is pretty much unaware, do we not?

The Way of the Eagle

Does the eagle mount up at your command and make its nest on high? (Job 39:27 NKJV)

I've spotted Eagles at different times while on my hikes along these various trails, both in the deserts and in the mountains. Perhaps we'll have the good fortune to catch a glimpse of one today. I was hiking along Rush Creek near June Lake in the eastern Sierra Nevada a few summers back. It was there in a somewhat remote and picturesque area of the high country that I had a most unique encounter with a *Golden Eagle*.

The Greek word for Eagle is *aetos*, which means, to blow as the wind or become one with the wind. The Psalms teach us that the way of an eagle in flight is too wonderful to understand (Psalm 30:18,19). I had just rounded a bend in the trail when I saw the Golden. She was soaring at eye level, above the canyon, just about 30 feet west of where I was journeying along the high trail.

It was a very large Eagle, so I judged her to be female. She was incredibly close to me. She slowed, almost stopping in mid-air. She was riding the wind, correcting for every deviation of its velocity, all the while seemingly investigating me. She was looking right at me! At one point I believe, or at least would like to believe, that our eyes actually met. It's hard to tell if they're looking directly into your eyes, but just having the Eagle behold me was an honor in itself.

I didn't move a muscle or even twitch a finger. I was thinking, 'the good Lord has indeed blessed me in allowing me to witness such a grand and glorious wonder so close at hand. I am indeed humbled by His kindness!' I was suspended in time, hopeful that the encounter might last a little while longer. I was overwhelmed at the Eagle's control—fascinated by it.

Then, in a moment, in the twinkling of an eye she dipped a wing and turned off, headed down along the canyon to pick up speed. I estimated that she was flying somewhere between 50 and 60 miles per hour. I soon caught her in my binoculars and tracked her until she was out of sight. How majestic and graceful she was!

I've known Eagles to attain speeds in excess of 100 miles per hour while in a dive. They can hold those speeds while maintaining focus on the object at which they are diving. They are so well coordinated they can avoid in flight collisions at that speed and can actually drag just a fraction of an inch of talon across the back of another bird, sending it spiraling to the ground in complete shock. I've seen them close their talons, as if making a fist, to strike their prey as they swoop on by. Pilots have reported seeing Golden Eagles in flight above fifteen thousand feet.

Eagles have tremendous vision. You and I, according to medical science, have some two hundred thousand of what they call *visual receptors*, per square centimeter, within our eyes. The Eagle has 1.6 million receptors per square centimeter; eight times that of a human. That makes for an extremely high visual resolution or 'optical clarity', in simpler wording. Let me illustrate:

Imagine sitting in the very last row of the Dallas stadium during football season—I mean who can afford closer seats, right? With a pair of binoculars I might be able to catch the main action of the game. From that same distance an Eagle can individualize every blade of grass on the playing field. An Eagle could read three-inch letters on a billboard one mile away.

They can see small fish jumping out of the water five miles out to sea. They can spot fish in a swiftly flowing stream from thousands of feet in the air. They have remarkable vitality. An Eagle weighing about twenty pounds has enough strength in its talons to break both of the bones in a man's forearm, just by grasping it firmly. Any small, unsuspecting prey would be crushed instantly under that kind of power.

If you recall, I had an operation on my stomach a few years back. I learned something about the Eagle's talons from my surgeon, after he had stitched me up. He informed me that surgical needles were modeled after Eagle's talons. They are specially crafted to pierce the flesh and not to tear it. I was thankful to the Lord that day for His unique design of the Eagle's talons, and for the both informed and skillful surgeon who knew how to use that particularly well-designed needle.

When an Eagle soars it is not by his or her own strength. They effectively extend their great wings and are lifted by the rising currents of air. They just simply make themselves *available to the wind*. I too can soar within my own spirit like the Eagle, when I make myself *available to God and yield to His Spirit*. I have soared many times while just thinking about His greatness.

I have danced atop desert mesas and high mountain peaks. I see His greatness and feel His presence in all of His wonders. I feel it with each breath that I take along these hiking trails. I can also reach out and touch a variety of His different works at any time. This particular uplifting of spirit has been identified as the *Rocky Mountain High* by a songwriter, but it is much more than that. I feel kindred to the Eagle in this way.

The Eagle—a brilliant creature, extraordinarily graceful, with incomprehensible control, incredible speed, supreme vision and commanding strength. It's no wonder then that God pays grand tribute to their majesty. How well I have learned through my own experiences the immeasurable value of the following Biblical teaching:

Do you not know? Have you not heard? The Lord is the everlasting God, the Creator of the ends of the earth. He will not grow tired or weary, and His understanding no one can fathom. He gives strength to the weary, and increases the power of the weak. Even youths grow tired and weary, and young men stumble and fall; but those who hope in the Lord will renew their strength. They will soar (mount up) *on wings like eagles; they will run and not grow weary, they will walk and not be faint.* (Isaiah 40:28-31 NIV)

*

We've so much to learn from the creatures God has made—from Coyotes, from Jack Rabbits, from Locusts, from Owls, from Sheep, from Ravens, from Snakes, from wild Donkeys and from the Eagle. Actually, from every single solitary creature God has created upon the earth—insects, birds, reptiles, mammals, fish, you name it.

There is not one creature alive on the earth or in the sea that God has not individually, diversely and uniquely designed for a specific purpose. According to the Scriptures, each one of them could indeed *wisely* educate us. The Scriptures teach us that each and every one of them knows, honors and trusts in God, their creator (Job 12:7-10).

Being the highest order of creation on God's earth, shouldn't we humans all the more do likewise? Modern science has learned much about the habits and life-style of many of the earth's creatures. There are huge libraries stocked full of this particular type of information throughout the world. The problem however with modern science, and with most textbooks on the inhabitants of the creation, is that they fall short by failing to *recognize God* as the author of all things (Genesis 1:20-26).

Therefore, the best of the presently existing theories, reasoning's or arrived conclusions of mankind regarding the creatures of the earth are burdened with false or misleading information. In other words, you can't really trust them for complete accuracy. They represent no understanding of true origins and only scratch on the surface of understanding the qualities and abilities of any of these creatures. Discernment that considers God's time, perception, direction and purposes pertaining to what He has made is what's required at the highest level.

The Biblical book of Job, chapters 37 through 42, is a great place for the whole world to begin. Secular textbooks are useful, providing that you consider the information and apply it under the *proper light*, which is God's truth and eternal purpose. Most rewarding of course is your own personal observation of God's creatures in their natural environment. Your spirit will soar as you watch and contemplate the creature creations first hand, while you carefully and thankfully consider God's words:

Ask the animals, and they will teach you, or the birds of the air and they will tell you; or speak to the earth, and it will teach you, or let the fish of the sea inform you. Which of these does not know that the hand of the Lord has done this? In his hand is the life of every creature and the breath of all mankind (Job 12:7-10 NIV).

A sad note here: There's talk now that there are too many buffalo in the American west, and hunting is now permitted in some regions. The wolves also are endangered in this regard, around the world, because they think there are too many of them as well. They are now capturing the pups and actually shooting them in the heads at point blank range. People who can do something like this—God forgive me —deserve similar treatment.

Just recently, a group of employees from the Department of Agriculture (college educated) were fearful that there were too many starlings flying around in the New England states…So, they threw poisoned seed into their feeding areas. A few days later, the birds were dropping out of the sky by the hundreds—on the roadway, in peoples yards, in front of businesses, and into the local water supplies.

Do you think these things grieve the Lord in His heart? It all boils down to what you feel about Him—what you've learned about Him from the very start of your Hike on the Trail of Truth. What He has to endure for the sake of His chosen is unfathomable! The very next time you're out on the trail, consider the birds and animals. Watch them and learn from them. Talk to them. You *can* get their attention.

Many of them have not had the English language spoken at them, and most of them are fearful because humans many times hunt them. Their families may have been the victims of gunfire, and so they hesitate in trusting us. Some are dangerous because of this mistrust. It's best to stand still and speak gently. Do not approach them suddenly. If you're not inclined to stop and talk, then at least give them the courtesy of a "good morning" as you hike on by them. Move slowly in hope that you will not frighten them.

If you are a pet owner and in the habit of taking your pet for a walk or along with you on your hike, slow down a little bit and let that particular creature soak up the Creation. Let them wander around and investigate things. They like to sniff the grass, flowers, trees and brush. God gave them a great sense of smell, acute hearing and good eyesight, that they might enjoy His creation. They are aware of these gifts and are also aware of their source. Allow them to appreciate their surroundings in their own way. If you're in a hurry, don't take them with you. If they're on a leash, don't jerk on it in your impatience. How would you like someone to throw a rope around your neck and jerk on it? What goes around comes around.

Your concern for God's creatures honors their Creator. Therefore, do not intentionally crush the smaller species; the ants, the beetles, or any of the crawling things. Having a merciful and generous relationship with God's creatures will indeed draw you closer to Him. And by your standard of measure (the degree of your kindness) it shall be measured to you, and more shall be given you besides (Mark 4:24).

Again, the creatures know instinctively who God is, and they know much more about Him than you do, so remain humble in their presence. Animals are just one of the reasons we humans are without excuse for not knowing that God exists. The Scripture on the cover of this book bears that out. The entire creation cries out to you. That's what this writing is all about. Pay attention, for it will be both life and health to you.

*

Are you ready to explore the wilderness areas of your own, personal life—failure, doubt, affliction, fear, despair, loneliness, anxiety—jut a few of those difficult areas that each of us are prone to wander into? Gear up, for the Wilderness Trail is where we're headed...

Chapter Twelve...The Wilderness Trail

Welcome, Hiker, to the *Wilderness Trail!* This is one of the longer trails (chapters) on your journey through this book, but will indeed be well worth the hike. You're about to embark on an enlightening journey into the wilderness areas of your own life. There are a minimum of seven wilderness areas that each of us will encounter during our lifetime. The time spent in these areas can be as short as three days, or as long as forty years. Some have been known to spend almost their entire lifetime wandering in the wilderness.

Wilderness wanderings are the times in our life when God brings about circumstances or events to discipline us for better things, namely, to accomplish His earthly purpose for us, conforming us to the image of His Son. These wanderings usually encompass the difficult times of our lives, which may or may not come about by our own choice.

The most common include the wilderness of failure, the wilderness of doubt, the wilderness of affliction, the wilderness of fear, the wilderness of despair, the wilderness of loneliness, and the wilderness of anxiety. There are others, but we will only concern ourselves with these seven more crucial wanderings at this time. For a more in-depth look at this journey, consider my book; *Hiking Life's Difficult Trails.*

We will be taking several day hikes (perhaps a few nighttime ones as well) into this vast, wilderness country of our lives. These particular hikes will help you to understand the absolute necessity for your wilderness wanderings, as well as serve to better equip you in facing and dealing with them. You will perhaps come to better understand your true need for God.

Sometimes it feels like God backs away from us when we wander into hard times, but that's not true, as you are about to discover. The only requirement for this most important journey is *courage*. Are you ready? Then grab your hiking staff and let's head out...

Wilderness of Failure

Failure Peak is cold. Winter stays long this high. From here you can see most all of the other wilderness areas—their crags, their canyons, their thick forests and their regions of parched desolation. These wilderness areas don't appear too inviting when you're on failure's peak, but it all depends on how your eyes look at things. One can actually see beauty in all of these areas when looking through the eyes of understanding. Riding out the storms sent your way is indeed a humbling experience, yet can be a remarkable journey of learning as well.

God has said: *And you shall remember all the way which the Lord your God has led you in the wilderness these forty years, that He might humble you, testing you, to know what was in your heart, whether you would keep His commandments or not* (Deuteronomy 8:2 NASB).

The whirlwind of the wilderness is a time when we learn to take God seriously. He means what He says. His purpose is to insure our ultimate good. Is that not true love? Since we so desperately need His counsel it is then indeed wise to pay attention to each of His words.

We know that failure has many forms and magnitudes. It can be devastating to one's emotional well being. It can result in a long time spent in the wilderness. It can destroy, but it can also teach, correct and build up again. For most of us accepting failure can be quite difficult. Within the mainstream cultural attitude of the United States failure is a fault—a defect in one's personality or ability. But among the poor and the enlightened it's the norm.

However, how we feel about failure doesn't really matter because, by God's standards, it's par for the course. You will fail many times during your journey on earth. You are prone to wander—it's your nature. Mankind is but flesh, and failure is his/her nature (Genesis 6:3, Psalm 51:5). God allows failure because that is how He gets our attention. And we will continue to fail because we so desperately need His attention!

Failure comes on a daily basis. We usually see the greater failures, but we seldom pay attention to the smaller ones. Ever think a bad thought, or say an unkind word? Both are failures. Again, it is impossible to get through a day without one. The law (word) of God was instituted to shed light upon our failures; to heighten our awareness of them and to teach us to be sensitive to them.

Unfortunately, we don't usually comprehend our smaller failures until we are quite mature in age. What do we do then, when we realize that most of the good opportunities in life have gone—passed us by— when we've become bitter and filled with remorse? What do we do when the major and smaller failures come together all at once and drive us into the wilderness of despair? To avoid any of these consequences, how should we respond when we find ourselves in the wilderness of failure? Actually, failure is a great opportunity to commune with God.

Your failure in any area of life is merely a step in the right direction. And, not every failure is necessarily a failure against God. If, for instance, you fail an employment examination, it has nothing to do with the kingdom of heaven. If you fail a driver's test the result is the same; it has nothing to do with qualifying you for eternal life. But failure, whether against God or not, can draw you toward God in seeking an answer, a solution, or some type of comfort. In fact, failure can lead to the most important discovery of your lifetime; *Apart from Me,* (Jesus speaking of Himself) *you can do nothing* (John 15:5 NASB).

Webster defines failure in several different ways: To prove deficient as to be totally ineffective. To be unsuccessful. To receive an academic grade below the acceptable minimum. To weaken, decline, or cease to function properly. To disappoint or prove undependable, or to omit or neglect. Any of these can motivate one to seek God. Any of these can be used by God to encourage one to seek Him. The bottom line is that failure is not a bad thing. It can be the best thing that ever happened to you—a grand turning point in life—a time when you begin to comprehend your desperate need to *focus* on God.

204

Failure is a wake-up call from God and can be the result of His discipline in your life. Through it He draws you to Himself. Therefore, a proper attitude regarding failure can make all the difference in the world. When failure dawns on your horizon, first of all, consider it normal. Consider that the purpose of your particular failure is to bring about understanding. Go to the Psalms and learn the attitudes of those who have failed before you. There is nothing new under the sun, so it is wise to learn from those who beforehand have experienced what you arc going through. Some outstanding readings are Psalm 13, Psalm 25, Psalm 51 and Psalm 139.

Correction leads to understanding and understanding leads to hope. Dissecting failure with these enlightenments is dealing with it before it perhaps leads you into other wilderness areas. You can avoid the anguish of doubt and affliction, the prisons of fear and despair, the deep waters of loneliness, and certainly the irrational behavior of anxiety by merely facing failure for what it actually is and then dealing with it accordingly and correctly. Should you have the patience to allow it to teach you all that it can, failure can be, as I previously mentioned, a significant turning point in your life.

To glean the most from failure is to be patient in and through each of its consequences. Satan attacks fiercely against one who fails. His goal is your ruin and ultimate destruction. Therefore, much knowledge in God and His attributes is your only hope in defeating your adversary in the realm of failure, or any other wilderness area. Ten thousand human counselors cannot help you in your recovery unless their counsel is based on God's truth. Self-help based on human philosophy is also not qualified to deal with your situation.

Again, only true knowledge—the knowledge of God—can help you deal with failure. So, while you are atop that lofty peak of failure, seek answers and guidance from the Most High. Sit down in remoteness and quietness and read the Scriptures. Trust in God and allow Him to speak to your heart. He will not fail you. Pour out your distress before Him and confess all of your anxieties regarding your failure(s).

This in itself will bring great relief to your spirit. Confession or acknowledgment of failure is the key that opens the door to the healing process. You will indeed sense a beginning to that healing immediately upon your confession/acknowledgment, which is its purpose. God promises that He will hear you. He also promises that He will answer you. He is the God who hears (Psalm 17:6).

Thank Him for His time spent with you. Look into the heavens and *trust*. Reach out and touch a rock or a tree and acknowledge His presence. Hike down from that peak with confidence and go on with your life, in hope. Depend entirely upon God and don't lean on your own understanding (Proverbs 3:5,6), for your failure was designed as part of His perfect plan for your ultimate success.

Open my eyes, that I may see wondrous things from Your law (Psalm 119:18 NASB).

Wilderness of Doubt

It is so easy to lose the surety of your way and wander into the Wilderness of Doubt. It borders the wilderness of fear, which can ultimately lead you into the wilderness of despair as well. Doubt is more common than most will admit. Some form of doubt enters our hearts on a daily basis. Doubt is always a part of our thoughts, words and actions; we just don't usually label it as such. Some say self-doubt is the worst—I don't think so. Self-doubt is probably the best kind of doubt there is.

The Scriptures themselves teach us, *Trust in the Lord with all your heart, and do not lean on your own understanding.* And, *The heart is more deceitful than all else, and is desperately sick; who can understand it?* (Proverbs 3:5 & Jeremiah 17:9 NASB). According to these truths set forth by your Creator, self-doubt becomes a good thing, for it can lead one to understand their need to depend on God and not on themselves! God wants us to be confident in what we believe about Him, not in what we believe about ourselves.

When you have doubt in yourself you are not timid or weak. You are not a coward or inferior in society. You are actually a fountain, capable of spewing the waters of eternal life. Yes, in spite of your doubts, words and actions that truly benefit others can indeed flow from you—it's just that perhaps your pump needs to be primed. To overcome doubt you need to understand that it's a part of your nature, and you need to learn how to recognize it and how to deal with it. You need to first consider that doubt can be a result of time spent in one or more of the other six wilderness areas that we are exploring.

In failure, there may be doubt that you can succeed. In fear, there is the doubt that you can overcome your fears. In despair, doubt plays a major role, for all things seem indeed hopeless. In loneliness, doubt sees you as a distant or unreachable person, seemingly unable to be motivated by any good thing. In anxiety, doubt causes you to first move one way then change course for another—susceptible to any wind that might blow. In affliction, doubt can break your spirit, shattering your hopes for any type of recovery.

Doubt is subtle and as you can see works in a variety of ways. It is dangerous ground—full of predators—those spirits of unrelenting doubt who seek to devour you. In your defense and preservation you must carry the staff of *truth*. Truth drives off and even slays doubt, like the staff of a shepherd drives off or slays the attacking wolves, bears or lions. God's word is complete truth (John 17:17). Unfortunately, doubt can cause us to not pay attention to this truth of God when we so desperately need to pay attention to it!

Webster defines doubt as: To be uncertain or unsure, to tend to distrust, to disbelieve. Doubt caused the crucifixion of Jesus. That's a most horrid consequence for doubt, is it not? Doubt is indeed your subtle enemy. Get hold of it before it leads you into any of the other wilderness areas. Understand that in this present world *all things* are uncertain or unsure. Death can come to you at any moment. Trust is a rare find on the earth and disbelieving in anything that has proved to be solid truth is common to our nature. We are prone to doubt—prone to wander in this wilderness.

On the other hand, with God nothing is uncertain; all His promises can be *fully* trusted, and belief in Him can lead one to eternal life. God's character and purposes are unchangeable. On an individual basis He will always do something out of the ordinary to assure you, in your particular situation, of His presence. He does this in group scenarios as well. It may be quite a small thing, but it will be out of the ordinary—not a normal occurrence—and most likely will take place when you are not fully or not even the least expecting it.

Sometimes however, though we are surely aware of a little help, we act as if we didn't get any; we keep right on pursuing our doubt until we fall again. It is usually then that we wonder why we didn't pay attention to our little miracle—why we didn't consider and act on it accordingly at the time. But, it can also be true that you may not recognize or become aware of what God has done to help you, in any particular matter, until later on down the road of life. And of course, some things will only be revealed after death, as there are certain doubts that can trouble us until that time.

Walking through doubt is like making your way through a strong wind. It takes a stern look on your face, a strong will in your heart, and a firm stroke or pull of your hiking staff—all of these things—with each step that you take. Only faith in God can give one this superior confidence, for He *is* confidence. He is the one who carries you through the wilderness of doubt. If you try to muster it (confidence) up on your own, you will fail. Doubt is not something you can deal with on your own. Commit God's promises to your heart and they will strengthen you.

No matter how far into any of these wilderness areas that doubt has banished you, you can find your way out through your knowledge of truth. Actually, a great measure of that truth is found in just these few words of Scripture: *We know that God causes all things to work together for good to those who love God, to those who are called according to His purpose* (Romans 8:28 NASB). You need to consider this particular promise of God repeatedly as you hike along in your struggle with doubt. One who doubts God's promises is considered to be like a wave of the sea; driven and tossed by the wind (James 1:6).

Only God's *promises* can give us the assurance that we are His beloved children and move us into an attitude that can overcome doubt. Believing in the one, true God can actually keep you out of the wilderness of doubt. That belief requires deep faith, which can be defined as your *belief in action*. Active belief not only embraces the aforementioned Scripture, but considers the following understanding as well:

Whatever God says throughout the Scriptures is true. Therefore, anything that disagrees with what His word says regarding any matter is obviously false. That's the final 'rule of measurement' against doubt. You need to act in accordance with that rule, which primes the pump that will allow living waters to begin to flow from you and nourish others.

Wilderness of Affliction

The Wilderness of Affliction can indeed be a lonely and desolate place. We usually think of affliction as something physical, but it can be spiritual as well. Afflictions of both types are of course a result of the Fall at Eden, and can be magnified by one's continuing in a life of sin. Some are born with a physical affliction while others may experience physical affliction at some later point in life. In either case, the plague of original sin and its consequences, in some form or another, brings about or has brought about affliction. It may not be one's own sin that's the culprit, but it is the ever-present consequences of universal sin nonetheless.

We must also learn that while physical afflictions are difficult for us to accept when they strike, they can be what are best for us. While we pray to be released from the effects of a particular sickness, injury or disability, God may have determined that we can serve Him better or be better off with certain limitations caused by an affliction, whether temporary or permanent.

Again, it is because of the fallen nature of the human race that we are prone to afflictions. There are many without physical afflictions and they are indeed fortunate, but we *all* encounter spiritual afflictions. We will live with them as long as we occupy the human body.

Physical affliction however *appears* to us to be the worst kind. We are each saddened when we encounter someone with any type of physical affliction, such as a deformity, a paralysis, a disease, an incurable illness, or a particular mental or physical disability. There are also within the physical realm the afflictions of poverty and hunger.

Most of us would endeavor to help someone in any of these conditions or circumstances, yet we usually remain blind to spiritual affliction, which is in reality the worst type of affliction, whether within ourselves or within anyone else. We'll look into that momentarily. Webster defines affliction as physical or mental suffering. He also uses the terms 'plague' and 'sickness.'

At the time of Christ there were those among the people whose specific physical afflictions gave them an opportunity to glorify God. In the case of a man blind from birth, Jesus' disciples asked Him, "Why was this man born blind? Was it a result of his own sins or those of his parents?"

Jesus then answered them: "It was not because of his sins or his parent's sins, but for the purpose that the power of God could be seen in him." Jesus then displayed the power of God and healed the man of his blindness (John 9:2-41). This man's whole life was bound up in one great purpose. Freedom from his physical affliction was born in a moment of time. Can you imagine what a great witness for God he became after that?

In the case of Lazarus, who died from a personal illness and was four days later raised from the dead, Jesus beforehand spoke of the true purpose for his illness: "This sickness will not end in death. No, it is for God's glory, so that God's Son may be glorified through it." (John 11:1-44) Lazarus' illness, death and resurrection was for the glory of God and identified Jesus as the resurrection and the life (11:25).

In another matter, God reminded the apostle Paul that his own physical/spiritual weaknesses allowed him to trust in God's strength and not in his own (2nd Corinthians 12:7-10). Paul then boasted in his afflictions, for he knew that through them God was glorified (*recognized as the Author of all that is good*). We can therefore conclude from these separate teachings that physical affliction can be allowed in one way or another for the glory of God.

Satan of course is the author of affliction. Physical afflictions are therefore much better dealt with when understood in this light. If you are afflicted physically, or know someone who is, you must consider this understanding and act accordingly—believe it, share it, and find hope through it. Affliction causes one to pay attention to God—to live one moment at a time, as we should.

There is purpose in all things. Faith in this understanding will lead to the enlightenment that serves to deal with the affliction and perhaps overcome it. You may not be able in this present world to physically overcome a particular affliction, but you can overcome it (i.e. deal with it spiritually) through some correct spiritual understandings. The Psalmist has said: *If Your law had not been my delight, I would have perished in my affliction* (Psalm 119:92 NIV).

Spiritual affliction is of a different type than physical affliction. It is at many times not recognizable. Spiritual affliction simply means that one rejects the truth that his/her life is directed and controlled by the human spirit—that the human spirit is one of depravity and needs a Savior. Psychiatry and psychology won't do, for they are not founded on this spiritual truth, but a product of the reasoning of mankind and subject to grievous error.

Rejection of God's truth is gross spiritual affliction. This gross affliction can be overcome by belief in God, yet even if we believe in God we will still be subject to other forms of spiritual affliction. This is because we will not be perfect (complete) until the Lord returns. We will in the meantime continue to suffer various forms of spiritual affliction due to our natural proneness to wander.

Satan is well aware of our inclination toward sin and works constantly against us. Another reason for our various forms of spiritual affliction is our lack of faith (*active belief*). We may be faithful in some things, but we cannot be faithful in everything. We must depend on God's daily forgiveness to 'take up the slack' in those areas in which we fall short. We are by no means within our human nature subject to the will of God and indeed cannot be (Romans 8:7).

In other words, we are prone to not obey His will (unfaithfulness). However, by acknowledging our daily failures to God we can strike a blow against spiritual affliction. The understanding that you will always fall short spiritually serves to keep you in a state of humility. This is a good thing. Know that a wise person indeed walks with his/her head bowed, for physical afflictions can come upon you at any time, and spiritual afflictions are with you at all times.

Realizing your own weaknesses (afflictions) also serves to make you aware of the weaknesses of others. It teaches you not to be so critical of the spiritual afflictions of others who make mistakes in life and fall into sin. Remember that anyone is capable of anything, no matter what his or her station in life. Your mercy upon them when they fall is a great encouragement and can lift them out of the pit of despair at a critical time. If you learn to show mercy you will obtain mercy (Matthew 5:7).

When others are afflicted physically or spiritually, it is up to you to extend to them mercy, kindness and helpfulness, as much as is within you. There are many ways to do this, as each of us are given various talents and abilities. Each person has something to offer the afflicted. It is exceedingly wise and beneficial to stand still and take the time to consider how it must be to walk in another's shoes. The smallest gift (sacrifice) that you offer could be the gift most needed.

If *you* have a particular physical affliction try not to despair. As I pointed out earlier, your affliction can be used for the glory of God. What you accomplish in your affliction may serve to show others particular strength(s) that God has given you. He is glorified through you. You may be without the ability to walk, but you may have the talent to teach or counsel.

211

You may be without sight, but through your blindness you may learn to see further by developing great spiritual insight that will encourage others. If you cannot hear or speak, it will not stop you from becoming a productive physical servant to another or to many others. If you are mentally retarded or restrained from physical activity by a particular illness, God can still be glorified through those who serve you. In your prayers regarding any type of personal affliction, whether physical or spiritual, keep in mind that there is a purpose for your life —for every life.

Pray that God will in your affliction reveal His purpose for you and help you to accomplish it. God can work through you as you submit to His will and may, in the process of your earthly life, remove your affliction(s) when and if they have served His purpose. Do not give up because of your afflictions. Endeavor to persevere. May you do this according to true faith. In God's sight the faith of His servants is the most pleasing thing there is. You can accomplish many things through your belief in His promises.

I have a friend who has been afflicted with cancer from birth, and this condition was not discovered until she was fifteen years old. At that time her doctors advised her that she would not live beyond the age of twenty. She is now well into her forties. She has undergone numerous physical operations, painful therapies, dealt with a variety of medical people; some kind, some indifferent, and has had to live every day of her life with an unimaginable anguish of spirit.

In spite of this arduous routine she manages to get through each day. How? Naturally my heart is grieved by her suffering, and one day I summoned the courage to ask her, "How do you cope with this— what keeps you going?" She told me that much of her life has been spent in encouraging others in similar circumstances. She explained that she found great comfort in her associations with these people. She said that as for her personal condition, she stopped asking God "why" long ago.

She said that she knew that there was a reason for her condition, and that she would just have to continue to trust in God, holding onto the hope of a change in her body on the day of Christ's return. She said that she was not afraid anymore and had accepted what she was dealt in life, and remains willing to accept whatever comes her way in the future. Suicide is not an option.

What an unselfish expression of trust! I was indeed happy that I could reply to her, "Your faith will be vindicated, and I am honored to have been allowed to hear your words in this matter. I am greatly encouraged through your faith. Thank you for sharing your story with me." I told her that I would speak of her faith in this book, and so I have.

Her name is Clare. Her life is a profound witness to one's personal, active belief in God's promises. She has dealt wisely and bravely with an extremely difficult, ongoing experience in the wilderness of affliction. No one can do this without help from above.

Wilderness of Fear

The Wilderness of Fear is full of darkened crags and dangerously steep terrain. A young servant once said to his blind, elderly master: "Of all things, to live in darkness must be the worst." The old man wisely replied, "Fear is the only darkness."

Indeed fear, like all of Satan's works, is dark and deceptive. It takes on a variety of forms, but it is *always* cloaked in darkness. One cannot see through fear. That is because it blinds us to the actuality of what really is, or to the reality of what can actually be accomplished. It seems also to be like an impenetrable wall. Since we refuse to see beyond that wall, we often fail to get over it, around it, or through it.

We usually find ourselves to have a fear of some type of failure or perhaps of loss, perhaps of pain, perhaps of heights, perhaps of closed in quarters or darkness itself, and of course there are a myriad of other things that we can fear. At present there are many who fear the future. However, I believe the most destructive form of fear is the fear of man himself.

This particular natural fear gives birth to many other forms of fear. By fear of man, I am referring to our natural fear of what others may think, or of how they may react to the way we think. We naturally long for the approval of others. Because of the fear of not having their approval, we wander into all sorts of calamities that take a toll on our lives. As a result we blindly follow the majority into many deceitful forms of *attitude*, which lead us into sin, depravity and destruction.

Rather than take a stand for what is right, we are prone to follow those who approve of what is wrong, even though we ourselves know it to be wrong. Fear of man is what causes wars among nations, who in actuality have every God-given reason to seek peace. If they endeavored to live just by what you've learned so far in this book they would surely seek peace. Fear promotes envy, jealousy, strife and hatred. Fear is always destructive, however there is one particular form of fear that leads to understanding and life. Webster defines fear in two ways—realization of danger, or reverence and awe.

The second definition is usually considered as the *fear of God*. The Scriptures teach: *The fear* (reverence and awe) *of the Lord is the beginning of knowledge*. This type or form of fear is most productive and can dispel all other fears.

We are encouraged; *God is our refuge and strength; an ever-present help in time of trouble. Therefore, we shall not fear, though the earth give way and the mountains fall into the heart of the sea, though its waters roar and foam, and the mountains quake with their surging* (Proverbs 1:7, Psalm 46:1-3 NIV).

To escape the wilderness of destructive fear, you must first realize that you are within its borders. Remember, fear is darkness, and you can be blind to its existence because it can masquerade as light (2nd Corinthians 11:14). Through the knowledge of God you can understand that you are capable of fear and that some form of it will always plague you. Acceptance of this truth leads to an understanding of fear as well as a respect for it.

By respect, I mean that you accept it as natural and that you deal with it according to true knowledge. Dealing with fear according to true knowledge understands that only an attitude that takes into consideration the many attributes of God can hope to expel fear. God is light, and in Him there is no darkness at all (1st John 1:5). An attitude that is fixed on this truth can walk through the dark wall of fear. This attitude can also stand amidst fear when there seems to be no way out. It can dispel the surrounding darkness and allow one to walk continuously on into ever brightening light.

To overcome fear is to be bold and daring in attitude. It is the sword of the Spirit and the shield of Truth that protects the one surrounded by and in battle with fear. God's words (which themselves *are* Spirit and Truth) are indeed powerful weapons in the hands of a skilled (knowledgeable) swordsman/swordswoman. These are the only weapons that have any hope of dispelling the darkness and deception of fear. No form of human psychiatry or psychology is as effective, for they are only temporary measures erected by men and incapable of withstanding the test of time.

214

Fear is not (contrary to popular opinion) a human weakness encountered only by the weak. It is not something that any particular form of psychological therapy can resolve in a short time, as I mentioned earlier. It is instead a reality of our nature that no one escapes, no matter who they think they are. In actuality, fear, in some form, is a lifetime defect. In dealing with fear, reading or memorizing Scripture is the most effective. What can be more powerful than the Spirit of God? Absolutely nothing!

The Spirit of God enables one to stand in the epicenter of an earthquake and not fear the outcome. It enables one to not fear the roaring of the seas, the awesome power of the wind, or the crumbling of mountains. The Christian understands that these 'fearful' things will happen as long as the earth exits in its present state of decay. This particular knowledge and trust in God is, again, most effective in dealing with *any* type of fear—fear of the physical or fear of a spiritual nature.

Many of our ancestors overcame fear; winning battles, conquering kingdoms and escaping great danger and personal tragedy through their belief and trust in God. The Bible contains many endearing stories representing the degree of faith that overcomes fear. It is wise to become familiar with these stories. When any type or form of fear overwhelms you, whether it be considered a small fear or a great fear, whether a little hurtful or life threatening, whether discomforting, devastating, or catastrophic, *remember* that your life is in the hands of the One who formed you.

There is no way that He is going to let you down, no matter how things may appear. God's plan for your life includes everything that happens to you. When He leads you to the edge of the cliff, trust Him fully and let go. Only one of two things will happen; either He'll catch you when you fall, or He'll teach you how to fly. Accept that truth and fear not!

Your faith in that particular knowledge is your hope of deliverance. Holding to this form of attitude is the only way to deal successfully with fear. No matter what happens, train your mind and your senses and learn to trust in God and not in yourself (Proverbs 3:5). Embrace this right attitude with all of your being. This will dispel the darkness of fear.

Wilderness of Despair

The Wilderness of Despair can seem so endless—bleak and desolate from horizon to horizon. Despair is the most common end result for a variety of consistent wilderness wanderings. When the bottom drops out of most of our expectations we usually find ourselves wandering in the wilderness of despair. But as we begin to explore this particular wilderness we find that it is not a strange place to be—we won't find ourselves alone. Many of the world's human inhabitants live continually in despair, and poverty is one of its root causes.

Television and the news media for the most part cater to the so-called middle-class or wealthy, and we tend to evaluate ourselves in the world through their eyes. But in reality, anyone with a job is wealthy. Anyone with food, clothing and shelter is even wealthier, and anyone who owns a home is exceedingly blessed! If you can look at things in this way—if you can realize that there are many, many people less fortunate than yourself—then it will be much easier for you to avoid the wilderness of despair—to hike right on around it toward wisdom.

Remember that the mind is deceitful and therefore must be trained. To 'count your blessings' are then not just words, but an assembly of decisive thoughts that provide an excellent means of avoiding despair. When you measure your blessings against those less fortunate, how can you even begin to despair? Webster defines despair as the complete absence of hope, or, to abandon all purpose or hope. But one can never be without hope if he/she has food and clothing. If this is all that we have we are fortunate indeed, for God has allowed us to be poor that we might become rich through the knowledge of Him.

The Scriptures teach throughout the Bible that the poor have the blessing of knowing dependence upon God. Sure, poverty is indeed a rough life, but if only for this life we have hope in Christ, we are of all people the most miserable (1st Corinthians 15:19). Knowing one's absolute need to depend on God is a rare find for any of us, and a multitude of understanding can come from it. It can transform your life and render you exceedingly valuable in the service of God, thereby making you rich toward Him.

This is the great advantage of being poor. For the poor who do not know God, their path is one of desperation and destruction. But, when a poor nation turns to the one, true God, there is hope and salvation. Unfortunately, many poor nations worship a false god. They do this because the god of this world has blinded their minds. They establish rituals and religions conceived by men, which do not honor the God of heaven for whom He truly is, and therefore suffer the consequences of their ignorance.

Envy, strife, hatred and despair and even war rule their spirits as they abandon the hope in and search of *truth*. However, God does not reject the poor who endeavor to seek Him *in truth*. Beyond the Muslims, the Buddha's, the Hindus and all other forms of religion there is *the truth*. The truth is *not* a man-made religion, but the *way* to eternal life.

Within a nation like the United States, which is not in the mainstream of poverty, think of some of the reasons that might lead you into the wilderness of despair. A death in the family? Some type of accident? Rejection by friends? A physical affliction? Unemployment? These causes for despair are indeed valid, but things could be much, much worse. There could be despair of life itself, which those of poor and ravished nations face each moment of each day.

Again, count your blessings. Consider those in deeper despair. Take the focus off yourself and look into the eyes of truly fathomless despair, such as extreme poverty, a homeless existence and starvation, or the ravages of war. Try and walk in the shoes of those facing these circumstances. Take what you have, even if it is very little, and go out there into your neighborhood and give it to the truly poor. There are also organizations established so that you can help the poor throughout this nation and in other countries as well. Blessing will indeed come back upon you, as that is God's promise (Luke 6:38).

I have personally experienced rejection, failure, a homeless existence, poverty, deep frustration and overwhelming anxiety, to name just a few despairing things, yet I have never been allowed to go without food or clothing. That's grace! I've been able to overcome the above-mentioned degrees of despair by considering the less fortunate. I've also made use of being allowed the privilege to focus on more meaningful things, which many people take for granted:

The beauty of God's earth from atop a high mountain. The way of a child with its mother. The loyalty of a puppy with its master. The sound of a rushing stream in the wilderness, and the intricate design in just a mere blade of grass. Reason to despair? I think not. Reason to rejoice? Exceedingly so!

217

This comes through the knowledge of God and the things He has made. *Woe is me* is replaced by just one moment of understanding through acceptance of the wisdom, glory and hope found in and through the Creator and His creation. Reaching out and touching any of God's wonders along a hiking trail is indeed great therapy in times of despair.

Endurance in learning and understanding, followed by realization and acceptance is the key to finding one's way through the wilderness of despair. Yet, know that your wandering in the wilderness of despair plays a most important part in your spiritual growth! Patience can bloom like a flowering cactus here—rich in color and magnitude. Isolation and desolation can become beautiful in the eyes of one who has made true spiritual discoveries. Hope becomes a refreshing oasis in a parched and weary land. Despair need not be master over you. You can be free of that wilderness.

So, what will you do with your despair? You can realize first of all that it gives birth to great knowledge and understanding. Secondly, you can learn to be merciful to others through it. You can give light to those in darkness. You can give encouragement to the faint-hearted. You can learn to understand your equality of spirit with the least of God's servants, which marks the birth of true humility. Most importantly, you can learn how little it takes physically and materially to live righteously—to love justice and mercy, and to walk humbly with your God (Micah 6:8).

Wilderness of Loneliness

The lofty peaks of the Wilderness of Loneliness are indeed inspiring, but should be shared with others. I have hiked much of the California high country, and done much of it alone. It is not wrong to want to spend time alone, but the wrong attitude about solitude can give birth to a loneliness that you will not willingly recognize. This particular loneliness can affect the way you function spiritually. It can indeed bring on life-changing discoveries and spiritual growth, but it can also produce attitudes that can plunge you into the wilderness of isolation and despair.

Webster defines loneliness as isolation, being without companionship or devoid of people. There are times when we need to be alone, but we were designed for companionship with others

(Genesis 2:18). For man God created woman, who was to become his most intimate companion.

There are those who have allowed members of the same sex to become their most intimate (sexual) companion, but this is of course contrary to nature and detestable in the sight of God. Those who live in this manner will suffer while here on earth, and if they remain unrepentant, will painfully forfeit any right to the kingdom of heaven (Romans 1:27, 1st Corinthians 6:9, 10).

Recently, television personality Oprah Winfrey had two men on her program who identified themselves as 'priests' of religion. One wore the clothing that we would expect a priest to wear, the other was dressed in a common suit. The discussion in that interview was centered on homosexuality. These 'priests' told Oprah that being 'gay' was a "gift from God."

Oprah's response was, "That's the first time I ever heard any priest say something like that!" The audience was silent and rightly so. Without question, God's word teaches that homosexuality is a product of human depravity—against the very nature of God (Romans 1:26-28). Do not therefore be deceived by the world's philosophies. The cities of Sodom and Gomorrah remain in ashes to this day because of this very perversion.

If the wilderness of loneliness has driven you into this type of relationship, you had better escape it as fast as you can. There is no sin in having a member of the same sex as your best friend, but when one lusts sexually after a member of the same gender they become of debased mind (Romans 1:28).

There are sins of mental depravity that you must literally run from to avoid, as they are considered by God to be the most shameful of lusts, which lusts completely disregard His sovereignty. Be alert to the fact that no one is incapable of being captivated and consumed by these lusts. No one! However, as all humans are capable of unnatural relationships, there are also those capable of no relationships at all.

There are those without wives or husbands and there are those without friends. The wilderness of loneliness is their continuous abode. Those who have made friends with God while in this wilderness are the only ones who have a chance to deal with it adequately, or to escape it completely. Jesus dealt with loneliness on a grand scale—there is no one who has matched the depth of loneliness which He encountered when He was betrayed by His own and put to death by those whom He loved.

In the very end, as He hung on that cross, He was offered a mixture of vinegar and gall to deaden pain, but chose instead to bear the full, indescribable agony of the world's sins and the death we so deserve. During His lifetime Jesus journeyed into all of the wilderness areas we are exploring here and then some. He understood their depths, while we are merely passing through them.

His antidote for loneliness, failure, doubt, affliction, fear, despair and anxiety was found in communion with His Father. He withdrew many times to lonely and desolate places to accomplish this. His entire three-year ministry was spent in thought of His Father and much of it in prayer to Him. This was His daily encouragement. Thoughts of His Father I'm sure were moment by moment. This was the way He dealt with the many wilderness areas that one can wander into while on the earth.

When He wasn't formally in prayer, Jesus went about doing good and healing all who were óppressed by the devil, for God was with Him (Acts 10:38). He never isolated himself from the needs of others. No one needs to be lonely. If you do not have friends, if you do not have a best friend, then you should consider having God as your friend.

Abraham, the great ancestor of the patriarchs, was indeed a friend of God. Noah too was a friend of God. David was himself a man after God's own heart. Anyone has the ability to become a friend of God. In fact, He can become your very best friend. We can become friends of God through the actions we take in our lives (James 2:23, 24).

We are made right with God by what we do, and not just by *believing* in Him alone. Anyone can believe—even the devils believe, and they tremble (James 2:19)! True friendships involve *action.* Jesus said: *You are my friends if you do what I command*, and, *Just as you want people to treat you, treat them in the same way* (John 15:14, Luke 6:31 NASB, underscored for emphasis).

Those life-giving duties are active, not passive. By becoming an active friend of God you have the power to establish great and meaningful friendships with others. As you become God's friend, through obeying the teachings He has given you in the Scriptures, you learn in time what it really means to be a friend to others. God can teach you compassion, which I believe is one of the most important ingredients in a friendship.

Jesus left us a fine example of compassion, for He did not hesitate to show mercy on anyone, from any walk of life, whether small or great. Though He was, according to Scripture, a lonely individual, He did not isolate Himself, but as I mentioned earlier, went about doing good to all those whom He encountered. Being lonely did not stop Him from being effective and should not stop anyone from being effective. Love becomes the key to being effective, and love is the essence of the ingredients in any meaningful and lasting friendship. Love is in fact the essence of God Himself:

Love is patient and kind. Love is not jealous or boastful or proud or rude. Love does not demand its own way. Love is not irritable, and it keeps no record of when it has been wronged. It is never glad about injustice but rejoices whenever the truth wins out. Love never gives up, never loses faith, is always hopeful, and endures through every circumstance (1st Corinthians 13:4-7 NLT).

Through the operation of this genuinely pure meaning of love true friendship can be established. If your mind dwells on these things while you offer friendship, and if you through the Spirit of God truly put your heart and soul into it, while at the same time keep a guard on your *natural* attitude and actions, then the one upon whom your friendship falls is indeed fortunate. Becoming a friend to others does not necessarily mean that your days of loneliness will come to an end. You may not receive in return the depth of love that you offer others.

Jesus was a true friend to all, yet His closest friends, who claimed utter loyalty to Him, fled from Him in his hour of need, leaving Him alone in the hands of wicked and cruel men, who sought only to destroy Him. You may have experienced or are yet to experience similar loneliness and betrayal, no matter how much love you give to others. This is the road of choice the Christian must travel, prepared to deal with the unexpected. Again, I want to emphasize your need to be a *friend* of God. *He* will not desert you, even in your darkest hour.

He was once however forced to desert (not intervene with) His only Son as He hung on the cross. Why? Think of all the sins that have ever been committed brought together in one nauseous mass! The very thought of it staggers our imagination. We cannot comprehend it. Enduring the horror of this awful burden the Son of God cried, "My God, My God, why have You forsaken Me?" (Matthew 27:46)

Christ actually tasted the hell we deserve, being separated from God the Father by the burden of mankind's sins. This suffering (separation and anguish) was far more horrible than the mere death of the body. The good news is that this will never happen again! You won't lose God's attention for one moment. Yet, loneliness is something that is within the nature of man, so there will be times when you *seem* unable to avoid it.

If loneliness has been brought about through sin in your life, my heart goes out to you. In this case, consider that God offers unparalleled forgiveness and your loneliness need not consume you; Jesus promised to always be with you (Matthew 28:20). Remember— it is only through His many great and precious promises that any of us in this earthly life may overcome loneliness and continue on in hope (2nd Peter 1:4).

Wilderness of Anxiety

I believe the Wilderness of Anxiety can be the most destructive yet yield the most profound learning experience of all your wilderness wanderings. Anxiety comes in many forms, most of them not at first recognizable. They can drain you physically, mentally, and rob you entirely of all common reasoning.

Anxiety can actually rob you of life itself. Anxiety wreaked havoc upon my own life. Lust is one root cause of anxiety. Another is simply the fact that we are a fallen race and anxiety is part of our makeup. In this particular realm there are those with great anxiety and those with little—it's just a matter of how the Potter has formed you, and where the adversary attacks you. All humans experience some manner of anxiety. Anxiety can be harnessed for good, but it is a strange force, always requiring understanding and control.

It can become quite out of control, and in this case the only solution is continual prayer. Medication and certain types of physical or mental therapy can be temporary controls, but only God can completely cure anxiety, and there are a variety of anxieties that He may not want to bring under what we call 'control' or 'cure,' because they ultimately serve His special purpose for us. Personal anxiety has always been my greatest 'thorn' in the flesh. Yet, it has taught me many things that I would have otherwise been completely ignorant of.

Webster defines anxiety as a state of uneasiness or worry, abnormal fear that lacks a specific cause, and being eager or earnestly desirous. But there are many forms of anxiety that we fail to label as anxiety, and anxiety is not really 'abnormal fear'—it is instead a *normal* consequence of failure, doubt, fear, loneliness, and despair. Affliction can cause anxiety as well.

Any of these forces singly or in conjunction with one another, seen or unseen, recognizable or not recognizable, can cause anxiety. Among the seven wilderness areas we are exploring, the wilderness of anxiety can be the most deceptive and devastating and, as I mentioned at the beginning, the most destructive.

One type of deception is *anticipation*. Anticipation is actually anxiety, though we may refuse to label it as such. But in reality, to look forward to something (anticipation) is to be anxious about it. This particular anxiety is impossible to avoid. Our only hope in any type of anxiety is to pray for patience. The answer to this prayer will give us the ability to accept our anxiety, but not to completely remove it. A form of it will always linger, again, because this is our fallen nature, and secondly, God's special purpose for us may require that it continue.

When anxiety becomes overwhelming, only acceptance of it and an absolute trust in God's plan for us will bring it into a somewhat controllable position. One needs to learn to beware of anxiety's deception, for anxiety can devastate and destroy. Yes, it is natural to worry (be anxious), but it is foolish to allow worry to enlarge beyond the scope of today. Too much anxiety will lead you into the wilderness areas of failure, doubt, fear, loneliness, despair, and even affliction. Yet, too much anxiety can also have a good result, in that it can lead us to seek God in an earnest way.

One should never assume that he/she is beyond the state of needing to learn something new in his/her spiritual relationship with God. Overwhelming anxiety may be the tool God uses to bring about a particular learning experience in your life. The devastating and destructive forms of anxiety come when we fail to see God's hand in our learning. If we fail to realize that God works *all* things in our lives together for good, then we may fail to see that He is using our anxiety for a particular purpose in conforming us into the image of His Son, which is His ultimate purpose.

Jesus endured great anxiety in His earthly life. Again, He wandered into each of the wilderness areas we have explored here. His knowledge of God and His faith in God brought Him through each of

223

them with victory. We can experience these victories as well. How do we recognize unrecognizable anxiety? Let us begin by considering our fears that lack a specific cause or *seem* to lack a specific cause. Experience teaches me that I am prone to anxieties or fears whose origins elude me. It is, of course, impossible to know the depth of depravity within the human nature (Romans 7:15).

However, through the spiritual enlightenment of the Scriptures, for example, Romans 7:14-25, I can identify anxiety when it rears its head. I can know that *some form of it* is seeking control of me, and I can endeavor, through the Spirit of God within me, to defeat it or at least bring it under some reasonable form of control or acceptance.

This is simply recognizing that there is the unrecognizable and dealing with it. This preparation for battle through *awareness* is all that one can do spiritually in dealing with deep, unrecognizable anxiety. We're usually not certain how anxieties will play out—we just have to trust in God while we wait for Him to work. Are these unrecognizable anxieties responsible for the grievous sins in some people's lives— murders, child molestations, homosexuality and other sins of a depraved mind?

I believe they can be, and I also believe that the evil spirits of the unseen world can enter a person, and control his/her thoughts and actions (Mark 5:9, Acts 5:16). The Scriptures teach that our greatest battles are with these rulers and authorities and wicked spirits of the unseen world (Ephesians 6:12). I believe, in this present day and age, that prayer is our only defense against them—individual prayers and/or the prayers of others *for* those of us who are afflicted with these deeper anxieties.

We can also counsel these people in truth, hopefully giving them an understanding that they can work with. Allowing them to think or believe that they are abnormal does not work. Sharing your own anxieties with others who are anxious removes their fear of abnormality and opens the door to healing. It is easier to gain one's confidence when you are truthful—when you inform them that *you* could become just like them—that their attitude and their situation could be your own, for all are under sin.

Once their confidence is gained in this manner, then they are ready to be instructed in the things that pertain to their only escape. (Galatians 6:1) It is wise to learn to comprehend that no matter who we are or how strong we think we can be, Scripture teaches that we are *all prone* to anxieties brought on by the great deceiver. Personally, I consider the wilderness of anxiety to be most responsible for the growth and maturity of sin.

It is a catalyst in strengthening lust. I believe it to be the most difficult of all the wilderness areas of our lives—fighting against all of our resolve to do what is right. From my youth I have experienced sometimes unbearable anxiety. I have fought and struggled against it many times. Some battles are won, while others have the enemy falling back for a short time, and then attacking even more violently—pulling and tearing at my resolve.

However, I have also found that when its pull is the strongest it can be controllable through changes in thought and intense prayer. It's a matter of just saying 'no' to its lure, its pull, its ability to overwhelm, and meaning 'no'! It is a matter of depending on the Lord for the great strength needed in that endeavor, which you *cannot* muster through your own will. Only God can hold one back from sin (Genesis 20:6).

You need to earnestly believe in God—trust in all that He has promised. It has been said that anxiety itself is simply unbelief in action. That is a profound comparison. However, whether you believe or not, you'd better run when you are dealing with overwhelming temptation—run like the wind or get caught in the whirlwind! Few escape, and no one escapes without God stepping in.

Our proneness to anxiety is strengthened when we doubt the promises of God. The Scriptures warn us against this doubt by teaching us to remember: *Do not be anxious about anything...* (Philippians 4:6 NIV). You must therefore train your mind and your senses to dwell on God's word and to think also about His wonders (created things) when anxiety rears its head (Colossians 3:16).

Learn to dwell on the *promises* of God, which particular trust allows you to become a partaker of the divine nature (2nd Peter 1:3,4). In other words, you are a child of God, a part of Him through your belief and trust in Him, and it is through this union that you are being conformed to the image of His Son; a partaker of the divine nature.

So, keep on believing and trusting—that's the best advice I can give you. Be advised also that you'll truly have to work at these things —belief and trust. It is indeed a fight of great proportion against the sin nature. We are prone to unbelief and distrust; therefore we are inclined to be blindly anxious. That's just the way it is in the wilderness of anxiety. Your patience *will* be tested here. Remember that we are all put to the test, and it never comes in the form or at the point we would prefer. Wait on Him for deliverance—trust God to do what He will in His own time. May the Lord strengthen you!

I want to remind you that there is one other way that may help you to endure and even escape the wilderness areas of failure, doubt, affliction, fear, despair, loneliness, and anxiety—each of the areas we have hiked through. There's the dance, if you're so inclined; a cry to God against the dark forces that have imprisoned you.

Don't be timid; it's okay to be a spiritual person, for the wicked spirits of this world are indeed real—God's word declares them your *only* enemy. The Native Americans are wise about these things. The creation has always been their teacher. Though many of them have never read the Bible, they have learned to honor all of God's creation, and wisely dread the forces of evil, which they know abound. There knowledge of these things makes most other cultures appear pretty foolish.

Okay, if you've climbed to the top of a hill or found a secluded area, you're more than ready! Let's do it—(any tune you desire, preferably Native American). "Hey-ah, hey-ah, hey-ah, hey-ah, hey-ah, hoi-yah-oooh." Repeat that chorus. "Oh, Grand Father, how long will you look on? Do not be far from me. Rescue me from their destructions.

"Stir up yourself, and awake to my vindication, to my cause, my God and my Lord. Vindicate me, O Lord my God, according to Your righteousness, and let no one rejoice over me. Let them not say in their hearts, 'Ah, so we would have it.' Let them not say, 'We have swallowed him up!' Ah-ho, ah-ho, ah-ho, ah-ho, ah-ho." Repeat that chorus. (A prayer of deliverance; random thoughts from Psalm 35.) You're now a true American.

I first told you about the 'dance' way back down the trail in chapter 2, remember? I was out in the middle of nowhere in the Arizona Desert, remember? What I didn't explain to you at that time was, the Native American, whose family name was Wild Horse (but he went by the name of John), was on a stand of red rock (in Monument Valley) and was engaged in the 'dance.' He was carrying a Walkman and was wearing the headphones.

That's right—and he was dancing to a Native American song that he was listening to (in the quietness of the desert I could hear the headphone speakers). Naturally I had to investigate. He welcomed me, shared his wisdom and inspiration, and I've been doing the 'dance' ever since. Thought you might like to know. (I found out later that Robert Mirabal had recorded the original song; 'The Dance; Music from a Painted Cave.')

*

It's been an incredible trek. Thanks for taking the time to hike along with me on the *Wilderness Trail*. I sincerely hope this trail has helped you to understand more about yourself and your personal wilderness wanderings—more importantly, that you may have some ideas regarding how to deal with them.

Feel free to come back and hike with me again. You might want to bring a friend or two along with you next time. Wilderness wanderings of some type are always a part of our lives, and we need to stay informed concerning them, as we are prone to forgetfulness.

*Let me remind you once again that I have dealt with these wilderness trails in even greater depth for you in the pages of my book, *Hiking Life's Difficult Trails*, which is now available. There is also a 'High Country Hiker's Edition' of the same book, which contains a perpetual devotional for each day of the week, located in the last section of that particular edition. Don't miss out!

Chapter Thirteen...Hiking into the Bible

Note: I have chosen to designate this thirteenth chapter (appropriately numbered) the *X-files* of the book—you may choose to not believe what I am about to tell you along this journey, but I can assure you that everything that's talked about here *is out there*—I've seen the evidence—I've been there.

These *X-files* however have *nothing* to do with little green men in flying saucers. I only label them *X-files* because of the unbelievable measure of doubt surrounding their existence. With that same regard (doubt surrounding its truth), many people today consider the Bible to be the *X-files*. Gear up for an illuminating hike...

The photograph associated with this chapter (above) is an actual photo (taken by me) of the 5000-year-old remains of Noah's Ark as it appeared in 1991. Take a good look at it, dear reader, and let not your heart be troubled—be instead joyous! Go ahead—stick your tongue out at the skeptics and the non-believers.

The Ark is located some 8 miles southeast of Dogubayazit on the *mountains of Uratu* (Ararat) in eastern Turkey, about 10 miles from the Iranian border. The Ark rests at a 6,300-foot elevation on the northward slope of a mountainous ridge, some 14 miles south of Mt. Ararat itself. In 1959, a NATO survey pilot took the first aerial photo of this site showing an incredible outline of a ship, high on a mountainside in a mudflow.

His discovery caused quite a stir. Newspapers in Turkey and the United States carried the story that year, and in the summer of 1960 an archeological team from the U.S. mounted an expedition to the site. The team spent two days there, and upon finding no wood or obvious artifacts indicating the remains of a ship, reported at a news conference that they felt the object was likely only a natural formation.

Actually, the weathered condition of the ship camouflaged its true identity. This first expedition did not understand *what* to expect—they were looking for an intact ship, not the mere outline of a ship or the petrified remains that were hidden beneath tens of feet of soil and rock. Photographs of the expedition were carried in a story by Life magazine in September 1960.

Incredibly, yet typical of an unbelieving world, no one returned for any further investigation until 1977, when the late, Biblical archeologist Ron Wyatt and his two sons made the trip. Wyatt returned in 1979, and made two visits again in 1984. Based on his observations he was fully persuaded that the site contained the remains of Noah's Ark. The main difficulty in proving this claim in 1977 was that the majority of the boat shaped object was buried beneath tens of feet of soil and rock—the result of a massive mudslide in the area.

But then, in late 1978, an earthquake caused the soil surrounding the object to fall away from its sides. With the soil removed from its outer surface, the object took on the more recognizable shape of a boat, which is obvious in the 1991 photograph above. The general consensus of theologians and skeptics is that the Ark was supposed to have landed on the top of Mt. Ararat—how could it be 14 miles away at a lower elevation?

First of all, the Bible says that the Ark came to rest "upon the *mountains* of Ararat"—plural. The word in the Hebrew text translated Ararat is *Uratu*, which was an ancient kingdom in the region. Furthermore, many early historians attest that the remains of the Ark were visible in their day and could be visited on a routine basis by travelers who journeyed through the area.

For example, Berosus, a 3rd century BC Babylonian historian, says, "But of this boat that grounded in Armenia some part still remains in the mountains of the Gordyaeans (Kurds) in Armenia, and some get pitch from the boat by scraping it off and using it for amulets." The famous 1st century historian, Josephus, mentions that a plant called *amomum* grew in abundance at the Ark site. Amomum grows prolifically today on and around the site discovered by the NATO pilot.

Travelers could not have routinely visited the Ark if it were on the 16,946-foot summit of Mt. Ararat, nor can amomum grow in the ice and snow at that elevation. Furthermore, *common sense* tells us that many animals leaving the Ark would not have been physically able to descend the steep slopes of Mt. Ararat itself. Ark hunters today are still searching Mt. Ararat itself, apparently not even considering God's concern for the disembarking of the animals, nor the fact that the Bible does not put the boat's resting place upon that particular mountain.

In 1985, David Fasold, an expert on ancient ships, explored the Ark site with metal detectors. Tests conducted by Fasold and his associates indicated that there were lines of metal underground at the site. These lines are thought to represent rows of nails or spikes. They form a specific pattern both lengthwise and across the structure. The ones running lengthwise converge at points at either end of the site—clearly consistent with the construction of a boat.

Also, the visible shape indicates that the structure is the remains of a large boat. Evidence in the surrounding area suggests that the Ark came to rest several hundred or perhaps as much as 1000 feet higher in elevation, and was later carried to its present location by a mudslide. It appears to have grounded on an upward protruding outcrop of bedrock. During the course of the mudslide the interior of the boat was filled with mud and rock.

This pressure would have caused the sides to be forced outward, resulting in the splayed condition of the structure now visible. The bedrock outcrop on which the boat grounded is now exposed at the surface, extending from the west side approximately to the center. The surveyed metal lines bend sharply around the rock outcrop. This suggests that the boat's bottom structure was damaged when it struck the rock.

The starboard (right) side of the boat was probably facing the outcrop during the mudslide when it was forced into it. When the boat struck the outcrop, a portion of its lower midsection impaled itself on the rock. The mudslide continued to move the stern (rear) portion of the boat 90 degrees or more in the natural down slope direction of the slide. This movement continued to damage the boat, the rock pinnacle grinding its way upward through the hull, slowing the boat's descent until it could slide no more. The outcrop halted any further movement of the Ark within the mudslide, and it remains imbedded at its present location.

Some samples collected at the site are approximately 90% iron oxide. This evidence suggests that the metal detected *is in fact* iron. The grid of metal lines demands that the site contains a *man-made* structure and the shape is clearly that of a boat. Fasold, using a piece of high technology equipment known as *subsurface interface radar*, obtained a three-dimensional image of the underground structure.

This image revealed a measurement of the structure consistent with the Biblical dimensions of the Ark. The depth of the structure matched the measurement of 30 cubits (52 feet using the Egyptian cubit of 20.8 inches) given by God to Noah. The length and width (splayed) of the boat are in agreement with the measurements recorded by Moses in the book of Genesis; approximately 520 feet by 86 feet. (Genesis 6:15)

The cross beams were determined to be spaced every 9 feet to center. The radar also revealed rooms and 3 tiers or stories to the structure. A very interesting artifact found on the site reveals a piece of petrified wood with a spike or pin through it. On one side of the piece is a washer and there's a round head on the pin—clearly an ancient rivet. A piece of fossilized animal antler was taken from the inside of the boat, pulled out through a hole drilled into the side of the structure. Fossilized animal dung was also recovered. Wyatt had a piece of petrified wood taken off the deck of the boat. It was shown on CNN news in 1991.

In the immediate area, scattered on the face of the land, miles from any body of water, are at least 13 anchor stones. An anchor stone is simply an ancient anchor made of stone, with a hole in the center at the top of it, by which it was hung from the side of a ship using a length of very heavy rope. The size of each of these stones is approximately 8 feet tall by 3 feet wide by 14 inches thick, and the average weight is 8700 pounds. These stones, used by ancient ships, were lowered into the water to stabilize the ships in heavy seas, not to stop the ships from moving.

Similar stones have been found on the floor of the Mediterranean and other seas. These particular stones found in the vicinity of the Ark have petroglyphs on them, which depict the flood in many ways. Some have eight crosses on them (symbols of Noah and his family), indicating that early Christians may have revered them as memorials of the flood. The crosses are Byzantine, which indicate a time period after 300 AD. One stone bears the symbol of Nimrod, the builder of the tower of Babel, which event took place some 200 years after the flood (around 2200 BC). Other inscriptions indicate that Knights of the First Crusade may have visited the area.

There is a small village nearby, *still known* as the 'village of the eight.' In front of an ancient house there were two tombstones. Carved on the stones are a rainbow and eight symbols of Noah and his family, above an ancient petroglyphic portrayal of Noah's death on one marker, and that of his wife on the other. The graves were found looted shortly after their discovery. A very large piece of petrified wood was also found in the area and is believed to be a portion of the covering of the Ark, which Noah removed after the Ark came to rest.

A visitor's center was opened at the site by the Turkish government in 1989, however, political corruption and current unrest in the area has made travel to the site very difficult. Further excavation has not been possible to this date.[1] The discovery of Noah's Ark is one of the most important archeological finds of all time and is a testimony to the trustworthiness of the Bible. There have been many other discoveries that also serve to bear up this trustworthiness. Unfortunately, many people remain blind and refuse to accept the reality of these things, pride being their foremost deceiver.

*

The fate of Sodom, Gomorrah and the cities of the plain from Genesis 19, rained upon by fire and brimstone, is no fairy tale. It was an historical event that occurred exactly as the Biblical account presents it. The remains of two of these cities can be seen on the southwestern side of the Dead Sea, just below Masada.

There are no roads into the affected areas and walking through the ash is difficult but well worth the trek. Numerous ashen formations amid tons of ash containing imbedded sulfur balls and scattered salt formations are all that remain of these cities that were destroyed by fire and brimstone (sulfur) from heaven (Genesis 19:12-29). There are ashen remains of a variety of towers, sphinxes, buildings and city walls. It is an incredibly revealing site for the believer and truth seeker.

From testing the sulfur in this area it is estimated that these cities burned at temperatures well above 4000 degrees Fahrenheit.

Temperatures in this range would vaporize gold and melt stone. There is no sand or dirt at these sites, but only ash—right down to the bedrock. There are sulfur balls of various sizes throughout these ashen remains. Brimstone, or sulfur, found at these sites is contained in round pellets, some the size of golf balls. Many have been tested and are found to be 95.7% sulfur. Their round shape indicates beyond doubt that they passed through the atmosphere.

Lab tests have confirmed that the *quality* of the sulfur found in this particular area is unprecedented in the world. Scientists have pointed out however that sulfur evaporates at a lower temperature than stone, such as marble, and therefore do not understand how sulfur balls could remain intact at this site.

In reply, it is obvious that sulfur balls continued to rain down upon the ashed cities after its initial super-hot firestorm burned everything up. These sulfur balls embedded themselves into the initial layers of soft ash and were cut off from oxygen. A resulting chemical reaction formed capsules around them, allowing them to be preserved in the ashen layers. Tests on the ash itself confirm it to be sulfuric ash, actually heavier than the material it replaced. Rain, wind and erosion have very little effect on this type of ash.[2]

Unique salt formations have been observed in the area of these ashen remains. The Bible says that, as Lot's wife fled from Sodom, she looked back on the destruction and was turned into a pillar of salt (Genesis 19:26). Josephus, a 1st century historian (mentioned earlier), claims to have seen her remains, as did Clement of Rome and Irenaeus in the 2nd century. There are additional eroded salt formations in the area described by Josephus that remain to this day—were others who fled perhaps turned into salt? Considering the *context* of the Biblical narration I would assume that there very well might have been.

At one time, according to Scripture, the vast area of plains upon which these cities were constructed was well watered and bore much fruit, like the Garden of Eden (Genesis 13:10). But today those cities and gardens are but ashen remains. The Bible tells us that this area would continue to bare witness as an *example* of the judgment of God upon human depravity—and so it has (2nd Peter 2:6).

An interesting note however—Jewish tour guides, who work at the ruins of Masada, high above these ash formations, refuse to accept the idea that the remains below them are those of Sodom and Gomorrah.[3] Their attitude is of course typical of those who are without knowledge concerning the works of God. Unfortunately, their ignorance is passed on to all who visit Masada—most people assume that 'tour guides' know everything.

Consider, if you will, what tour guides and even many geologists teach about the Grand Canyon, about Yellowstone and all other such wondrous places. They have very little knowledge concerning the truth about these places, especially when it comes to describing the age of something or how it was initially formed. A lack of credible knowledge in the things of God is one's worst enemy, and will eventually destroy him/her. Note also that a misunderstanding of origins has a disastrous effect upon all of the 'sciences.'

*

The location where the children of Israel crossed the Red Sea under the leadership of Moses is found on the Gulf of Aqaba, Saudi Arabia, *not* on the Gulf of Suez nor its lakes to the north, where many misinformed scholars suppose that it took place. At the Gulf of Aqaba location (Nuweiba) there is an underwater land bridge, where parts of coral covered human and animal (horse) skeletons have been retrieved. Several coral covered chariot wheels, axels and chariot boxes of Egyptian construction have also been found.

The underwater land bridge is the only one of its kind within the Red Sea, which confirms the Biblical account of the "dry ground" or "path" in the midst of the walls of sea water that God provided, allowing the children of Israel to escape from the pursuing Egyptians. The prophet Isaiah called it "the road," which God had made in the sea for the redeemed to cross over (Isaiah 51:10). This path is also mentioned in Psalm 77:19. The very existence of it is in itself a clear explanation for how the Israelites could have crossed over on "dry ground" amidst walls of water on either side.

The Israelite people had camped on the west side of the gulf just prior to crossing the sea at this point. This particular area where the land bridge is located is the only area of land along the entire Gulf of Aqaba large enough to support the 1-2 million people of the Exodus. A mountain range borders this land area, Migdol (*fortification*), overlooking the sea, which is impassable to the west.

The Israelites came south into this area via a passage to the north. This entire geography is described in detail in Exodus 14:1-4. The Egyptians could have therefore only pursued them from one direction, which helped in providing the Israelites protection and escape (Exodus

14:19,20). 500 years after the actual crossing of the Red Sea, King Solomon erected two stone pillars, one on either side of the sea, to commemorate this crossing site.

These two matching pillars were found across from one another at the site of this path in the sea. Inscriptions still visible on one of them indicate that King Solomon had placed them there. The one on the Saudi side (with the inscriptions) has been removed since its discovery, probably by thieves of ancient artifacts. A marker has replaced it. The pillar on the Egyptian side is still standing, near Nuweiba, but any inscriptions have weathered away over time. Powerful storms are more frequent on that side of the Gulf.[4]

*

Thousands visit the traditional Mt. Sinai in the southern Sinai Peninsula each year. Unfortunately for them, it is not really the Mt. Sinai of the Bible. The Bible *clearly* tells us that Mt. Sinai is in Arabia (Galatians 4:25), and so it is—standing statuesque above a broad desert plateau, a mystifying relic of antiquity in a land the Bible calls Midian, east of the Gulf of Aqaba.

The real Mt. Sinai is Jubal al Lawz (*mountain of the law*). The first thing one notices upon approaching Jubal al Lawz is its startlingly visible and mysteriously blackened peak. On the summit of the mountain, the dirt and rocks are burnt into a black and shiny marble glaze from the fire of God described in Exodus 19:16-19. These rocks atop the mountain can be broken in half, revealing an inner core of plain, brown granite—clearly not of volcanic origin.

On its craggy slopes are a mind-boggling array of ancient man-made structures and tantalizing geologic formations that come *right out of the pages of Holy Scripture.* There is a sprawling plain at the base of the mountain that would have provided an ample campsite for the Hebrew people, a primary feature missing from the area of the 'traditional' Mt. Sinai at St. Catherine's Monastery.

Near the base of the mountain, a quarter mile into the plain, there is a huge altar of stacked granite. Etched onto the altar are distinct shapes of cows and bulls, resembling the Egyptian Hathor and Apis bull gods. Cattle have never been a domesticated livestock in Saudi Arabia. The cattle memorialized in stone here were driven there by the Israelites at the time of Moses. This is the site where Aaron, Moses' brother, formed a golden calf from molten gold and made offerings on the altar, proclaiming, "Oh Israel, these are the gods who brought you out of Egypt" (Exodus 32:1-5).

At the very base of the mountain there are orderly piles of stone markers, arranged at four-hundred-yard intervals in a perfect semicircle about the mountain. These are referred to in Exodus 19:12, where the Lord ordered Moses to put *boundary* lines around the mountain so that the people would not go near the mountain, beyond the markers, where they would be put to death. Seeing is believing— these evidences speak for themselves and generate more than just awe. I have seen them, and I know.

At still another point at the foot of the mountain is a huge, V-shaped altar, clearly man-made. This was an altar of worship, built by Moses to include twelve stone pillars that represented the twelve tribes of Israel. To this day, twelve hand-hewn stumps remain there, the pillars themselves toppled over and broken into sections of which the majority still lay in disarray near the altar.

In recent years this entire region has been fenced off as a restricted archaeological site. Posted 'no trespassing' signs in both English and Arabic threaten the death penalty for any violations of the order.[5] This is of course Satan's work, hiding the truth from the world through the hearts of men. This is indeed sad, yet far worse than that is the darkness that surrounds the hearts of so-called 'believers' who don't actually believe in *any* of these evidences that I am presenting to you within this chapter.

Some of these unbelieving 'believers' have been educated by the world's collegiate system and are even referred to as *Biblical scholars*. However, they ignorantly refuse to accept the realities of God's truth, even when the facts and evidences are combined right before their eyes. Their pride and irreverence dominate our educational systems worldwide. You and your children are the victims of their madness and folly. I was fortunate—I learned more from my mother regarding the things of God, who died when I was 14, than I did in all the years I attended college.

*

If you are not familiar with the rock at Horeb (*drought* or *desert*), it is located on the approach to the rocky western slopes of Sinai (the true Sinai) in a camp called Rephidim (Exodus 17). This was the rock that Moses struck with his staff to fulfill the promise that God would

236

provide water in that parched, desert wasteland for the 1-2 million people of the Exodus. The split rock is indeed there, along with the evidence that the rock itself erupted like a great geyser, creating deep furrows of water erosion that are still visible to this day.

The rock sits in a shallow depression at the mouth of a ravine. It is a towering pillar of rock, split laser-fine down the middle, the split approximately nineteen inches wide from top to bottom. Its appearance alone is indeed a wonder, but the rock's inconceivable location at the crown of an ancient head-water is most impressive! It appears as if the riverbed indeed sprang from the rock itself. There are water polished boulders in this natural stream bed that runs down from the split rock; an ancient watershed furnishing clear evidence of a fast-rushing stream, indeed large enough to serve the Hebrew multitude.

While enroute to this rock at Horeb (Mt. Sinai in Arabia), the Israelites camped at a place called Elim (*terebinths*). The Bible states that there were 12 wells of water and 70 palm trees located at that particular campsite (Exodus 15:27). The 12 wells and numerous palm trees are still there in that remote area to this day.[6] This oasis is only a few days walk from Jubal al Lawz (Mt. Sinai), exactly where the Bible says it should be. What more can I say? Again, the trustworthiness of the Bible is indeed enlightening, to say the very least. Again, these evidences provide great encouragement to believers of the truth.

*

Most of us have heard of the *Ark of the Covenant*. Remember Indiana Jones? Jones was the fictional archeologist of the blockbuster movie, Raiders of the Lost Ark. He indeed seemed to be the type of man we would want to employ to locate the Ark. His character and adventures have inspired many into new and renewed interest in Biblical artifacts, and that's a good thing, because they are the only *truly valuable* artifacts of any type.

The discovery of Biblical artifacts is now on the increase. Ancient cities mentioned in the Bible, once believed to be non-existent by skeptical critics, have more recently been unearthed. The true Ark of the Covenant was discovered in 1982, before Indiana Jones ever came into existence on the screen. Very few people have known about the actual discovery of the Ark, due to the nature (Satan's rule) and corruption of the unbelieving world in which we live.

The Ark was thought to have been carried away from Jerusalem sometime around 587 BC, when the city fell to King Nebuchadnezzar of Babylon. But, it was not carried away. It was in fact hidden in a cave, with other temple furniture, perhaps under the direction of Jeremiah the prophet. This cave, or 'room,' was part of an ancient stone quarry, later called *Jeremiah's Grotto*. The cave is located beneath the actual Calvary escarpment, *the place of the skull*, on Mt. Moriah in Jerusalem.

A little history: The Ark of the Covenant was the only piece of furniture within a back room of the *original* Hebrew Tabernacle, or tent of meeting. This room was separated from the front room by a curtain or veil and known as the *Holy of Holies*. The front room pieces of furniture included the *altar of incense*, the *seven-lamp candlestick*, and the *table of shewbread*. The Ark (within the Holy of Holies) was a wooden chest, overlaid with gold, and at one time contained the Ten Commandments on stone, a pot of manna that never spoiled, and Aaron's rod, which once had budded miraculously overnight.

The top of this Ark was called the *Mercy Seat*, which was a flat portion between two golden cherubim overlooking it. The High Priest alone could enter inside the Holy of Holies only *once* each year to make an annual sin offering for himself and for the people. Here, the blood of animals was sprinkled onto the *Mercy Seat* as an atonement for sin. This information regarding the atonement is indeed important for you to understand as I attempt to explain to you the location of the Ark, as well as the significance of its discovery *within* that particular location.

Keep in mind now that the Ark was hidden in a cave or chamber that existed in Jerusalem about 587 BC. In that year or near about the city was completely destroyed and its inhabitants hastened away into captivity. That the invading armies *did not discover* the whereabouts of the Ark is indicated by the fact that it is *not mentioned* in the list of treasures that had been broken and carried off by the Babylonians (2nd Kings 25:13-17, Jeremiah 52:12-23).

The table of shewbread, altar of incense and the seven-lamp candlestick are also *not among those mentioned* in the list of articles captured. The Holy Spirit inspired these Scriptures, which detail the list of treasures carried off; therefore the accuracy of that list is unquestionable.

Now, gather together the mental paints and brushes in your mind and create a picture of what I am about to relate to you; as I relate it: The city (Jerusalem) has been rebuilt upon several times since the destruction of 587 BC, each time *over top* of the previous ruins. In 1979, an excavation began atop previous ruins at the Calvary escarpment (place of the skull) or Golgotha, where Christ was crucified.

No known excavations had ever taken place in this particular area since the crucifixion. The traditional site is *not* located here, where some believe it should be. This particular location was actually being used as a dump. That is so typical of men who are ignorant of God's truth. Forgetfulness of God over time plays a major part in that ignorance.

An old friend of truth and Biblical archeology, Ron Wyatt, headed the 1979 excavation, which was one of many projects he was involved with at that time, and on through to 1989.[7] Excavating tens of feet down (below ground level) from what he believed to be the approximate site of Calvary, his team discovered the walls of a small structure surrounding what he believed to be the original crucifixion site. This building (structure) was apparently constructed during the first century to memorialize the location.

Within this structure, in the center of the rock floor, there were four cross-holes. Three were in parallel, a fourth was found under a small stone covering, elevated somewhat behind and centered on the other three. Black spots, later positively identified scientifically as human yet *unusual* bloodstains, were found near this elevated cross-hole; in a crack in the bedrock floor, underneath the small stone covering.

A *large* round seal stone (used for sealing ancient tombs) was also found within the room, lying flat on the floor, just a short distance in front of the cross-holes. This stone is now believed to be the one rolled in front of Christ's nearby garden tomb. It appeared to be memorialized here as well. Note: The nearby tomb is not the *traditional* site of the Garden Tomb, yet evidence indicates the site as authentic—a garden with a tomb in it, near the actual cross site (John 19:41).

This evidence includes physical identification of the hand-hewn track in which the stone was placed and rolled in front of the tomb, and also evidence that the tomb was sealed with a *Roman* seal, indicated by the location of unique impressions on the stone wall of the entrance on either side of the opening. That a round stone for sealing the tomb was not found *here*, but instead discovered nearby within the walls constructed around the cross-holes, is significant in determining that it must have been considered sacred by early Christians.

Over a period of time the Wyatt team's excavations continued below this room. In 1982, they discovered another room or chamber, some 20 feet below the cross-holes. Though a difficult work, Wyatt was able to make his way into this chamber, through a small but negotiable opening in the rock. His ability to move about in the chamber was hindered, due to numerous large rocks and debris that filled its interior.

He would later come to understand that an earthquake had nearly buried this chamber in rubble, yet he was destined to find some items that had been shielded from the damage caused by that eruption. In this chamber, just under a layer of large rocks, some dry rotted timbers were observed. Under the timbers, Wyatt found the dry rotted remains of animal skins. He discovered that the animal skins were covering a gold veneered table, which had a raised molding around the side, consisting of an alternating pattern of a bell and a pomegranate.

This table had the *appearance* of an object described in the original Tabernacle and used in the Temple of Solomon; the *table of shewbread*. Later, what appeared to be a golden *alter of incense* and a *seven-lamp candlestick* were identified within the chamber, covered and protected in the same manner.

Other objects were also observed, some of which appeared to be related to the original Tabernacle furniture. The greatest find was a large stone case to the rear of the chamber. It had a flat stone covering on top, which was found to contain several cracks, and had, at some point in time, split into two separate pieces. The smaller section of the stone covering had been somehow moved aside, creating an opening in the stone case.

Black spots were scattered on the top of the stone covering. Samples of these 'spots' were later scientifically identified as *bloodstains*, of the same type found at the cross-hole. Immediately above the stone case there was a crack in the rock ceiling, obviously caused by an earthquake. This crack in the rock was directly above the open lid on the stone case.

Beneath the opening and inside the stone case was what appeared to be the golden *Ark of the Covenant*. Black spots of the same type found on the stone covering were observed atop what appeared to be the *Mercy Seat* of the Ark, between two golden cherubim. Ron Wyatt, Biblically informed and excited by what these discoveries might reveal, carefully fed a tape measure up into the crack in the ceiling just above the ark, which continued up a crevice, running through some 20 feet of solid rock.

The end of the tape eventually appeared within the *elevated cross-hole* in the room above, and was pulled up by an utterly amazed member of the research crew. Ron Wyatt later told me that he nearly passed out at that time—he said it was hard for him to breathe. The most *overwhelming* realization of this entire discovery is summarized as follows:

(a) As Christ hung on the cross there was a great earthquake, just at the time of His death. (b) Sometime later, a Roman soldier thrust a spear into Jesus' side as he hung on the cross, and His blood was shed for the remission of our sins, fulfilling Old Testament prophecy.

(c) His blood then ran down from His pierced body, onto the base of the cross, into the recently cracked rock, and followed a crevice some 20 feet down into the hidden chamber. The blood splashed onto the broken covering atop the stone case, assumed to have broken during the earthquake, where it spattered inside the opening and onto the *Mercy Seat* of the one, true *Ark of the Covenant*; thereby fulfilling forever the Old Testament law regarding the sin offering (Matthew 27:50-52, John 19:34, Hebrews 9:22,23, Leviticus 16:14-17).

Wyatt concluded, as any reasonable man would, that 600 years before Christ would die, God arranged to have His earthly throne, *the Ark with its Mercy Seat*, hidden deep within the earth, just below where His Son would die on the cross. Upon this *Mercy Seat* Christ's blood would fall, acknowledging the claims of God's *eternal* Law. The prophetical presenting of Christ's blood to His Father was *perfectly* fulfilled; no human hands presented the blood offering, and no one was in the room save the Spirit of Christ, the true High Priest.

In the earthly service, as I mentioned earlier, the Jewish High Priest offered the blood atonement once each year, sprinkling it privately onto the Mercy Seat. This was according to the Law of Moses, a foreshadowing of what was to come. Hundreds of years then passed. Christ, the true *High Priest*, was now dead—slain on the cross

241

—His body later pierced by the spear of a Roman soldier. Yet, His Father had arranged that, even in His death, Christ would 'sprinkle' the required blood—the blood of the lamb slain from the foundation of the world—upon the *Mercy Seat*.

I was told that Wyatt was only able to see the top portion of the Ark—the two cherubim and the Mercy Seat. He had taken several photographs of the Ark from a position near the small chamber opening, but when developed, the entire group of photos came out blurred.

I have examined *one* of these photographs—the best one. The blurred image *appears* to be the top of the Ark, as described in Exodus 25:17-21. For some unknown reason the photographs are currently not available to the public. I believe a corrupt influence is presiding at this time, which may be according to God's purpose.

Ron Wyatt passed away in 1999. Informed archeologists were at that time unable to locate the hidden chamber that he had described in his notes and drawings. Some deeper areas within the excavation had collapsed. Recent excavations as late as 2006 have still not located the hidden chamber, yet, other artifacts of 1st century Roman origin have been recovered.

The chamber containing the cross-holes within its center has been located and excavations in that area have increased. 2006 is currently the last date that information has been made available on the progress of that work. Artifacts dating back to the time of King Solomon have been unearthed. These artifacts, found below the 1st century level (Roman era), would indicate to me that they are part of a cherished collection, placed their by Jeremiah around 587 BC, which helps to validate Ron Wyatt's theory and discovery.

The stone tablets, upon which the Ten Commandments were written by the finger of God, are believed to still be within the Ark itself, in the yet undiscovered chamber that Ron Wyatt made his way into. But due to bureaucracy, political corruption, greed, violent unrest in the area and other *providential* happenings, including mysterious and untimely deaths, these ancient Temple treasures remain unearthed to this day, well guarded amid the broken rock walls of their underground tomb.

There are those who believe that God does not at this time want the contents of the underground chamber further revealed. But, *who can know the mind of God?* (1st Corinthians 2:15,16) However, there are a few others who believe that eventually this tomb will be completely excavated, and that the whole world will be able to physically see this profound evidence. Unfortunately, in my opinion, I don't think any revelation from this excavation is going to matter to the majority of the world.

They don't care about the ark of Noah, which is sitting right out in the open—in plain sight, nor do they recognize the real Mt. Sinai, even though several books have been written about it, explorers have visited the site, and indisputable evidence has been presented. So, I ask you, why should they care about the Ark of the Covenant?

Why have all of these particularly profound Biblical archeological discoveries, and many more throughout the earth, remained 'silent' to the majority of the world? *Why* hasn't more of the world reacted positively at the present time? The late Ron Wyatt was an exceptional man and we owe him an unprecedented respect for his supreme contribution to God's children.

These discoveries are indeed *unquestionable proof* regarding the accurate testimony of God's only written word, the Bible. As I mentioned earlier, Ron Wyatt died in 1999. David Fasold has embarked on that journey as well. Both men have since been betrayed by the world they knew—their very own people.[8] Betrayal is not uncommon among men—or among 'beings' of greater honor. God was betrayed, also by His very own; the angels who rebelled.

His Son, who later came to earth, was betrayed by his own as well, those who were his closest of followers. Satan never sleeps, yet the world seems always to be asleep. Where is everybody? Where are their minds? Why are they so stubborn in their unbelief—and why are there many professed Christians who doubt these profound evidences as well? What's it going to take to awaken people out of their sleep—out of their hardness of heart?

Jesus gave His *true* followers this answer: *The secret of the kingdom of God has been given to you. But to those on the outside everything is said in parables so that, they may be ever seeing but never perceiving, and ever hearing but never understanding; otherwise they might turn and be forgiven* (Mark 4:10-12 NIV).

This simply means that the *true followers* of Jesus will see and understand the evidences of His truth. Those who do not follow Him in *truth*, as well as those professed Christians who are actually of the world, will be spiritually blind to the truth and not be allowed to perceive it. Though the truth may be right in front of them they will not be able to see it, nor will they be able to understand it, nor will they be able to comprehend the significance of it.

God has blinded them to truth because they refuse to accept truth. He allows them to have what they love, which is the love of that which is *not* truth (Romans 1:28). This is because, in their heart of hearts, which only God can see, they truly just don't care about it. They don't really want it. It's not important to them. The sin nature has hardened them against it.

This is, sadly, the unfortunate condition of a vast majority in our world today. There are many professed Christians within this majority. The world's interest is not centered on the things of God. *The heart is deceitful above all things, and desperately wicked: who can know it?* (Jeremiah 17:9 KJV) And among Christians, Satan is out there to deceive, if possible, even the very elect (Mark 13:22). Beware! You don't know the power of the dark side.

*

You've been allowed a look at some profound physical evidences regarding the teachings of the Bible. Archeology continues to produce overwhelming evidences as to the trustworthiness of its contents. The writings of the Bible itself have been proven without question to be inspired by God. And, on the human side, how the Bible has come down to us is a story of high adventure and unequaled devotion on the part of more than a few men and women.

The Bible did not just happen nor has it been preserved through the years by mere chance. Living in a day when books are written and printed by the thousands, we are apt to overlook the intense drama that lies behind the emerging of our Bible. The fact that there are 66 books bound into the single volume that makes up the Bible tends to obscure its origin.

We'll spend some time in chapter 14 discussing the written documents contained in the Bible, and how they have come down to our time. We're now approaching the trailhead at Discovery Trail. It is the next to the last trail that you will hike on our journey together, but certainly one of the most significant. It is there, among the great rocks along that trail, where we can gain some uplifting and needed insight into the history of the Bible, its preservation, and its incomparable message of salvation.

About one-quarter of the way up that trail, and adjacent to it, is a huge boulder known as *Discovery Rock*. Carved into this unusual stone are petroglyphs—telltale clues that can provide answers to many questions. Discovery Rock is a good place to take a break, to drink some water from your canteen, to relax and to prepare yourself for some difficult terrain beyond the rock itself.

The inscriptions on the rock will come to life along that journey. I will be there to point them out for you, and attempt to open your eyes as to the significance of each of them. Are you ready? Then let's do it —let's continue along together in one another's company and hike the Discovery Trail...

Chapter Fourteen...The Discovery Trail

Welcome to the Discovery Trail. The history of the Bible spans thousands of years, taking us to various regions of the world and into the hearts of countless people, whose first love was the Word of God. The 'human side' of the Biblical record is conditioned upon the development of writing and the history of materials used in the making of ancient books.

Archeologists tell us that *stone* is the material upon which the earliest writing has been found. Discoveries have taken place in most every region of the world. The oldest writings found are in picture form and known as hieroglyphics. These pictures represent a word, syllable or sound, and came about as the result of a gradual deterioration in human memory that began after the Fall in Eden.

Upon being separated from God and the Tree of Life, mankind began to lose the unlimited memory retention that was a part of their original makeup. Picture writing was developed that they might record information, or events, and have the future ability to recall the specifics of that information through picture (hieroglyphic) portrayal. However, as time went on, picture portrayal alone was not enough to stimulate the mind in recalling all of the original information surrounding any specific pictograph.

With the gradual decline in memory retention, detailed writing was then developed so that mankind could better express their thoughts and ideas, and record a more comprehensive record of what was taking place at any particular time. The early Egyptians are credited with being the first to develop an alphabetic system of writing. Their alphabet was not just one of letters, but of syllables and sounds, as some of their earlier pictographs represented.

Alphabetic writing has evolved to its present state from this original effort. A variety of different alphabets now form the basics for all world languages, each having a unique form and history of its own. The world is currently, for the most part, into the computer age. E-mail writing abounds worldwide and direct oral communication is pretty much a thing of the past. Though writing is an excellent way to communicate, it would have never been needed had Eden not been defiled.

God had planned for His behavioral law to be written on our hearts —displayed through our mental and physical actions—*living communication*—but that is unfortunately not the way things have turned out. In fact, modern science tells us that at this time in history we use only a small portion of the brain. In spite of this mortal wound, no computer, no matter how 'technically' advanced, will ever be able to reproduce the coded information in the brain, or function in the unique and unfathomable way that the brain does—it remains a great mystery, understood only by its Designer.

As practically everyone knows, the Ten Commandments were first written in the Hebrew alphabet and on stone. In the countries of early Assyria and Babylonia the predominant writing material was clay. Huge libraries of clay tablets have been unearthed from these regions. The tablets were originally written on with a stylus when soft and then allowed to air dry, or baked in an oven. Wooden tablets crafted by the ancients were also used for writing purposes. However, leather or animal skins played a most important role in the very early history of the Bible.

It was Jewish law that the Old Testament be copied on animal skins, which regulation surely incorporates an ancient tradition, perhaps having something to do with the sacredness of animals. Leather was used for hundreds of years in making copies of the Old Testament, and in some cultures to this day is the only material upon which any type of writing is done. Many Jewish scholars today still produce leather scrolls containing the Old Testament Law, which scrolls are read from in the synagogues and in public gatherings. However, New Testament letters were originally penned on papyrus sheets.

The papyrus plant grew in abundance along the Nile River in Egypt. Papyrus sheets were made from the stems of the plants, and were actually used long centuries before Christ, eventually making their way as far as Greece and Rome. The production of papyrus sheets required great skill, but are subject to deterioration over time. These sheets were often glued together to form rolls of papyrus, some up to 30 feet in length. The longer of the early New Testament letters were undoubtedly in this scroll form, perhaps carried around in a bucket or similar container by their owner(s) (2nd Timothy 4:13).

By the first or second century AD, the papyrus roll began to give way to the papyrus *codex*. A codex manuscript is simply what we know today as a book. It was not long after the birth of Christ that men began to put papyrus sheets together in a book form instead of joining them end-to-end to make a roll. The book form was easier to carry and could contain more written material than the average sized roll or scroll.

Vellum, or parchment, made from specially treated animal skins, eventually replaced papyrus and became a prominent material in the making of books. Vellum was used for more than a thousand years in making copies of the New Testament. These copies were of course hand written and laboriously re-copied by hand, thus making them quite expensive and hard to get. Government authorities as well as religious leaders worked together to appoint the best scribes, who were held responsible for making accurate copies of the New Testament.

These selected scribes would gather in a room called a *scriptorium*. Within the scriptorium one scribe would read aloud the authenticated Scriptures, while the other scribes worked to create the handwritten copies. The number of copies made depended of course upon the number of scribes working in the scriptorium. Actually, many copies were made in this way during the centuries that followed Christ.

There are over 5000 ancient handwritten copies (manuscripts) that defend our modern translations in an extraordinary way, coming from *all parts* of the world. This in itself is sufficient guarantee against any collusion or purposeful manipulation of the texts by various scribes. Dedicated scribes who copied out early Biblical manuscripts sometimes made mistakes in their copying, as no human hand is perfect. But these were trivial matters, such as the misspelling of certain words or the omission of smaller words, such as 'and' or 'the,' which were the result of common errors in both writing and hearing.

They did their work well. Scribes were indeed aware of their integral duty to posterity. Variations in their manuscripts where smaller words have been omitted or added are noted in the margins of some of our more modern translations, such as the New American Standard version and the New King James version. The careful Bible student will avail him/herself to these variations so as to be better informed in their study and application of the Scriptures

(Note: more precise translations of particular words, based on recent archeological discoveries relating to applicable languages, are also noted in the margins of these more modern versions of the Bible).

An event of immeasurable significance took place in about 1450 AD. A man by the name of John Guttenberg perfected a method of printing in Germany that would prove to be indeed practical in the making of books worldwide. No longer would the sacred texts of the Bible have to be produced laboriously by hand. The first major work to emerge from the 'press' of Guttenberg and his associates was the Bible. The year was 1456.

The Bible would now be available to scholars in many lands in its original Hebrew and Greek languages. These scholars would soon offer to the common man more modern translations, based on these original languages. However, dictatorial church authorities of that era did not want the Bible in the hands of the common man. Anyone found translating the Bible into common languages fell prey to some of the most horrific crimes in history.

Religious leaders, who dominated the times, committed tyrannical acts against scholars, forcing them to flee for their lives. Their work had to be done in secret—while in hiding. When caught, some were literally burned alive at the stake. One man's bones were dug up several years after he had died, burned in a public ceremony, and scattered over a river to show the disdain of the church against his work.

The Bible as we have it today has come down to us at the expense of the brutal torturing and killing of both men and women dedicated to the spiritual education of the common man. We can thank God for those who had a part in the survival and preservation of this book of life. At a time when even the very reading of the Bible by the common man was punishable by death, countless people who yearned for enlightenment endeavored to persevere. *We* are enlightened as a result of their gallant efforts and final victory. If you own a Bible you indeed possess a great treasure.

The Dead Sea Scrolls, discovered in 1948 in the caves of ancient Qumran near the Dead Sea, are extraordinary evidences on the Old Testament text. These texts date back as far as 100 BC and confirm in a most remarkable way the text of our modern Hebrew Bible. The text scrolls discovered at this site are at least 1000 years older than the oldest of our previous Hebrew manuscripts!

Fragments from every book of the Old Testament have been found. These scrolls are currently housed at the Hebrew University in Jerusalem, Israel. There are other documents from this find that tell us something about the everyday life of the citizens of Qumran, who authored the scrolls. The entire discovery was nothing short of sensational.

If you're carrying a Bible in your backpack, and I hope that you are, you'll want to pull it out and hold it in your hand and observe it for a moment. The fact that all the books of the Bible are bound together in one volume tends to obscure its origin. The Bible is in fact a library, and like a library, did not come into existence at any one time or place.

The 66 books of the Bible came into being separately and under varying conditions. That the Bible is like a library is implied whenever we use the word *Bible*, derived from *biblia*, meaning, *the books*. The Bible is no ordinary collection. There is no other book like it in the history of the entire world.

Originally written in Hebrew, Aramaic and Greek, the Bible is a treasure house of sacred books that ultimately owes its origin to Him who is the author of all things. Although about forty different people of varying backgrounds, castes and cultures had a part in writing the Bible over a period of 1600 years, it contains a remarkable unity of message and harmony of purpose.

This harmony is no accident. These writers were guided by *Divine Wisdom*. Therefore, the Bible is the mind of God in human language. You are holding in your hand a copy of the most priceless treasures on earth. You will do well to treat them as such from here on out. Since the Bible is God's *only written revelation* to us, we owe it to ourselves to study it on a daily basis, for when Jesus comes again each of us will be judged by the contents of the Bible (Revelation 20:12).

It is the only book that reveals the truth about mankind; where we came from, our purpose while on the earth, and what we are to believe and do to live with God eternally. The Bible is also in perfect harmony with all known secular history. In addition, the geographical references to rivers, lakes, physical terrain and distances are absolutely correct. It is my plea that you will give yourself a chance to know more about this book of life.[1]

The most important message in this book of life is that of *salvation* (becoming a Christian). The Bible is a map—a spiritual trail map—designed and drawn by the hand of God, according to His compass. You and I, in the providence of God, become its hikers. Like any hiker using a map to arrive at an ultimate destination, we will journey quite some distance and make many discoveries along the route to that destination.

The way is narrow and there are many difficulties to encounter (Matthew 7:14), but the Bible is God's step-by-step trail map to our salvation and the *only* accurate map to daily living and eternal life. Belief in this particular truth is absolutely essential. Our faith in this matter will either justify or condemn us in our relation with this book. This journey is far more involved than the average modern-day teacher or preacher would allow you to believe.

On the radio and television today we hear of several different ways that one can be saved and live with God eternally. Each broadcast offers something a little different. Some portions of their teachings are indeed accurate, while other portions of their teachings, especially in regard to salvation itself, are the doctrines of demons (1st Timothy 4:1). Though salvation is one of the Biblical doctrines that should be more readily understood, it is at the very top of the list of those doctrines that are perverted and misunderstood, which ignorance causes even further misunderstanding of other Biblical concepts.

I know why it is misunderstood, but for me to convince *you* why it is misunderstood might be difficult, so I will let the Scriptures themselves do the talking. You do not have to have any letters before or after your name (Dr, PHD, etc.) in order to understand the concepts of the Bible. Furthermore, what you may have learned at a particular

251

theological seminary or school of the Bible does in no way guarantee your mastery of it.

The Psalmist has said: *I have more insight than all my teachers, for Thy testimonies are my meditation* (Psalm 119:99). Understanding the Bible depends upon the time *you* spend at meditating upon its teachings. The teachings of the Bible are entirely spiritual, and only through spiritual application do these teachings come to life. You *can* know more than your earthly teachers. I hope that you will gain this particular understanding.

The Bible teaches that one day a famine will come upon the land—not a famine for bread or a thirst for water, but rather for hearing the words of the Lord. People will stagger from sea to sea, and from the north even to the east; they will go to and fro on the earth to seek the word of the Lord, but they will not find it (Amos 8:11,12). Sometimes I wonder if that time is not upon us?

We've reached that point on the trail—that huge boulder adjacent to it—known as *Discovery Rock*. I spoke of it at the end of the previous chapter. You're going to look at some inscriptions, so to speak, that are etched into the Rock. The Rock is of course God's word. The inscriptions are His eternal teachings—things that never change—immutable things.

Go ahead and sit down next to the Rock. Take a break and drink some water from your canteen. Relax for a few moments—when we continue the hike you'll have some time to consider some of the spiritual inscriptions as I bring them to life. I'll put everything out where you can see it—one principle at a time. You've hiked a long way through this book to reach Discovery Rock. The trail is difficult from this point on.

There are some who will continue the hike for a short time (a few more paragraphs—perhaps even a few more pages, I hope), but then suddenly decide to turn back. The winds of doubt and the storms of indifference blow hard along this narrow section, and these elements will cause them to lose heart. The Discovery Trail is a challenge—no doubt about it. But now is not the time to quit. You've come this far, and the end of the trail *will* offer you a stunning panorama that can change your perspective on all things—change your whole life for the better.

Go for it. Hiking is all about challenges. A sincere effort will be rewarded—don't turn back just because the going may *initially* seem to you a little questionable. Remember chapter 10, your hike into the desert? Remember the sign in Death Valley that read, *Hike or Die?* Make the right choice—as far as I'm concerned; the only wise choice. Are you not seeking the truth—your connection with God? The Discovery Trail may actually be where you to find it.

When the early church began its outreach, Philip the evangelist was prompted by the Spirit to join up with an Ethiopian eunuch, who was traveling home from Jerusalem and intently reading the Scriptures (writings of Isaiah) while aboard his chariot. When Philip approached the eunuch (a complete stranger to him) he asked him if he understood what he was reading.

The eunuch's reply was, "Well, how could I, unless someone guides me?" (Acts 8:30-31) That's the purpose, dear reader, of this chapter—of this entire book—to guide you. I hope that you possess the attitude of the Ethiopian eunuch, who was *willing* to listen to a complete stranger, who had approached him from nowhere, in the middle of the desert, and whom he eagerly welcomed.

I'll begin by saying that you cannot add to or take away from the Bible. Men who do so produce something different than what the Bible says. You cannot plant corn and reap tomatoes. Every seed brings forth after its own kind. The Bible contains the *seed* (word) of God (Luke 8:11). You cannot therefore plant what *is not* in the Bible (impure seed) and end up with or reap something *that is* in the Bible (pure seed). The word of God needs to be taken quite seriously.

You shall not add to the word, which I am commanding you, nor take away from it, that you may keep the commandments of the Lord your God, which I commanded you (Deuteronomy 4:2 NASB).

This warning is repeated in Deuteronomy 12:32, in Proverbs 30:6, and in Revelation 22:18. It is implied in many other Scriptures of both the Old and New Testaments. Consider that in the very beginning of human life, as we know it, just *one* word was added to God's words, which word changed the entire course of humanity; God told Adam and Eve that if they ate of the tree of the knowledge of good and evil that they would surely die. The devil added, "You will *not* die" (Genesis 3:3,4). *One word* changed their destiny.

That particular destiny has been passed on to you. Again, God is sovereign and needs to be *taken seriously*. Adam and Eve failed to do that. Many teachers today do not take God seriously and add *several* words not found in the Bible when they expound on salvation, 'wrestling' with the Scriptures to their own destruction (2nd Peter 3:16). I listen to radio preachers often. Many of their teachings are accurate to the core. Yet, one must beware.

Consider the city of Berea, mentioned in Acts 17. We are taught that the Bereans were a fair-minded or *noble* people, who *searched the Scriptures daily* to see if the things that Paul and Silas were proclaiming concerning Jesus were true. As a result of their research many of them became believers. They had allowed the Scriptures to convince them of truth, *not* the preachers who proclaimed it, though the preachers in *this* particular case had taught them accurately.

In Acts 18 there is the story of a man in Ephesus named *Apollos*, an eloquent man, fervent in spirit, who spoke and *taught accurately of the Lord*, though he knew only the baptism of John. Here we have a man who taught accurately, though he was lacking in a particular area. He was kindly approached about his inaccuracy by a husband and wife —Aquila and Priscilla—who explained to him *the way of God more accurately*. He did not quibble with them, but went on with even more encouragement, greatly helping others who had believed in the Lord Jesus through grace (Acts 18:24-28).

A short time later, while passing through Ephesus, the Apostle Paul ran into some disciples who may have been previously taught the way of the Lord by Apollos—before he had been corrected by Aquila and Priscilla.

When Paul found them, he asked them, "Did you receive the Holy Spirit when you believed?"

These men then answered Paul, "We have not heard whether there is a Holy Spirit." (Someone had taught them, but obviously in error.)

Paul then said to them, "Into what were you baptized?"

They answered, "Into John's baptism." (Possibly indicates that Apollos had been their teacher.)

Then Paul said, "John indeed baptized with a baptism of repentance, saying to the people that they should believe on Him who would come after him, that is, on Christ Jesus." Now when the men heard this they were *baptized into the name of the Lord Jesus*. These men, twelve in all, learned from Paul the correct doctrine regarding salvation, by grace, and then responded accordingly. (Acts 19:1-7)

As I mentioned earlier, I often listen to radio preachers. I read many Christian books and examine many Christian tracts. I have watched and listened to a few television evangelists as well. Unfortunately, I have discovered that nine out of ten present-day writers/teachers/preachers currently teach the way of salvation inaccurately, like Apollos had originally done. I love these teachers. I equate some of them with Apollos—fervent in spirit and individually, in many respects, teaching accurately of the Lord.

Yet, with regard to salvation, I believe that nine out of ten have 'missed the boat' so to speak—they were not aboard the Ark when it was delivered by the waters of the Great Flood, they did not pass through the Red Sea with Moses, and they apparently do not fully comprehend the meaning of being 'born again,' which concept Jesus presented to Nicodemus.

Their inability to comprehend the 'born again' concept is quite understandable, for Nicodemus did not understand what Jesus meant at that particular time as well—we'll discuss that shortly. I have written 'kind' letters to the nine folk's I am talking about, but have received as of the date of this writing *no responses whatsoever*. Remember—if you can't get hold of them, why trust them?

Be advised that I have heard each of these teachers expound on false teaching. They each admit that there are those within the circle of Christian teachers who do teach in error, however, the nine I am referring to here fail somehow to include themselves among that group. I believe it is because they are perhaps unaware of their own capability of teaching in error. Anyone can teach in error if they do not *thoroughly* understand what they are teaching.

I am inclined to give them the benefit of the doubt here and claim that they do not thoroughly understand what they are teaching. There are actually many who teach the way of salvation inaccurately, in fact, I would estimate that nearly 90% of the world's Christian evangelicals (nine out of every ten) teach this particular doctrine in error. That's a lot of folk's!

I don't believe it to be intentional, which is one of the reasons I am about to expound a little bit on the subject. Unfortunately, their misunderstanding of salvation has also led to their diverse conclusions regarding the second coming of Christ—but that is a another matter, and an extremely important one, which I hope to discuss in my very next book, Lord willing.

Their misunderstandings regarding salvation have also caused them to pull some of Jesus' teachings out of history and apply them to themselves and to their followers, which teachings actually do not apply to any of them. They haven't learned to *handle accurately the word of truth* (2nd Timothy 2:15 NASB). Some also have the mistaken idea that Jesus is going to establish a physical kingdom upon this present earth at some point in time.

This one concept, born through an impulsive attempt to unravel the book of Revelation, has led to a myriad of misunderstandings, which I am sure Satan is exceedingly happy about. His arrows of deceit have indeed struck their targets. Remember, his most fierce arrows of deceit target all *believers*, and also strike those who *want to learn to believe* —in God, in Jesus, and in the Bible (Revelation 12:17).

Fortunately, Jesus has informed us that His kingdom is *not of this world* (John 18:36). It is in fact spiritual in nature, like all of His teachings. We live in a generation where sensationalism abounds. There are many, many false teachings that have sprouted from this chaos. I would like to tell you about them in detail, right now, but first things first and then perhaps we can hike along together in that next book and discuss these things.

Of the ten individuals I've listened to, save well-known author/teacher/radio program host, Max Lucado, I am not sure of their particular reasons for teaching the salvation doctrine as they do. I'm not trying to put Mr. Lucado on a pedestal, for we all sin. Yet, remember that only one leper out of ten returned to thank Jesus just after he had cleansed all ten of them from leprosy (Luke 17:11-19).

Why the other nine did not return to thank Him, I am not sure, but perhaps they did not really know who Jesus was. Perhaps they did not understand the authority of His works. Perhaps they did not understand the deeper significance of their cleansing. Or, perhaps they did not consider the thanklessness within their own hearts.

There are also at least four possible explanations for anyone today teaching salvation in error. (1) A misunderstanding of Biblical dispensations, (2) a misunderstanding of the attributes, works and gifts of the Holy Spirit, (3) a failure to understand the significance of water in the 'new birth' process, and (4) perhaps no in-depth understanding of the deceitfulness of the human heart, namely their own.

Each of the nine individuals could be a victim regarding just one of these topics, or perhaps confused as a result of all of them. I am sure by this time that you are wondering, "What the heck are you talking about when you say, 'missed the boat'?" and, "What is in error concerning the way that these particular teachers and many others present the doctrine of salvation?"

First of all, the Bible represents three periods of history, or dispensations. The first period is considered to be the *Patriarchal age*. This period covers Old Testament history from the Creation until the time of Moses and the Exodus from Egypt. During this dispensation God spoke directly to the fathers of the households; such as Adam, Noah, Abraham, etc.

The second period of Old Testament history begins with Moses and the Israelites receiving the Law in the wilderness, and continues through the life and times of Jesus, until His death on the cross. This is usually referred to as the *Mosaic age* because God gave His law through Moses, which law came to an end with the death of Christ (Colossians 2:14).

The third period, the *Christian age*, bears the name of Christ, who is its central theme. This age began just after Jesus' death and resurrection and will last until He comes again. Then time, as we know it, shall be no more. In the Christian age, God speaks to men through His Son, for the gospel (*the good news of God*) came through Jesus Christ.

Once a person sees this overall picture of the Bible, he/she is able to understand, appreciate and study it more intelligently. Both the Old and New Testaments are very important to the Christian, but the New Testament books are the Christian's guide for today (Hebrews 1:1,2), the Old Testament having been fulfilled in Christ.

However, it is extremely important to understand here that Jesus was born, lived, and died under the Old Testament period of history—both according to and under its Law. Matthew, Mark, Luke, and John, though considered New Testament writings, are actually historical biographies of Christ that *took place* during the Old Testament Period —the Mosaic age. Jesus always told those who listened to Him and those whom he healed to offer the sacrifices commanded in the Law of Moses (Luke 5:14, etc.).

Jesus announced during this historical period the coming of His kingdom, which was 'at hand.' But it was not until His death on the cross that the Old Testament Law (or covenant) actually came to an end (Colossians 2:14). Understanding this truth will allow a Bible student to better comprehend the conversations that Jesus had with a certain group of His followers—namely, "the twelve." There are some specific things that He told them that have never and will never apply to other men/women—in any age.

Secondly, there is a great deal of misunderstanding in the world today about the Holy Spirit and the way He operates in this Christian age. This is partly because an accurate Scriptural view of the Holy Spirit's influence is something not hastily acquired. It requires not a little reading, much thought, and more than natural caution to avoid falling into error. Anything less than the most *thorough investigation* is sure to miss the mark (the truth).

Without an understanding of the work of the Holy Spirit in each Biblical age, it is impossible to understand His overall revelation to us in the Scriptures. After all, the Scriptures were written entirely through His influence (2nd Peter 1:20,21, 2nd Timothy 3:16). I suggest you read this particular paragraph (also the previous paragraph), one more time, for emphasis.

The Holy Spirit is a Divine Person-Spirit, a member of the three-person-spirit Godhead. By 'person,' I mean that He has personality—that He possesses life, individuality, character, influence, knowledge, thought, will, power and ability. He is not impersonal—a glorified 'it.' I do not mean that one God is three Gods. Rather, I mean that there is only one infinite Spirit Being, but within that spirit essence there are three personal distinctions, each of which may be called God, each capable of loving and being loved by others, and each having a distinct part to play in the drama of salvation.

The Holy Spirit possesses all the characteristics of divinity: eternity, absolute power or authority (omnipotence), above and independent of the material universe (transcendence), and knowing all things (omniscience).[2] The Holy Spirit was active in several ways in the Old Testament Period.

He was involved in the creation of the universe and of mankind. He worked in the lives of men and women to heighten their abilities and powers, giving them the wisdom and skill to guide armies, build the tabernacle, interpret dreams, govern nations and resist God's enemies. He inspired the prophets to make known God's will and to reveal future events. He inspired the writers of the Old Testament Scriptures and enabled them to produce a true and accurate revelation of God.[3]

A wise man has said, that from Creation to Incarnation was the *age of the Father*. From Incarnation to Pentecost (33 AD approximately) was the *age of the Son*. From Pentecost until Christ returns is the *age of the Holy Spirit*. This does not mean that all personalities of the Godhead were not and are not active in all periods, but merely that one person of the Godhead worked more prominently in each period. There are at least 264 references to the Holy Spirit within the New Testament writings, including 59 in the gospels, 57 in Acts, and 131 in the Epistles.

The New Testament in its entirety speaks of four 'measures' or 'manifestations' of the Holy Spirit. They include (1) the *unlimited measure* (John 3:34), which only Jesus is said to have received, (2) the *baptism of the Holy Spirit* (Acts 1:5), which I will expand upon in the upcoming paragraphs, (3) the *miraculous* gifts (*Charismata*; at least nine different gifts in all), given to Christians *only* by the *laying on of the Apostle's hands* (Acts 8:18 &19:6, 2nd Timothy 1:6), and finally, (4) the non-miraculous gift (*Dorean*; Acts 2:38, Romans 8:9-11, Galatians 3:27, Ephesians 3:16,17), which refers to the indwelling of the Spirit, which God gives to all believers upon their water baptism into Christ (Acts 2:38).

The Holy Spirit was completely identified with the life and teachings of Jesus. He was conceived by the Spirit, baptized with the approval of the Spirit, anointed with the Spirit, able to perform signs by the Spirit, and raised from the dead by the Spirit. Only of Jesus is it ever said that He received the Holy Spirit without measure.[4] After Jesus' resurrection from the dead, He promised to send the Holy Spirit to work with the Apostles in an especially unique way, *never promised to other men*.

The Spirit was at work through them in the establishment and building up of the church and in the inspiration of the New Testament writings themselves, which were completed before100 AD.[5] The Apostles were 12 in number at first (Acts 1:26) and later numbered 13, with the Apostleship of Paul, who was confronted by Jesus on the Damascus road and just three days later became a Christian through a man named Ananias, whom the Lord had appointed for that special purpose (Acts 9:17,18).

Through the Holy Spirit these men were given miraculous divine reassurance, miraculous divine guidance and miraculous gifts, including the power to speak and write the inspired word, the power to speak in the differing languages of their hearers (tongues), the power to confirm the inspired word though miracles, and the power to bestow certain miraculous gifts on others *through* the laying on of their own hands.

These particular abilities are referred to in the Scriptures as the *baptism of the Holy Spirit*, and at first fell only upon these appointed men. Jesus referred to it in Acts 1:5, calling it by that name. Some have referred to it as the baptism of fire (Acts 2:3,4). About 10 years after the baptism of the Holy Spirit upon the Apostles, this same manifestation of the Spirit fell upon a man named Cornelius, a Gentile, and fell also upon all who were in his house listening to Peter as he taught them the word of God (Acts 10:44-48).

This was a special baptism upon the Gentiles, but the *same* (Acts 11:15) as that which fell upon the 12 Apostles at the very beginning of the church on the day of Pentecost, 33AD. Peter confirmed his witness to this special baptism, when he later informed the other Apostles in Jerusalem of this miraculous event (Acts 11:15-18). This second miraculous baptism of the Spirit completely fulfilled the Old Testament prophecies regarding the Holy Spirit falling upon *all flesh* (Jews and Gentiles), which fulfillment signified the end of the *miraculous* baptism of the Holy Spirit throughout the church age (Acts 2:16-21, Joel 2:28-32).

Again, certain miraculous gifts were given other followers of Christ, but *only* through the laying on of the Apostles hands (Acts 8:18, etc.). There are many denominational religious groups today that fail to discern this most important understanding. Their religious practices are centered on human emotions, not on faith. All of the Apostles died before 100 AD. The ability to pass on any or all *miraculous* gifts of the Spirit died with them.

Do not be deceived—no one today has this power. Miraculous gifts were used only to *confirm the Word* as Christianity took root. These specific men were endowed with 'all truth,' as Jesus had promised them (John 16:5-15). These gifted men *were* the Word (John 17:20, Galatians 1:11,12). Through *their* Word (all truth—God's Word) we now have the confirmed Word in written form—the 27 books of the New Testament. Any revelations beyond 100 AD are strictly from the imaginations of men (deceitfulness of the heart), not from the Spirit of God.

260

Thirdly, we have our aforementioned teacher's (nine out of ten) possible failure to understand the significance of *water* in the 'new birth' process (salvation). You asked earlier about 'missing the boat' and 'what is their error'? In relating this particular principle I will answer those questions for you. First of all, let us understand that the words 'new birth' appear nowhere in the entire Bible. The words 'born again' are only mentioned twice, and are actually translated (from the Greek language), *born from above* (John 3:7, 1ˢᵗ Peter 1:23).

The Bible does indicate however that being born from above— being born again or regenerated or re-born—is actually being *spiritually born*, not of corruptible seed but incorruptible, *through the word of God* (1ˢᵗ Peter 1:23). Salvation is received through being born again—Jesus told Nicodemus that, unless one is born of water and the Spirit, he could not enter the kingdom of God.

One *must* be born again. That principle is simple for us to understand—no 'new birth'—no salvation. The terms (must be born again) could not be any clearer; I believe all Christians can agree on that. If not, they need to read it again, aloud, with their eyes open and their ears more attentive. What Nicodemus could *not* understand I will talk about shortly.

What is being taught from the pulpit in much of the Christian evangelical world today is as follows: When the question is asked of a minister, pastor, church leader or teacher, "What must I do to be saved?" the answer people get is similar to this: "Just accept Jesus Christ as your personal Savior." This statement is found nowhere in the bible, nor is it even hinted at, yet it is a common answer, heard in many churches and broadcast on radio and television throughout the World. Those who proclaim this answer sometimes further add, "And the Holy Spirit will guide you into all truth."

With regard to the latter, being 'guided into all truth,' only the Apostles were at first guided into all truth (John 16:13), and they left us the New Testament, which when added to the Old Testament *is all truth* for the Christian today. I explained this when we talked just previously about the Holy Spirit. No man/woman today can 'know all truth,' *except* through a study of the Scriptures and the help of the indwelling Holy Spirit (*Dorean*) in those studies.

Only the Apostles, at first, were given a miraculous degree of the knowledge of God, known then as 'all truth,' that they might bind on earth the teachings of God (Matthew 16:19 & 18:18). This they did in

261

their own generation and then recorded it for succeeding generations. Again, when Jesus spoke concerning 'all truth' (John 16:7-15) He was speaking to eleven disciples, who later became His Apostles, *not* to you and I in this 21st century. This is one of those areas of Scripture where teachers today fail to 'handle accurately' the word of truth (2nd Timothy 2:15).

Luke and Mark (John Mark), who were not Apostles, were also among the writers of the New Testament (Mark, Luke and Acts). We can logically assume, from the history related in Acts (the only Biblical book containing a history of the New Testament church), that these men were able to know 'all truth' through the laying on of the Apostle's hands; Mark through Peter and Luke through Paul, who himself received the baptism of the Holy Spirit through Ananias, whom Jesus had empowered for that very purpose (Acts 9:17,18). Paul was appointed as an Apostle as *one born out of due time* (1st Corinthians 15:8,9, NASB).

There was no written New Testament when any of these men began their ministries and travels for the Lord. They *were* the New Testament in the flesh (so to speak) before it was ever written, through the *miraculous knowledge* (all truth) given them by the Holy Spirit. Jesus sent them into the world to teach the world (John 17:18). He also prayed for those of us who would in the future believe on Him through *their word* (John 17:20,21).

Their word is the 'all truth' found today in the New Testament. The early Christians continued *steadfastly in the Apostle's doctrine* (Acts 2:42), which serves to convert people from all walks of life—all religions and philosophies—to Christianity. We are to do the same— their doctrine (*teaching*), by the authority of Jesus, is the 'pure seed,' the *only one* that leads to salvation and eternal life.

With regard to the 'just accept Jesus as your personal Savior' teaching, not found in the Bible, individuals continue to respond to this invitation, believing that salvation is theirs. If they would but consult their spiritual trail map more closely, they might indeed find themselves on a road *toward* salvation, but *not yet* at that destination.

They would instead find themselves on a wide road and in the company of millions of other people, who have also not *carefully studied their maps*, but instead have allowed someone else (a preacher, teacher, talk show host, etc.) to do the navigating. Allowing another's map reading or compass orientation to determine their course for them, they have been unable to locate the narrow trail, as the Scriptures warn:

Enter through the narrow gate. For wide is the gate and broad is the road that leads to destruction, and <u>many</u> *enter through it. But small is the gate and narrow is the road that leads to life, and only a* <u>few</u> *find it* (Matthew 7:13,14 NIV, my emphasis on 'many' and 'few').

These are actually the words of Jesus Himself. If I had never read the Bible, this particular statement would *certainly* cause me to search diligently for the 'narrow way,' which is obviously not the common way of today. I would have to break away from the multitude and do some serious searching, even if I had to do it on my own. I trust Jesus, but unfortunately I cannot trust men.

So, dear reader, let us search the Bible, find the way, and then attempt to try and convince others. (If you've come this far in the reading of this chapter and haven't yet turned back, that's good! The winds of doubt and the storms of indifference have not yet deterred you—stay diligent, attentive, and stay the course. The ability to come to your own conclusions has not and will not be taken from you.)

The Christian age began on the Day of Pentecost, 33 AD. At that time the *very first sermon* was preached to a multitude of Jews from many nations, in fact, from *every nation under heaven* (Acts 2:5). Peter had been given the *keys* to the kingdom of heaven, in that he was appointed to preach the first sermon ever delivered on the subject of salvation (Matthew 16:19, Acts 2:14).

He would unlock the door to Christianity (which door is Christ; John 10:9). That was his purpose, and that is exactly what he did. His answer to the question posed by his hearers, "What must I do to be saved," was indeed different than that of many of our present day teachers, who may honestly attempt to bring others through the door, yet fail to make use of the keys given Peter (Galatians 3:27).

When the multitude heard Peter's sermon they were cut to the heart, and having realized that the crucified Jesus *was indeed* their Savior, they responded, "Brothers, what shall we do?" (Acts 2:37) Peter's immediate answer was *not*, I say again, *not*, 'just accept Jesus Christ as your personal Savior.' In fact, it should be obvious that no one can 'accept Jesus Christ' in his or her fallen condition.

Come now, let us reason together; our hearts are deceitful above all things and desperately wicked. We're not qualified to accept anything —slaves of sin. Jesus is instead the One who does the 'accepting' when one *obeys* His will in becoming a Christian, for Peter's answer was, "Repent and be baptized, *every one of you*, in the name of Jesus Christ for the forgiveness of your sins. And you will receive the gift (*Dorean*) of the Holy Spirit" (Acts 2:38).

The hearer's conversion involved a change in attitude and a step forward in faith, allowing themselves to be baptized in water (Acts 2:41). At that time the Holy Spirit (*Dorean*) began to dwell in the fallen heart of each of those being so baptized (Acts 2:38). The Holy Spirit then bore witness within their spirits that they had become children of God (Romans 8:16).

Their shackles had been broken—they were free. This is initial salvation in a relatively easy to understand method, for Jesus had previously instructed the Apostles, "*Go into all the world and preach the good news to all creation. Whoever believes and is baptized* (an act of faith) *will be saved, but whoever does not believe* (not acting in faith) *will be condemned.*" (Mark 16:15,16 NIV, clarification added).

Even with Jesus' clear teaching, some people today have difficulty believing or knowing that they are saved—I will discuss that shortly. All New Testament conversions recorded in the historical book of Acts involve water baptism.[6] This was the practice for many years until *uninspired* men changed that practice as early as 150 AD.

Furthermore, all the letters of the New Testament (Romans thru Jude) were written to various congregations of people who were water-baptized believers of Christ. Certain sentence constructions in the Scriptures imply that there were a few people in some of the congregations who had not yet been baptized (example: Galatians 3:27), but unsaved newcomers seeking truth are common in any congregation of Christians.

Many will say here, "Some Scriptures say *faith* is all you need, while others will say all you have to do is *believe*." Both are emphatically true. But first, one has to be taught *what* faith entails, and, be taught *what* to believe. Faith without acting upon that faith is dead, being alone. And even the devils believe—and tremble (James 2:14-26).

The foundation of these 1st century words goes much deeper than our modern English usage. Faith is not just standing still and hoping something happens, which is what this 'accepting Jesus' teaching (again, *not* in the Bible) is all about. Faith is instead putting into action the *truths* you have been taught to believe. I'll take that to a 1ˢᵗ century depth for you:

The Bible teaches that faith is the assurance (or substance) of things hoped for, the conviction (or evidence) of things not seen (Hebrews 11:1). That's God's definition of faith. That is why Abraham's faith included *doing* everything he was told—*going* where he was sent, etc. He raised a knife over his son and was about to kill him, because of his *assurance* of a promise and a *conviction* in his heart that God could raise his son from the dead in order to fulfill that promise.

That's faith! Action—that's what the Greek word entails. And his was a 'work' of faith, not a work of the Law. Faith is not a work of the Law. Faith is an *attitude* that motivates one to believe and obey the commands of God because one trusts in His promises. Works have to do with the traditions of the Law, *not* with *obedience* unto faith. (We all know that Abraham's faith resulted in God sparing his son—stopping any downward thrust of the knife—whew! God loves it when we're faithful.) Belief? Now that's a shallow term in our generation; meaning that one simply *says*, "Oh yea, okay, I believe."

1ˢᵗ Century belief is when someone decides to mount a tightrope and push a wheelbarrow atop it, above and across Niagara Falls. When anxious crowds of onlookers shout, "Yea, yea, we believe you can do it," the tightrope walker looks down at them and shouts back, "Prove it!" The great crowds become silent, save for one young boy amidst them. The lad works his way forward, much to the amazement of the crowds, and shouts up to the man on the tightrope, "I'll prove I believe —I'll get into the wheelbarrow!"

That's 1ˢᵗ century belief—Biblical belief. There are those today who skim across an ocean in a sailboat and claim to know all about that large body of water. They know nothing unless they explore its depth—go to the bottom and examine its roots. So it is with having a Biblical perspective of what belief is, and a firm comprehension of what you believe in.

Faith's hall of fame (Hebrews, chapter 11) teaches us without exception that all of its members both *believed* and *acted in faith*, which established their faith. The Scriptures teach that when Abraham *believed* God, it was credited to him as righteousness (Romans 4:3). This belief includes all of Abraham's *actions* by faith. He was not

265

credited for standing still and doing nothing. He was not credited for sitting underneath a terebinth tree and daydreaming.

He was credited because his faith and belief were alive and breathing—motivated to both obey and do God's will. Our words mean nothing. It is through our obedience to God that our faith is made perfect (James 2:22). So, yes, you *are* saved by faith, and you *are also* saved by believing. They go arm in arm, and now, you know *how* they go arm in arm and hopefully your eyes are open to what they mean.

In addition to carefully investigating Biblical word meanings, you have to be careful of what you might be taking out of context, especially when searching the Scriptures regarding salvation. You need a more accurate compass reading. One of the most common mistakes with Biblical interpretation is not knowing *whom* God is speaking to at any particular time, and not understanding *why* He is speaking to them as such. Contrary to popular opinion, He is not always speaking *directly* to you, the reader, but is instead at times revealing a matter *for your benefit* it one way or another.

The majority of the religious leaders of Jesus' time rejected the way he presented the truths of God. Though professing to understand the Scriptures, they had little understanding concerning them. Has this attitude changed in the 21st century? Of course not—there's nothing new under the sun. Jesus is the author (or source) of *eternal salvation* to all those who *obey* Him (Hebrews 5:9).

Baptism is not a 'work.' It is instead a result of a belief in and an act of faith upon the promises of God. If Jesus said, 'be kind to your neighbor,' would you not have to actually *do that* in order to establish faith? Merely *thinking* in your heart about being kind to your neighbor is not faith—it has not yet been established.

Water baptism actually identifies one with Christ through His death, burial and resurrection. Nicodemus could not understand being born of 'water and the Spirit,' because Jesus had not yet died, had not yet been buried, and had not yet risen from the dead at that time. He would have come to learn what this being 'born again' meant, after the first sermon was preached on Pentecost. Being 'born of water and the Spirit' is both a physical and Spiritual operation.

A shadowy reflection of this new birth was seen in the days of Noah and in the time of Moses. This is perhaps one place where a majority of our present day teachers 'miss the boat.' The Bible teaches that only a few people (in the days of Noah), eight in all, were *saved*

266

through water. There is also an antitype, which now saves us—baptism (not the removal of the filth of the flesh, but the answer of a good conscience toward God), through the resurrection of Jesus Christ (1st Peter 3:20,21 NKJV).

Baptism does not remove our sinful nature, but it does confirm for our *conscience sake* that we have obeyed God in becoming His children, through the resurrection of Jesus Christ. This is your *assurance* of your own particular salvation. Under Moses, the children of Israel were 'baptized into Moses' as they passed through the Red Sea (1st Corinthians 10:1,2). For the Israelites the entire ordeal of the Exodus resulted in both a physical and spiritual identification with their leader.

In the Christian age, baptism represents both a physical and spiritual identification with the death, burial and resurrection of Jesus Christ. It also represents the washing away of sins by the Blood of Christ, through the word of God. You see, the word of God actually does the cleansing; therefore if you allow the word of God to cleanse you through your obedience to it, you are saved! There's more to baptism than just water, but without water there is no salvation (John 3:5), because the water represents your burial and resurrection with Christ.

The waters of baptism actually symbolize the grave from which you arise and begin your walk in newness of life. It is an act of faith, which becomes a witness to your salvation—that's just God's way. When one is baptized into Christ he puts on Christ (Galatians 3:27). At the same time he/she is *baptized into His death* and therefore obtains merits provided through the death of Christ (Romans 6:3). In this same act of obedience, one is *buried* with Christ and *raised* to walk in newness of life (Romans 6:4). He/she is also planted in the likeness of Christ's death, to come forth in the likeness of His resurrection (Romans 6:5).

By the grace of God, the *old man* (or self) is *crucified* (or done away), and the body of sin destroyed, that one might not be a slave to sin, for if you have died you have been freed from sin (Romans 6:6,7). God has delivered you from the power of darkness and has transferred you into the kingdom of His dear Son, in whom you have redemption through His blood, the forgiveness of sins (Colossians 1:13,14).

This is the 'spiritual' side of being born again and entering into a spiritual kingdom, the part that Nicodemus could not understand many

267

years before when Christ had spoken to him about it (John 3:1-21). You see, in your fallen condition you *cannot* 'just accept Jesus Christ as your personal Savior.' That is a concept added to the word of God (not printed in it) by men. Jesus is the One who does the accepting and accepts you *only* through your obedience to His teachings.

Paul goes on to remind the Corinthians of their obedience to the teachings that changed their lives—gave them new birth—which is also your assurance, dear reader, when you become as the Corinthians:

But thanks be to God that though you were slaves of sin, you became <u>obedient from the heart to that form of teaching to which you were committed, and having been freed from sin</u>, you became slaves of righteousness (Romans 6:17,18 NASB, underlined for emphasis).

By *obeying* Christ through the teaching surrounding water baptism they had been spiritually united with Him in His death, and washed free of sin through His blood—*born again of water and the Spirit*—born again through the living word of God, not the teachings of men. By obeying this teaching they had become Christians through *faith*, *believing* on the Lord Jesus Christ. They were purified—free of past sins, able to rise from that watery grave and walk in newness of life. This was not a work of the Law, which Law was dead, but instead an act of faith in the promises of God.

Being saved does *not* produce in you some mystical feelings from heaven. Although there is joy in heaven (Luke 15:7) and varying emotions within the penitent believer, salvation is a result of faith (action), *not* of feelings. You cannot 'feel' that you are saved, nor can you 'see' the Holy Spirit coming upon you in the form of a dove, nor can you 'feel' the Holy Spirit dwelling within you after you are baptized. Do not depend on your feelings—they can go up and down like a roller coaster. You can only *know* that you are saved and only *know* that the Holy Spirit dwells in you, and that particular knowledge comes *only* from the word of God and not from the teachings of men.

When one truly understands how he/she is freed from sin by Jesus' blood, baptism becomes the greatest, happiest and most meaningful event in his/her life. You are justified by faith. When you plant corn, you will reap corn. Every seed brings forth after its own kind. I stressed that point earlier. Likewise, when you plant the pure seed of the word of God into a repentant heart, you will reap a pure Christian, just like those of the New Testament, who were saved by the blood of

Christ, through the waters of baptism, according to the operation of the word of God. That is 'walking by faith.' That is your confidence.

Let us now build upon that confidence—firm it up. You're on the high ridge trail of this third principle (significance of water), nearing its panoramic summit. You've hiked well—I am indeed proud of you. The tears in my eyes are welling up, for illumination is about to descend upon you...

God is *precise* in *all* things. We discussed this in chapter 9, when we investigated the stars of the universe. We learned something of what disasters could befall us, had He not been so exceedingly precise. He is *the great engineer* who made all things with such *infinite precision*, that understanding how the universe works is unfathomable to the finite human mind.

On a much, much smaller scale, we do not even know how the human brain works! Yet, consider the preciseness of *human* engineering that makes a watch tick. You can be sure that there is a blueprint (a manual of instruction or precise notes) on the watch designer's workbench, which is a *witness* that verifies his finished work as being accurate.

God's blueprint—His manual of instruction/precise notes for us (the entire human race) is His word, which verifies His work as being accurate. Be assured then that whatever God does His word becomes a *witness* to it. His word backs up (verifies) everything that has ever happened according to it, and will continue to back up all things that are going to happen according to it.

His word assures us there are indisputable witnesses that testify to the relationship of Jesus the Son to God the Father, and these witnesses confirm Jesus as the 'Son of God.' The heavenly witnesses are the Father, the Word and the Holy Spirit. The earthly witnesses are the Spirit, the water and the blood (1st John 5:7,8). The Holy Spirit is part of each group, which confirms His presence both in heaven and on earth.

The very same witnesses also testify as to whether or not *you* are a child of God. They are the *only* witnesses that can give you the *confidence* and *assurance* of your salvation (confidence and assurance; does that sound familiar? That's *faith*). But, what do they actually testify of in order to give you that confidence and assurance? They testify, first of all, that you have obeyed God in becoming a Christian —that you have followed the lead of Jesus:

269

Just before He began His earthly ministry (and just as you are to begin your Christian life) Jesus went into the wilderness to be baptized in water by John the baptist. John felt unworthy of being the one to immerse Him, but Jesus instructed him to allow it to be so, *in order to fulfill all righteousness.*

In other words, though He was without sin, the righteousness of God demanded His baptism, for it is God's way, and foreshadowed the New Covenant. When Jesus came up out of the water, the Holy Spirit descended upon Him in the bodily form of a dove. Three years later, in death, Jesus shed His blood on the cross for the remission of *our* sins.

Secondly, and for your benefit, the testimonies of the earthly witnesses had been established. The Spirit, the water and the blood agreed as *one*, confirming Jesus as God's son. The heavenly witnesses are *one*, and also agree. Through water baptism, a portrayal of Christ's death, burial and resurrection, *you* are also *fulfilling all righteousness* —fulfilling it in God's way, according to His Word—His infallible witness. You are identifying yourself with Christ—becoming one with Him—a part of His body, whose blood was shed on your behalf.

This is your new beginning, and Jesus was the one who actually showed you the way, even *before* Peter announced it. Is that *marvelous*, or what? A great leader is not above doing what he expects his followers to do. Oh, the depth of the riches of both the wisdom and knowledge of God! (John 13:13-15, Romans 11:33)

Christ is now in you, for when you are baptized into Christ, you put on Christ through the indwelling of the Holy Spirit, who came upon you when you rose from that watery grave, and who allowed you to walk in newness of life.[7] God knows that you have obeyed Him in righteousness through this *submission to His will.* His earthly witnesses—the Spirit, the water and the blood—will testify forever of your salvation, as will the heavenly witnesses—it's just that simple. You are a child of God, as is Christ, through the testimony of indisputable witnesses.[8]

Again, that is both your confidence and assurance of salvation. Through indisputable witnesses your name is written in the Lamb's Book of Life, which leaves no room *whatsoever* for doubt (Philippians 4:3, Revelation 21:27). Are the witnesses to *your* salvation the Father, the Word, the Holy Spirit, the water, and the blood? Most people who claim salvation in a manner *not* in accordance with the Scriptures always reach a point in life, often more than once, where they have

270

doubts about their salvation. I have counseled many. Their confusion is indeed justified…

Other people have told them, "Oh, I know when I was saved; I felt God come over me," and so on. By the time the doubtful person asks several people what they experienced, each will have given a different answer or 'revelation.' The doubter then becomes *seriously* in doubt, wondering why nothing special ever happened to him/her? They look back on their lives and try to find something to fit the bill. If they don't find it they imagine it, and what they've imagined becomes their 'testimony.' These are the ones who believe the Holy Spirit is a glorified 'it.' They think He's a 'special feeling' of some sort or another.

The heart is deceitful above all things and desperately wicked. Don't rely on it for discovering your salvation. The early Christians knew when they were saved. They never doubted. Though *drawn toward* God in *various ways* (which may be in this modern day and age termed, 'a testimony'), they were all *saved* in the *same way*—the only way—through the living Word of God. They had obeyed from the heart that form of teaching that had been delivered them, which *assured* their salvation (Romans 6:17).

They were not 'feeling' oriented—believing that they were individually accepted by God in some 'miraculous' manner, at some particular time or place. They were instead all alike—each one baptized and each one justified by their faith and through their faith. God shows no partiality (Acts 10:34). The Father, the Word, the Spirit, the water and the blood had testified for each of them, and testifies in the same way for those of us who become Christians today.

God saves you in the same way that He saves everyone else under the New Covenant. There are those who site the 'thief on the cross' as one being saved without baptism. We don't know anything about the life of the thief, other than he was born, lived and died under the Old Testament Law, before the burial and resurrection of Jesus, and before the ushering in of the New Covenant. Therefore, Jesus could do with him as he pleased.

Dear reader, the New Covenant has ushered in 'God with us' (Matthew 1:23). This is because, with our baptism into Christ and the Holy Spirit taking up residence within us (Acts 2:38), we remain with Christ and He remains with us. Prior to the New Covenant this relationship did not exist. That is why Jesus said that, though John the baptist was the greatest man ever born of woman, one who is in Christ (His spiritual kingdom) is greater than John (Luke 7:28). The New Birth under Christ applied to no one until it was ushered in by the Holy Spirit through Peter's first sermon on the day of Pentecost, 33AD.

Peter was the only one who had the 'keys to the kingdom' (Matthew 16:19). He unlocked the door on that wondrous day (which I pointed out to you earlier), which door is Jesus, the Christ Himself. All who seek eternal life must enter through Him. All who are baptized into Christ will be clothed with Christ (Galatians 3:27). That spiritual entrance into Christ is explained with no small amount of detail in Romans 6:1-18, which we previously hiked through, and is accomplished through the physical act of baptism (vs. 3 and 17).

You've reached the summit of this 3rd principle. Do you now perhaps understand the significance of water—God's giver and sustainer of life? Can you see this sustainer of life in vivid operation from the very foundation of the world—through Noah, through Moses, through Jesus, through the very first Christians to you? Jesus did—He's God's Son!

Are you a child of God as well? *Unless one is born of water and the Spirit, he cannot enter into the kingdom of God* (John 3:5 NASB). Have your spiritual eyes now been opened, or do you stand among nine out of ten who I believe remain in darkness? In the future, when someone tells you that you can 'just accept Jesus Christ as your personal savior' for salvation, you should now be able to respond with this:

"Dear friend, Christ will not enter into you until you enter into Him, and, until you are cleansed from your sins, that will simply just not happen. You must be baptized into Christ in order to be freed from sin. He will afterward dwell within you through the Holy Spirit, for when you have been baptized into Christ, you have put on Christ—He has accepted *you*. Your faith should therefore not rest on the wisdom of men, but on the power of God." (Acts 2:38, Galatians 3:27, 1st Corinthians 2:5)

If you, dear reader, are still in doubt; if you are uncertain or perhaps standing on the fence, then you are one who needs to consider God's words: "*My thoughts are not your thoughts, neither are your ways My ways,*" declares the Lord. "*For as the heavens are higher than the earth, so are My ways higher than your ways, and My thoughts than your thoughts*" (Isaiah 55:8,9).

If your eyes have indeed been opened, then Jesus has been vindicated through you, by His words; "*I praise You, Father, Lord of heaven and earth, because you have hidden these things from the wise and learned, and revealed them to little children. Yes, Father, for this was Your good pleasure*" (Luke 10:21).

The fourth and final explanation regarding misunderstanding the teachings on salvation encompasses the *deceitfulness of the heart*. You've learned much about this subject as you've hiked through the pages of this book. You saw *deceitfulness of heart* at work in the Garden of Eden and you've been taught many Scriptures concerning it. You've learned that Satan's primary method of seducing men and women to do evil is that of *deception*.

You've walked through the majority of my life and saw it in actual and vivid operation. Because of that journey you have surely examined yourself and seen *deceit* and *deception* in your own life. You've hiked into the Monuments—the wonders of creation, where you examined the flood evidence, seeing and learning how the world is *deceived* by what is falsely called *science* (1st Timothy 6:20 KJV).

You've seen the wisdom of the animals; having been *deceived* all your life into thinking that man was more knowledgeable in his concept of God than they. You've hiked the Wilderness Trail and learned of the *deceitful* attitudes that can destroy your life. You have hiked into the Bible and seen the actual physical evidence of its truth, which the *deceitful hearts* of men blindly and ignorantly reject.

No human heart is immune to deception—one can also be deceived into thinking that he/she has not been deceived. You can now understand how any of the aforementioned teachers (the nine out of ten), and many others, could be *deceived* into thinking that what they are teaching is true. These folk's are Satan's primary targets. You may ask here, "What about all those people who follow them—what is their fate?" I am not their judge. But Jesus has said, "*If the blind lead the blind, both shall fall into the ditch*" (Matthew 15:14 KJV). Again, you need to take God's words seriously.

The problem is that people are like sheep and ignorant of that fact. They follow one another, not knowing where they might be going. Most people do not really read the Bible for themselves and if they do, they sometimes continue to allow a blind guide to lead them, believing that their teacher/preacher knows what is right. Many times sincere guides, who are blind to their false teachings regarding the new birth, do teach other things that *are* right—it happens everyday on television, on radio and from the pulpit.

You can be fooled (deceived)—you need to again consider how your adversary (the devil) operates. He paints a beautiful picture in order to hide a speck of mold in the center of his canvas, but in time the mold will destroy the entire painting. As I mentioned earlier, I have written letters to particular teachers and have received no response. This troubles me.

If Jesus were on the earth and I wrote Him a letter, He might even stop what He was doing and come to my home immediately. He was a very personal teacher and took time for anyone who approached Him. I continue to give these teachers the benefit of the doubt, as perhaps a member of their staff did not consider what I had to say to be important and did not present my letter(s) directly to their boss. It is indeed difficult to get past the bureaucracy of mankind, especially in the world of modern 'religion.'

When it comes to the Bible people are not usually willing to listen, especially if they have a *preconceived* idea of how something should be. Pride, tradition, and material success are usually the culprits here. No one wants to admit that they are wrong and no one wants to change something that they have been doing a specific way for years—that's human nature. It is also *deceitfulness of the heart*. Besides, Satan does not want a popular evangelist to sing a different tune, for his (Satan's) deception would be unmasked and *many* of the previously blind would have new sight to find their way.

To Satan, that would be like the eruption of a major volcano. Truth would be spewing out all over the world. No—he would do all that he could to quench that eruption—to put out the fire and stop the flow of lava upon his domain. He is the ruler of this world and the archenemy of Christ and the truth. Christian leaders and their followers are his primary target: *Then the dragon was enraged at the woman and went off to make war against the rest of her offspring—those who obey God's commandments and hold to the testimony of Jesus* (Revelation 12:17 NIV).

Recently I conducted an experiment. There is a small congregation near my home whose preacher is a knowledgeable man, but teaches by the common opinion that one can be saved by just 'accepting Jesus into their heart.' His belief is that baptism is some 'act' that one should do at some time to confirm his/her commitment to Christ, but that it's not really necessary for salvation. There are twenty-one people in the congregation. I was allowed to persuade them to read the 14ᵗʰ chapter of this book, which at that time was in manuscript form, and just completed to about this point.

I made 21 copies of this chapter and gave a copy to each of them. As a result, three were baptized into Christ and eighteen remained undecided after one month. About one out of ten—does that ratio sound familiar? I really believe that 90 percent of them did not complete the hike—the challenge was too difficult. You know—winds of doubt and storms of indifference, unfamiliar ground—some just don't stay the course.

That's too bad. If they wait perhaps until it's too late, they may have to explain themselves when the time comes for explaining. I for one would not want to be in their shoes. If Jesus said that one *must* be born of water and the Spirit (John 3:5), then I would certainly want to search the Scriptures to find out what He meant. I believe we've done that together here, have we not?

Baptism is an *easy* thing to do. It only takes a few minutes, and anyone can baptize you, saint or sinner, provided that *you* yourself understand the concept of baptism—what it represents—and provided that the one baptizing you (submersing you in water) proclaims (by the authority of Jesus, found in Matthew 28:19), "I baptize you in the name of the Father and the Son and the Holy Spirit."

If you do not understand what baptism represents, and you don't have it done according to Jesus' instructions, then you cannot honestly establish that it was done by faith and through faith. Though they *do* need to get it right, the wise person baptizing you is *not* the one who is highlighted in this submission—*you are*, and your submission is to God, not to men. *Note*: Be sure to use enough water—baptism is a 'burial and resurrection' from a watery grave (Romans 6:4).

Just a week ago I listened to one of the radio preachers mentioned earlier in this chapter. I tuned in that day because he was scheduled to teach from the book of Acts, regarding Peter's sermon on the day of Pentecost. When he got to Acts 2:37, he spent a little time defining how 'pierced to the heart' the men must have been, who uttered desperately, "Brothers, what should we do?"

He was reading from the New Living Translation. He then read, beginning at verse 38, "Peter replied, Each of you must turn from your sins and turn to God,"—He stopped there, just at the comma in the

275

sentence, then expounded on repentance and on turning to God for quite some time, but never read the rest of the verse, which reads, '*and be baptized in the name of Jesus Christ for the forgiveness of your sins. Then you will receive the gift of the Holy Spirit,*' which concludes verse 38.

Why did he do that? Why did he stop and not read and expound on the most important portion of that verse? Is it easier to leave baptism out? Is he afraid to declare the whole counsel of God? Does he not know, has he not read? Does he just leave things the way they are because the money keeps rolling in from people who want to purchase copies of his lessons as they are? Does he fear going against the multitudes that spread an incomplete gospel to the world? The early Galatian church experienced the preaching of a perverted gospel (Galatians 1:8,9):

Paul warned them, "*But even though we, or an angel from heaven, should preach to you a gospel contrary to that which we have preached to you, let him be accursed.*" Paul repeated immediately the same bold statement—said it twice. He wanted it made known that what the *Apostles* had taught and preached was in no way to be *added to or taken away from*.

He blamed the 'pleasing of men' as the reason behind the false teachings. It is not a difficult thing to be sure of your salvation. You don't have to believe me, and you don't have to believe your regular Bible teacher. But you do need to continue *steadfastly in the Apostles doctrine* (Acts 2:42). Jesus prayed that you would believe in Him through *their* word (John 17:20). A seed brings forth after its own kind.

Finally, Jesus said, "Not everyone that says to me, 'Lord, Lord,' will enter the kingdom of heaven, but only those who *do the will* of my Father in heaven" (Matthew 7:21). It is God's will that you be saved. He sent His son to make it possible. He gave His *inspired word*—His trail map—to show you the way. A great compass also—His creation —helps point the way. He holds out His promises to encourage you. He is waiting for you to surrender your life to him. But the choice, the final ascent to that summit, must be yours.

276

I hope your time on the Discovery Trail has increased your understanding regarding the narrow way to the summit. Satan does not want you to discover the narrow trail, but Jesus is waiting for you at the gate, and I believe you now know how to enter in—how to begin your journey into eternal life.

By the way, congratulations on completing the Discovery Trail! You've evidently got what it takes to negotiate the difficulties found on these higher trails. There's one more ahead—*the Mountain of Believing*. I'm confident that you can handle it...

Chapter Fifteen...Trail's End
The Mountain of Believing

You're not supposed to read the last chapter first. That would be like reading the final book of the Bible before you read the other 65 books—a grievous mistake. It is true that the mystery surrounding the prophetic book of Revelation, the Bible's final writing, draws attention to it, yet hundreds of authors who have written on it (expressing a variety of opinions) have been unable to interpret it correctly. Many of them have never read any other portions of the Bible.

So it is with this book—you will not deal rightly with this last chapter until you have read with much attention the first 14 chapters, nor will you comprehend its most important teaching. If you are one of those attempting to read this last chapter first—hoping to discover something about this book—looking for a reason to either reject it or to consider it—then you are indeed chasing after the wind.

That's like being airlifted onto a high mountaintop and foregoing the exhilaration and illumination of a challenging hiking experience. If you are not one of those attempting to read this last chapter first, then I commend you on your wisdom and integrity, and I apologize for this brief but necessary delay in the chapter's opening.

I thought I would conclude this writing with a hike up the Mountain of Believing. I realize that we have hiked a long way together, but in learning about God enlightenment never ends. The trailhead is just south of the Discovery Trail; in fact it begins just where the Discovery Trail ends. It's a good hike for you—I think a needed one, so take some refreshment and then we'll start the climb. We will consider the Mountain of Believing from four elevations—Base Camp, the Early Ascent, the North Face (rock of promises) and the Summit Ridge.

Base Camp

The *Mountain of Believing* is a no-nonsense climb. True belief itself is an exceedingly high mountain that must be climbed from Base Camp. Let's talk about this that you might better understand what I am saying and where I am going. Actually, believing in God is a *gift*. As a gift freely given to you, your personal belief in God now becomes a matter of your own maturity into understanding (Hebrews 6:1-3). You have been given a gift and you have to work with it.

Since we are incapable of spiritually believing without God's gift, it is obvious that the understanding involved with this gift and concerning this gift requires intensive training and an unlimited amount of time—perhaps a lifetime. The *emotion* of initial belief that God exists, that He is real, is only ground level or *Base Camp* belief. God requires that we grow with our gift—that we mature in our faith. We must therefore climb a high and difficult mountain toward spiritual maturity from Base Camp.

The Mountain of Believing itself is steep. The ascent trail to spiritual maturity is narrow and there are numerous places along that trail where climbers have stopped to rest—places where many remain resting, not able to or not wanting to continue the arduous journey. Their faith is limited—sometimes misguided, hindering their belief, and as a result true *spiritual maturity* cannot take place within them. Bottom line; they have not realized the extreme value of their gift.

A growing Christian—one increasing in faith and belief—will encounter many people like this at these resting places as he or she continues on their upward journey. Maneuvering around them on the narrow trail can sometimes be difficult, but never impossible. Here are some of the difficulties you, as a true believer, may encounter:

There are a myriad of beliefs out there in the world. There is however, in spite of world opinion, only *one* true God, who is extraordinarily revealed in nature and Scripture through three distinct personalities. These are the Father, the Son, and the Holy Spirit (Matthew 28:19). There is also only *one* way, according to Scripture (which is God's *only* written revelation to us), to approach this Godhead...

Jesus has said: "*I am the way, the truth and the life. No one comes to the Father except through Me.*" Yet, He also said; "*No one can come to Me unless the Father who sent Me draws him. Everyone who listens to the Father and learns from Him comes to Me.*" In addition, the apostle Paul said, "*No one can say that Jesus is Lord, except by the Holy Spirit.*" He also said, "*If we are led by the Spirit of God, then we are the children of God.*" [1]

First of all we can know, according to the word of God, that no one, no matter what his or her ideas, philosophy, religious belief or personal background, can come to God *except through Jesus Christ.* That overrules the vain attempts of *many* people involved in/with various world religions, who think they know how to approach the God of the universe. Secondly, no one can come to Jesus unless he or she is *drawn* to Him by the mercy of God the Father. Again, belief is a gift.

Thirdly, everyone who *truly* learns from the Father *comes to Jesus.* Fourthly, no one can claim that Jesus is Lord, except *through the Holy Spirit.* And finally, only if we are led by the *Spirit of God* can we claim to be the *children of God.* Any world religion or philosophy or idea that teaches anything other than what I have just outlined for you here is obviously a false and vain religion or philosophy or idea, and rightly, according to Scripture, should be considered as such.

Coming to God and believing in Jesus is *unquestionably* a matter of God *allowing* it to be so (Ephesians 2:8). Once again, believing in God is a *gift. True belief* in God then becomes an *individual honor* that for reasons only God knows is not given to every creature (Romans 9:15). You must learn to treat it as such. If you are a *true believer*, you must endeavor to learn the value of such good fortune in your life. You have indeed a most precious gift—you are in fact chosen of God (Ephesians 1:4).

Near the Mountain of Believing you will find many so-called believers who have no concept of what you have just learned. A little further up, at *Base Camp* itself, you will find many new believers who know there is only one God. They are not necessarily short-time believers. Many there have believed in God for a long period of time, but their faith and belief have not matured. They haven't understood their *need* to climb further up the mountain. They remain at Base Camp where they can and do encourage new arrivals, yet their own personal desire may be to not continue any further.

They often *feel* that they *do not need* to precede any further. Unfortunately they have not realized the true *in-depth value* of their gift. They are, shall we say, 'content' at their particular state of belief. The reasons for their contentment vary and many camping there are not necessarily 'honestly' content. Some are content with the basic concepts of salvation:

They have believed and have been baptized into Christ, but no longer continue to study the Bible and learn about their Lord and His individual purpose for them. Many others there have also believed in Jesus but have not yet been baptized, and so the Spirit of God does not dwell within them (Acts 2:38). Personal feelings, no matter how strong, *do not* confirm the indwelling of the Spirit of God. Only the Word can justify the presence of the Holy Spirit. I dealt with this concept in the previous chapter.

In the meantime, there are also some truly converted Christians at Base Camp who have not started up the mountain because of their fear of leaving the world behind. They hold to the philosophies and scientific teachings of the world and do not totally accept the truths of God. Their level of belief is indeed a 'Base Camp' level. There are non-baptized believers who have actually ascended to higher levels on the mountain than true believers because they desire to continue their learning.

Although these individuals are unaware that they are not truly Christians by *obedience to the faith* (Acts 5:32), each one *can* mature somewhat by applying Biblical principles to their life. They are however limited as to the distance they can ascend on the Mountain of Believing. Not having laid a true foundation at Base Camp, much of their understanding or misunderstanding is based on the trickery and deceit of Satan. They continue to learn, but never come to the knowledge of the *truth* (2nd Timothy 3:7).

They are not against Christianity, but they lack the knowledge of the most vital elementary doctrines of its teachings. In time they can become hardened in their own personal beliefs, thus failing to understand their need to renew their minds and become like little children (Romans 12:2 & Matthew 18:2-4). They also lack the ability to *purely* influence new believers, causing many to continue to live in error of the truth.

The point of this entire writing is for you to learn and to understand that the *strength of your belief* in God requires a *firm foundation* of *truth*, and a *continued ascent* in your *learning*—an ascent on the *Mountain of Believing*. The more you learn of God through experience in understanding *truth*, the stronger and more effective your belief in Him and His care for you will become. Sincere belief, from a heart that is guided by the Spirit of God and not the popular teachings of men, is given a most profound guarantee of success (John 15:7,8).

Your prayer life will improve. Your ability to understand your own needs and the more important needs of others will become exceedingly more evident. Your ability to understand the Scriptures and bring them to life will embrace your heart and mind. Life will take on *new meaning* and an *ever-increasing hope*. The peace that passes all understanding can be available to you. Let those of you then whose desire is truth courageously depart from *Base Camp*, open your hearts and minds, and begin an illuminating ascent with me on the *Mountain of Believing*.

The Early Ascent

If you have been given the gift of belief and you have left Base Camp and begun your ascent on the Mountain of Believing, then you are embarking on an incredibly eye-opening, thought provoking, life changing journey. As you ascend on to *spiritual maturity* you will begin to leave the world's concepts behind and below you. The basic philosophies and false scientific teachings and beliefs of the world do not compare in any way with the truths of God, yet they make it extremely difficult for the truth to be taught and understood.

For instance, the age of the earth, along with the formation of mountains, rivers and canyons, is completely misunderstood by most modern scientists and hundreds of thousands to millions of believers. But, the accurate knowledge of these things should be basic or indeed in the process of becoming basic to the true believer. I am going to give you a few examples of some *basic truths* that you will need to learn to believe in *before* you get too far up from Base Camp.

Without these understandings your further ascent on the mountain will be indeed slow going, difficult, and eventually impossible. First and foremost is the understanding that God's only written revelation to us (the Bible) is *absolute* truth, and *anything* that disagrees with it can only be interpreted as being misrepresented, misunderstood, misleading, or false. If you have progressed to *this point* of understanding, which does take some study time and experienced reasoning, you should then as a believer have a *firm grip* on the following truths:

1) The Lord formed the heavens we can see and the present earth upon which we live, with all of its full-grown plants, fish, birds and animals, in six (6) literal 24-hour days. He also made the planets and the stars and the sun and the moon to give light upon the earth. All are in perfect order, according to His plan. All things of nature including plants, animals, birds and insects upon the earth are in perfect harmony, depending upon one another for continued existence. All things point to a supreme intelligence as creator. True scientists tell us that if one studies the physical sciences long enough and hard enough, he/she is *forced* to come to the aforementioned conclusion. True belief looks *confidently* beyond the teachings of men.

2) On the sixth day of creation, from the dust of the earth, the Lord made man in His own *image* (a spirit being with creative abilities). He made a woman from the rib of this man, Adam, who was to be his helper and his equal. She was called Eve (*mother of all living*), and together they became the original ancestors of the entire world's human population. Unfortunately the couple fell from God's grace by giving into temptation, and were a part of the sad event that brought depravity, decay, disease and death upon the earth.

3) This present earth from the time of its habitable formation is less than 7000 years old. 1656 years after our earth's creation (around 5000 years ago), the Lord brought an overwhelming flood of waters upon a greatly populated earth, which destroyed all mankind, save 8 souls who were aboard an ark, and which reshaped the entire earth, resulting in the geography that currently exists. Many plant and animal species and sea creatures were buried into extinction during that cataclysmic flood, which accounts for present day coal and oil deposits as well as the fossil record.

Selected animals and birds aboard the ark are the ancestors of today's various species worldwide. From the surviving family of Noah and his descendants the people also began to multiply. They were eventually divided by language and race (through divine miracle at the tower of Babel) and continued to move about, populating areas of the entire earth. This post-flood population is still growing. Since everyone descends from the family of Noah, we need to realize that this relationship leaves us with the duty to respect, to honor and to care for one another—worldwide.

4) Since Satan is the ruler of this world (Matthew 4:8,9 & John 12:31), you cannot therefore trust in the wisdom, *nor* in the philosophies, *nor* in the majority of the educational systems of the various kingdoms in this present world. The world's population for the most part does not know their place on the earth, rejects the authority of God, and is ignorant concerning His attributes. They are inconsiderate of His sovereignty. Therefore, the wisdom of the world is mere foolishness in His sight (1st Corinthians 3:19). God is in control of earthly events and will eventually allow this present earth to be destroyed by fire, but will bring forth a new earth where only goodness dwells (2nd Peter 3:10-13).

5) Following the life-giving attitudes of a man called *Jesus*, the Son of God, is the only way of true wisdom and life for the entire believing world. No one anywhere in the world can come to God the Father, regardless of his or her beliefs, except through a belief in and submission to the saving will of Jesus Christ (John 14:6). It was His ultimate sacrifice on a Roman cross that paid the sin debt for the entire world (1st John 2:2). All peoples of the world are under the curse of sin and Jesus is their only hope of redemption from it (Romans 3:23,24).

Fact: If you doubt any of the five truths I have listed above (a very small list I might add), please don't take offense, but you are just not yet a *true* believer in God. If you cling to the false sciences, deceptive philosophies or vain religions or traditions of the world and call yourself a believer in God, then you are unfortunately only deceiving yourself. I'm not trying to be hard on you here, but your life is passing away and your need is to develop an eternal attitude—to become a *mature* believer. For if in this life only we have hope in Christ, we are of all people the most pitiable (Philippians 2:5, 1st Corinthians 15:19).

The Early Ascent from Base Camp requires that you acknowledge *who God is*, and that you trust in *what He has proclaimed* and *not* in the concepts, theories and conclusions of unknowing or unbelieving men and women of the world. Know that the 'knowledge' (wisdom) of mankind within this world is pure foolishness to God. If you want to increase in faith and belief, then you must courageously turn from the world in your thinking and follow the truths of God. You must be *transformed* by the *renewing of your mind* (Romans 12:2).

You may, at first, find truth difficult to follow since you were educated by the world. All of us have been educated by the world. Its affect in many cases is similar to 'brainwashing.' This may seem a harsh term, but *keep in mind* that God has said that Satan *is* the ruler of this world, that this present world is fading away, that it will be destroyed, and that *truth* will be all that remains (2nd Peter 3:10). Renewing your mind with what is true and right and everlasting and then acting positively on those realizations is the *only* thing that will save you or anyone else.

It's time now to ask yourself; have you truly begun the Early Ascent from Base Camp? Without learning to accept and learning to trust in the five minimum understandings I presented to you, you will be unable to grow properly in your faith and unable to climb any higher *spiritually* on the Mountain of Believing. But, know that belief in the *truths* of God can indeed set you free, that you might indeed benefit from your climb. Jesus Himself said, *"If you abide in My word, you are My disciples indeed. And you shall know the truth, and the truth shall make you free"* (John 8:31, 32 NKJV).

In this world we are indeed slaves—slaves to the world's teachings and slaves to the consequences of those teachings upon and within our earthly lives. But in Christ and in His *truth* we are made free—free to embark on *learning* the truth, free to reject the teachings of men, free from the condemning judgment of God, and spiritually free to live our earthly lives until the end, learning from God alone, trusting in God alone, serving others through God alone and looking forward to *eternal life*. What unparalleled *assurance* we have in trusting our Creator! Do not therefore be deceived through trusting in yourself (Proverbs 3:5,6).

The North Face *(rock of promises)*
If we have overcome our fears of doubt regarding the Bible itself and we know that it is true, and if we have courageously disregarded the concepts, theories and error-filled conclusions of false science, it is

285

now that our Early Ascent from Base Camp is complete. It is time to climb on *toward more mature understanding*. It is time to approach the North Face, which I call *the rock of promises*, so named because our entire Christian experience; birth, initial growth, maturity, ultimate salvation and eternal life, is based *entirely* on God's *promises* (2nd Peter 1:3,4).

I'm going to repeat that thought by saying that every step we take in life trusting in God is based 'one-hundred (100) percent' on His promises. However, even though we've come this far up the mountain through believing and acting *on* those promises, the chances of us *turning back* to our former thoughts and ideas can become much greater. Our trust in God can be thwarted. Satan wages a constant battle within us and around us to turn us from God. The more knowledge, faith and belief we accumulate, all the more fiercely he fights against us to produce apprehension or doubt.

"For we are not fighting against people made of flesh and blood, but against the evil rulers and authorities of the unseen world, against those mighty powers of darkness who rule this world, and against wicked spirits in the heavenly realms." (Ephesians 6:12 NLT)

Satan does not want you to learn anything or believe anything that will be detrimental to his hopeful reign over your personal life. He is the prince and ruler of this world. He will accuse you for the remainder of your earthly life, while God will continue to test your faith—to purify you as choice silver. Therefore, difficulties in your life *will* increase. Some believe that God will not send as many difficulties your way once you become a Christian. God never sends difficulties your way, but Satan does. He will endeavor to make your life extremely miserable after your conversion. Before that he could care less.

Since your ideas toward the world have now changed considerably, you are going to lose the confidence of some close relatives, perhaps even those within your own household. You may also lose the close friendship you have with some of your associates. In addition, the further up the mountain you climb, the fewer true believers you will encounter, for *narrow is the road that leads to life, and only a few ever find it*. Bottom line—the Christian path of life is extremely difficult on this earth. The end rewards however will be exceedingly great.[2]

The most difficult portion of your climb up the Mountain of Believing comes when you reach what I am calling the North Face or *the rock of promises.* You will reach the foot of this area when you have climbed over the aforementioned rocks and obstacles we have encountered since we arrived at Base Camp. You have believed in many of God's teachings and promises thus far or you wouldn't be where we are now. Yet, this particular face of the mountain, the *rock of promises*, is even more difficult to ascend.

It has been a foot trail so far, but now you are going to need both your hands and feet, some ropes and lots of *courage, faith* and *hope*—the no-nonsense stuff. Due to the *immeasurable* weakness of human nature—our natural heart and mind—many of God's promises seem notably difficult to comprehend and to hold on to. But remember, we count on His promises through *faith, not by sight* (2nd Corinthians 5:7). We move ahead, not always sure where we're going—but we have to get going—trusting in Him. When the north wind wails along the face of the mountain and threatens your foothold here you must struggle against it and continue your climb.

While ascending a steep, rock face as the rock of promises is, I would like you to imagine that there are several *pitons* hammered into the face of the rock at various intervals along the ascent. Climbers' pitons are wedged shaped for hammering into small cracks in the rock. The outer end of the piton is usually in the shape of a ring or hook, for securing your carabiners (self-locking rope holders, similar to D-rings) as you make the climb. Once pitons are hammered into place they usually remain in the rock for use by future climbers.

We're going to imagine the piton placements as the individual promises of God, which you are learning to trust in on your ascent up the Mountain of Believing. Each piton represents a different promise that you must ascend to, hang onto with your rope, understand *or* accept, and then continue on up from. Do you have a mental picture? Great! You will have a great distance to climb up this rock of promises before reaching the backbone—the ridge of faith that ascends toward the summit. I hope that your climbing gear is in good shape for this North Face ascent.

When you first became a Christian through being water baptized into Christ, the Bible teaches us that your past sins were forgiven—washed away by the living Word of God, through the death of Christ (Romans 6:3). When you arose from that watery grave the Bible also teaches that the Spirit of God entered your life (Acts 2:38). These promises of *forgiveness of sins* and the *gift of the Holy Spirit*, I believe, are the greatest of God's promises in the entire Bible. And because they are so great, sometimes we humans have difficulty in believing that these *promises* are actually true—we encounter times of 'spiritual weakness.'

One reason for this is that, after baptism, we are still *capable of sin* and still continue to do so, even after we have been given the *promise* of a new life! Our *nature* to sin does not change through baptism, only our *position* with God changes. We still sin and if we say that we do not sin, we only prove ourselves to be liars. However, though we continue to unwillingly sin, the blood of Christ faithfully and justly cleanses us from all unrighteousness as we confess our sins and pray through the intersession of the Holy Spirit, who helps us in our weaknesses to walk in God's way; having the intersession of Jesus on our behalf.[4]

These are *promises*—we won't 'feel' them happening, we just have to count on them as truth. Another reason we may doubt the promise of forgiveness is the fact that we may bear lasting *consequences* from our past sins—consequences that war violently against our ability to accept forgiveness. We talked about consequences of sin a little bit in chapter 7. The consequences of sin are unrelenting. Contrary to popular belief forgiveness does not remove consequences, but only allows us to *accept them*.

We cannot bring back the person we murdered. We cannot bring back the wife and children we deserted through adultery. We cannot get out of prison for the robbery we committed. We cannot return to the job we were fired from. We usually cannot undo the words we spoke in anger or the damage we committed through rage. We usually cannot win back the hearts of those we've hurt or lost through our sin(s).

In other words, the consequences of our sins will continue, whatever they are, even though God has forgiven us of the sins themselves, for God has *promised, "Do not be deceived, God is not mocked; for whatever a man sows, that will he also reap"* (Galatians 6:7 NKJV). Consequences can totally break the spirit of a man or a woman. Life can become painfully unbearable for the forgiven sinner, due to the *unforgiving consequences* of sin. All the suicides that have *ever* been committed throughout the world are the direct result of an inability to bear the consequences of sin, no if's, and's or but's about it.

A third reason we may doubt the promise of forgiveness is that other people usually don't truly forgive us the way God does. God forgives us, totally removing our sins, even from His memory! People usually don't forgive us to that extent. Somebody will always continue to point the finger at you. Someone will always be there to put you on a guilt trip.

Fortunately, God doesn't think like people do. His ways are far above our ways, as are His thoughts, His intentions and His judgments. No one can know His mind or be His counselor.[3] The fact remains that His compassion never ends. He forgives us of our sins. His mercy is new *every* morning (Lamentations 3:22-24).

I believe the forth reason I'm going to give you here is the most profound. We cannot grasp an understanding of God's true and everlasting forgiveness of sin because we *cannot forgive ourselves*. I have searched the Scriptures for many years, but have not found an example of anyone who could honestly forgive themselves. I heard a renowned man once say that it was an impossible thing to do. So far, I agree with him. I believe with all of my heart that we can *learn to accept* the *consequences* of sin, but I don't believe we can ever completely forgive ourselves for the sin(s)—not if our spirits have truly been broken and our hearts remain contrite.

On the other hand, some people use the crutch, "Well, I'm only human." Though that is true, it will not remove the scars from the heart, nor from those hearts scared through our sin. These crutch-walkers have not *truly acknowledged* their sins. Jesus died a horrible death for our sins. He bears our scars as well. How can anyone forgive himself or herself for that? However, what the inability to forgive ourselves should accomplish is to allow us to see our need to serve God more willingly and fervently—for those who have much to be forgiven of will in turn love much, and those who have little to be forgiven of will love little (Luke 7:47).

I have learned that personal pain develops humility. Though the pain of my former sins mentally cripple me, I would not have learned how to depend upon God without that pain, nor would I ever come to understand the depth and utter depravity of my sins and the irreversible damage they have caused. I would not be able to fathom any part of the crucifixion of Jesus. It is the guilt of sin, the pain of sin, the remorse of sin and the consequences of sin that teach me who and what I really am. That makes the *joy* of God's forgiveness exceedingly joyful! This joy is a most humbling experience to the truly remorseful.

It is this deep anguish within my soul that serves to bring change to my heart of stone, produce healing in my soul, and build character through the Spirit of God working within me. That particular anguish of deep repentance was one of the reasons King David was called, by God Himself, *a man after My own heart* (Acts 13:22). Consequences are indeed tough to live with. The piton then which represents God's forgiveness, this very first on the rock of promises, is indeed a difficult one to climb on past, is it not? Actually, it all depends.

It all depends on your attitude. The problem is, if you do not get past it you're going to be stuck right here on the North Face. You will not be able to climb any higher on this rock of promises. You will be unable to explore the magnitude or depth of any other of God's precious promises. There are indeed many enriching promises on ahead of you, so you need to get above this piton by learning to accept who you are, what you are, and how God deals with your sins. He forgives them—doesn't hold them against you. You need to deal with them as well—to consider your failures as stepping-stones to maturity. God knows your remorse, and loves you exceedingly for it (Psalm 51:17).

You need to take a new grip with those tired hands and take a firm hold on your climbing rope, so that you won't fall back and hurt yourself. Now, straighten out those shaky legs—accept your failures as growing pains and climb on up—get past that piton. This may take some time and that's not really a problem. The key is in *knowing* where you are on the rock of promises, *acknowledging* where you are, and then having the patience to *remain* where you are until you have acquired the wisdom, knowledge, skill and courage to proceed upward. This particular process is simply a further development of humility.

This patience will result in an illuminating increase of understanding, faith and belief in your Christian journey. That particular illumination is the revelation of your growing dependence upon God, for you are *slowly learning* that without Him you can do *absolutely nothing* (John 15:5). Embrace that attitude, because few ever really comprehend their need for it—by the time they do their life is gone. The poor and the destitute are the lucky ones here. They hold the secrets of depending upon God. They know the way to priceless treasures, and their journey is most difficult. (Luke 6:20)

God has indeed given us many *exceedingly great and precious promises,* through which we gain the hope needed to continue this earthly life's journey. Among those most familiar to Bible students are His shelter through life's many storms, answered prayer, His watchful eye in maintaining our path, His helping hand during illness or death, His bountiful love, mercy and forgiveness, along with food, clothing and relief of worries and cares—actually everything that concerns us, including an inner peace that passes all understanding—and in the end, eternal life!

He has promised us vast, new heavens and a new earth, with unending peace among its inhabitants. I believe that this new world will be where our most precious dreams come true. These promises we've considered here are all found within God's written word, the Bible. Each of these promises requires *distinct elevations of understanding* on our part, just as ascending to another piton on the North Face requires a distinct movement—a calculated movement.

However, unlike the piton ascent, these levels of understanding are spiritual levels and not physical levels. We attain to these spiritual elevations of understanding *only* through our continued faith and trust in God—our continued ascent on the *rock* of *His promises.* He is holding the climbing rope that we cling to. It is true that our belief in these promises usually requires faith in things that are not necessarily seen. Yet, if we look at these unseen things *spiritually,* we *will* eventually be able to see them—to know them.

Traditionally, seeing has always been believing. After we ascend the rock of promises and climb onto the Summit Ridge there is in fact much that we will be enabled to see. Through the eyes of one humbled by their sins God gives true sight, opening their heart to understanding. His mercy then becomes their anchor (Psalm 25). When you do reach the Summit Ridge, know that you have been allowed a monumental accomplishment, and all the credit goes to your hiking partner—our Lord Jesus.

The Summit Ridge

The picture associated with this chapter (page 278) is that of the Devil's Backbone, a razorback ridge on the high summit trail of Mt. San Antonio (Old Baldy), the highest peak in southern California's San Gabriel mountain range. The Devil's Backbone is a hair-raiser, an extremely narrow trek across a steep ridge, yet it offers grand vistas of both the Lytle Creek drainage on the north and east, and San Antonio Canyon on the south. I nearly met with disaster here once but was saved by Dr. Mike Mucci, a fellow hiker, whose swift hand caught the frame of my backpack just as I had lost my footing.

I learned something that day about hiking on that spiny ridge—to place one foot directly in front of the other, and to carefully place my hiking boot on solid ground with each and every step. It is definitely a place that will heighten your awareness. We have the given means and ability to also heighten our spiritual awareness, through the things God has made and the faith which those things can generate. We can learn so very much through the visible things around us that can give us wondrous insight into the invisible things—see the supernatural through the natural. That's when our hiking boots are on solid ground.

The Scriptures tell us that from the time the world was created people have been able to behold the earth and sky and all that God has made. They can clearly see His invisible qualities—His eternal power and divine nature, and so they have no excuse whatsoever for not knowing God (Romans 1:20). The Summit Ridge is a place where correct, repeated Biblical reading, faith, belief and trust in God's promises mesh together with the creation, allowing you to see as you have never seen before.

The trek from Base Camp to the Early Ascent, to the Rock of Promises and on up to the Summit Ridge culminates in a foundation that cannot be shaken. From here you can learn to see the unseen at all times. This concept was profoundly revealed through the simple, everyday teachings of Jesus, the Son of God:

"Observe how the lilies of the field grow; they do not toil nor do they spin. Yet, I say to you that even Solomon, in all his glory, did not clothe himself like one of these. But, if God so arrays the grass of the field, which is alive today and tomorrow is thrown into the furnace, will He not much more do so for you, Oh men of little faith?" (Matthew 6: 28-30 NASB)

King Solomon to this day is by far the wisest man who ever lived on the face of the earth. His wealth and possessions also far exceeded those of the wealthiest men or kings upon the earth throughout his lifetime (1st Kings 3:12, 13). Yet, in all of his glory and splendor he was not arrayed (fashioned/adorned) as magnificently as a simple flower of the field. Have you ever examined up close the tiniest flower blooming in a field? From the Summit Ridge you can see vast fields of radiant flowers far below you, each one a little different.

You can see majestic mountains and diverse canyons formed by the hand of God. This is also the home of the big horn sheep, the owl, the hawk and the golden eagle. It is indeed an honor to view any of these creatures. The rocks, the trees and the varying plants of the surrounding terrain speak to you of the incomparable glory and wisdom of God in His creativity. Have you ever plucked just an ordinary blade of grass and examined it closely? The intricate design of water canals and matter in just a single blade is awe-inspiring!

How much more in unfathomable, detailed splendor then are all these wonders seen from atop the Summit Ridge! Since God has taken such extreme care in His array of these things, how much more care has He put into each of us individually, as human beings, His highest order of creation on the planet earth? How utterly fortunate we are to stand on this Summit Ridge where we can physically see and spiritually contemplate each of these things and all of these things.

How honorable it is to be able, if we are indeed able, to touch a great rock or even a small one! How satisfying to scoop up a handful of fine pebbles and grains of sand from your foot trail and sift them through your fingers! How comforting to feel the wind atop this high place! How artistically harmonious are the wind-shaped Bristle Cone Pine, the Lodge Pole, Jeffrey, Sugar, White Fir and the towering Ponderosa!

There are also within view here a variety of green and flaming yellow fern, which smother the banks of a melodious creek that winds among a great mixture of boulders and exquisite thickets of manzanita! There is the distinctly sharp scent of sage and incense cedar! At this elevation the sky overhead is a fierce blue, the air pure and clean—who cannot know that the hand of the Lord has done all this? (Job 12:9)

The wise man or woman who has studied God's Word, who has increased in faith and believed in His promises, who has ascended to the Summit Ridge in their faith, having seen the unseen attributes of God through the things He has made—he or she indeed stands near the very pinnacle of faith! He or she understands, in great depth, the value of God's creation and can take any part of it anywhere with them in their heart or picture it within their mind. He or she can use it to fight temptation, to sustain themselves through hard times, to be thankful in good times and to truly praise and honor God at all times. He or she can find great satisfaction and incomparable joy in teaching, helping and encouraging others.

If you have come this far in your faith, if you have reached the Summit Ridge, then you have indeed conquered many things. You have spiritually discovered the variety of talents which God has endowed you with for this very purpose. The peace of God, which surpasses all understanding, can become available to you (Philippians 4:7). This mature faith and trust can lead you confidently across the ridge and to the actual summit of the Mountain of Believing.

The summit of true believing is *putting your belief into action*. That *is* the pinnacle of faith. True belief will allow you to put yourself in your own place and to put God in first place, which is on the front line, first and foremost in your life—in your thoughts, in your words and in your deeds. True belief will allow you to walk with God as His friend. True belief will allow you to understand the more important inner needs of others and to freely give your life to and for them, as Jesus did.

It will allow you to give generously of the things God has so freely given to you: Compassion, Mercy, Forgiveness, Patience, Kindness, Gentleness, Meekness and Self-control. This is the fruit of the Spirit of God within you. This is love—the mind of Christ within you—the greatest attribute and the very greatest commandment of God. Indeed, welcome to the Mountain of Believing! Your many failures are no longer a problem because you have put your trust in God—your life, hopes and dreams into His hands.

You have accepted who you are. You can now experience for the first time *true freedom*. You are therefore no longer a scumbag, wallowing in the mire. Though you will continue to fail in one way or another, you have finally discovered what it is to be a child of the Most High God. And when the Lord returns, you will be made *perfect* —there will be no more failures.

*

Where are you on the spiritual Mountain of Believing? Are you at Base Camp? Have you started the Early Ascent? Are you somewhere on the North Face (rock of promises)? Have you climbed to the Summit Ridge? Have you crossed that narrow spine toward the Summit itself? Wherever you are, be sure that you take into view all that is around you. Share your discoveries in truth with others along the way. Live free, help the world to truly see God, and trust in your Creator.

Be patient in this endeavor. God in His own time will lift you up and you will know and can rest in the fact that He can indeed do all that He has promised! When you are out there hiking, respect everything that moves—even the tiniest of creatures. Respect everything you touch—especially those little pebbles or that blade of grass you might pick up and hold in your hand. Be consistent out there as well—occupy your time honoring God through appreciating His creation. Become one with Him.

Thanks for hiking with me on the Mountain of Believing. It is hoped that your journey has been one of illumination. May God enrich your spirit as you continue *Hiking the Trail of Truth*. I most sincerely hope to hear from you regarding your discoveries. I am not one of those authors that you cannot get hold of. You can reach me through e-mail at, hikemark@hotmail.com, or contact me via my trail phone, currently, 909-549-0068. I will respond to you immediately upon receiving your communication.

I appreciate your hiking with me through this entire book. Stories are important. I am exceedingly thankful that God has allowed me to live long enough to tell mine—to share it with you. He allowed me to be creative—to build a book—the construction of which spanned nearly a lifetime. It took Noah 120 years to build the Ark, and his entire life experience I am certain was illuminating, as mine has been and continues to be.

I hope I was able through this writing to shed some light on your path. I hope that you can find your spiritual home—your connection with God. I hope you can begin to see the supernatural through the natural. You have a map and compass now, and I hope that you will choose to share it with others. May God bless you.

Sincerely, *Mark S Taylor*

From
LONE WOLF LIMITED
A Division Of
M S Taylor Productions
1997-2011
PO Box 547, Lone Pine, CA, 93545

Epilogue
He raised me up, so I could stand on mountains...

Today, I was sitting on top of a large granite boulder, overlooking a spacious valley. It's a desolate area, not far from home. I was reflecting on life, something I have done quite often during these last months while weaving this story together. I was having a difficult time keeping my pipe lit in the wind.

It reminded me that somewhere along the road of life I found that I was dead, and struggled many years thereafter to come back to life again. I recalled at that moment one time when my son, Mitch, was very young. We made a batch of cookies, placed them in a cookie tin, and walked together down a long, steep hill in the Ohio country to deliver them to a poor and needy family, whom we didn't even know.

When we knocked on the door a man poked his head outside. I told him that we had brought his family some cookies. He opened the door and allowed us to enter. The family was quite delighted with our gift, and we stayed and visited with them for some time.

I'll not forget the feelings I had then, nor the warm emotions expressed by that family. I have come to realize that those feelings and emotions are life at its fullest. As I sat atop that boulder I began to wonder why my mind would suddenly bring to remembrance something like that. Now I know why:

My most crucial advice to you in your search for or walk with God, in spite of the stains of your sins, is that you learn to understand that you have great significance to Him. Whether you have great earthly accomplishments or seemingly no accomplishments, whether you are President of the United States or homeless on some lonely street in the filthiest part of town—you are important to God. He has given you many things of which you are the steward. How you handle any and all of these things is all summed up in stewardship.

All things belong to God. He has only allowed you their use. You need to allow this truth to become your guide to daily living. The Bible is full of heroes, both great and small, some so small that only one sentence in the entire one thousand one hundred eighty-nine chapters of the Bible is devoted to them, and many of them are unnamed. They are listed as "a certain man" or "a certain woman," or described in another way without name.

Yet, their contribution to God is significant enough to be mentioned by the Holy Spirit of God, who inspired the writers of the Bible to include their faith in the narrative. Some are mentioned only as "others" who did this or that, and are listed in faith's grand hall of fame (Hebrews, chapter 11). You can be a part of that list as well.

You may have come a long way in life, not knowing if you have ever done anything worth the Lord's attention. You may have accomplished something for Him, but amidst the struggles of life it seemed so insignificant to you that you have seemingly no memory or awareness of it. On the other hand, you may be a young person, just starting out in life, on fire for the Lord and expecting to accomplish great things. Whichever of these you are, God will use you only as He chooses. He may use you for great things or for just one, solitary small thing in your entire lifetime.

Bottom line—your life is not your own. God will form you as He wishes and will use you for His purpose, in His time, and what you do or have done with what you've been given will serve to glorify Him. That is His purpose for you. God can deal with your sins and He alone has the power to deal with them. Your personal efforts at anything or your failure in anything will neither enrich nor thwart his ultimate plan for you.

Trust then in Him alone. Don't depend on the world you live in and never trust in yourself. Let God lead. He will let you know that He is there, and will help you to serve others. You will find your fullest joy in Him, and in the end, eternal life. Would you like some better advice on top of the good advice? Acquaint yourself with the Psalms. One of my favorites is Psalm 25:

To You, O Lord, I lift up my soul. O my God, I trust in You; Let me not be ashamed; Let not my enemies triumph over me. Indeed, let no one who waits on You be ashamed; Let those be ashamed who deal treacherously without cause.

Show me Your ways, O Lord; Teach me Your paths. Lead me in Your truth and teach me, for You are the God of my salvation; On You I wait all the day.

Remember, O Lord, Your tender mercies and Your loving kindness, for they are from of old. Do not remember the sins of my youth, nor my transgressions; According to Your mercy remember me, for Your goodness sake, O Lord.

Good and upright is the Lord; Therefore He teaches sinners in the way. The humble He guides in justice, and the humble He teaches His way. All the paths of the Lord are mercy and truth, to such as keep His covenant and His testimonies. For Your namesake, O Lord, pardon my iniquity, for it is great.

Who is the man that fears the Lord? Him shall He teach in the way He chooses. He himself shall dwell in prosperity, and his descendants shall inherit the earth. The secret of the Lord is with those who fear Him, and He will show them His covenant. My eyes are ever toward the Lord, for He shall pluck my feet out of the net.

Turn Yourself to me and have mercy on me, for I am desolate and afflicted. The troubles of my heart have enlarged; Bring me out of my distresses! Look on my affliction and my pain, and forgive all my sins. Consider my enemies, for they are many; And they hate me with cruel hatred. Keep my soul and deliver me; Let me not be ashamed, for I put my trust in You. Let integrity and uprightness preserve me, for I wait on You.

(Verses 1-21, NKJV)

*

On September 14th, 2008, I completed the final portion of this entire writing. I was getting ready to print the whole thing out for a copy edit when my cell phone rang. It was a surprise call from Jenny (the wife of my youth). She and her husband were doing some traveling in the West and found themselves in Napa, California, not far from Petaluma, where I was residing. They wanted to come and visit me because they were so nearby. I hadn't seen them in six years, since the wedding ceremony of my granddaughter, Alicia, in southern Ohio.

I spent the evening of September 15th with them, and it was indeed a wonderful time, to say the least. Their visit was one of those 'little things' in life that I talked about in an earlier chapter—one of those small miracles that God sends your way to encourage you and to enhance life's journey. During the writing of this book my journey has been somewhat difficult, for obvious reasons. Yet, God chooses to encourage us at just the right moment in any of life's worthwhile endeavors. I was exceedingly honored by the method He chose at this time.

There will be critics out there, ignorant of God's truth, who will scoff at this book and make light of its teachings. But, there will be those out there for whom it was meant that will be rewarded. Being given the ability and encouragement to write it has honored me, though I consider myself unworthy of those gifts. At the present time I have no idea of who this writing was meant for—whether for just one person, for a few people or for many, yet I am confident that someday I will—that's just the way God works.

Dear reader, I earnestly hope He is working for you as well. The end time is near—obvious through the deteriorating conditions in our world. I hope this book will help you to be more accurately informed and prepared for that event.

Sincerely, *Mark S Taylor*

O God, You have taught me from my youth; and to this day I declare Your wondrous works. Now also when I am old and gray-headed, O God, do not forsake me, until I declare Your strength to this generation, Your power to everyone who is to come.
(Psalm 71:17,18 NKJV)

More books by this author: page 305

References and Notes
Chapter 1

1. Genesis, Chapter 2
2. Genesis, Chapter 3
3. Genesis, Chapter 6 vs. 5
4. Psalm 139:13 thru 16
5. *In The Beginning*, Compelling Evidence for Creation and the Flood, Walt Brown, PhD., Seventh Edition, copyright by Walt Brown, 2001, Center for Scientific Creation, Phoenix, Arizona; used for teaching by permission, p3.
6. Isaiah 14:12 thru 14, John 8:44, Luke 10:18, Revelation 12:4, Mark 5:8,9, Ephesians 6:12, etc.

Chapter 2

1. Revelation 12:9, 1st Peter 5:8, Matthew 12:26, Colossians 1:13, Ephesians 2:2 & 6:12, Matthew 25:41, Revelation 12:7
2. Theological note, New Geneva Study Bible, New King James Version, Copyright 1982, by Thomas Nelson Inc, p13.
3. Author's notes, Ohio Valley Christian Lectureships, 1976-78
4. Following Jesus' resurrection God the Father gave to Him all authority in heaven and on earth; Matthew 28:18
5. Book of Job, Chapters 38 thru 42

Chapter 5

1. Public information made available from Lone Pine Chamber of Commerce, 126 S. Main Street, Lone Pine, California, 93545.
2. *Mt. Whitney Guide*, for hikers and climbers, Paul Hellweg and Scott McDonald, copyright 1990, 1994, by Paul Hellweg and Scott McDonald, Canyon Publishing Co., Canoga Park, CA 91304, p13.
3. Public information made available from Lone Pine Chamber of Commerce, 126 S. Main Street, Lone Pine, California, 93545.
4. The teepee fire is based on the author's wilderness experiences in the High Sierra, Death Valley, and the Navajo Nation in northern Arizona/southern Utah.

Chapter 6

1. Malachi 2:13 thru 16, God's hatred against breaking faith with the wife of one's youth.

Chapter 9

1. *In The Beginning*, Compelling Evidence for Creation and the Flood, Walt Brown, PhD., Seventh Edition, copyright by Walt Brown, 2001, Center for Scientific Creation, Phoenix, Arizona; used for teaching by permission, p31.

2. Author's notes, Ohio Valley Christian Lectureships, 1976-78

3. Author's notes, A Special Study on the Great Flood, Sunset Extension School, Lubbock, Texas, 1991

4. Author's notes, Ohio Valley Christian Lectureships, 1976-78

5. Author's notes, The Flood and Science Documentary featuring Dr. Walt Brown, Church of Christ, Temple City, California, 1991. This information is also available from reference #**1**, part 2, beginning p85.

6. The Flood record, Genesis 7:17 thru 8:14

7. Genesis, chapter 1, verses 2, 6, 7, 9, 10, 20, 21 and 22. Water is used in performing miracles throughout the entire Bible.

8. *Astronomy and the Bible*, Questions and Answers, Donald DeYoung, copyright 1989, Baker Book House Company, Grand Rapids, Michigan, p55-58.

Chapter 10

1. Genesis 9:12 thru 17. As long as it remains, the earth will never again be completely destroyed by water. The present heavens and earth are instead reserved for destruction by fire on the final Day of Judgment, after which new heavens and a new earth will be formed, according to God's promise, 2nd peter 3:5 thru 13.

2. 1st Corinthians 3:18-21. Men are foolish in their theories regarding the geophysical earth and the solar system. God first created all things full grown; therefore determining age is impossible, save carbon dating, which was made possible by the Great Flood and accounts for history after the flood, a mere 5000 years ago. No accurate dating beyond that time period is possible and scientifically confirmed as impossible. Paleontologists and geologists are among the worst offenders of this truth. See also in reference to dating: *In The Beginning*, Compelling Evidence for Creation and the Flood, Walt Brown, PhD., Seventh Edition, copyright by Walt Brown, 2001, Center for Scientific Creation, Phoenix, Arizona; used for teaching by permission, p244-246.

3. Public information made available from Death Valley National Park, Death Valley, California 92328.

Chapter 11

1. *In The Beginning*, Compelling Evidence for Creation and the Flood, Walt Brown, PhD., Seventh Edition, copyright by Walt Brown, 2001, Center for Scientific Creation, Phoenix, Arizona; used for teaching by permission, p5.

2. Information on the animals, birds and insects discussed in this chapter is the product of the author's research, studies in Job (Chapters 38 thru 42), and personal experience over several years.

Chapter 13

1. All information on Noah's Ark was made available through the author's personal contact with Ron Wyatt himself, and, Wyatt Archeological Research, Cornersville, Tennessee, some of which is available on the Internet at wyattmuseum.com. Information was thoroughly investigated by the author in 1991, and is contained in the author's notes and on video.

2. Information based on author's personal research and notes.

3. Information based on author's personal exploration, research and notes.

4. Information based on author's personal research and notes.

5. *The Mountain of God*, the discovery of the real Mt. Sinai, Robert Cornuke and David Halbrook, copyright by Bob Cornuke, 2000, Broadman & Holman Publishers, Nashville, Tennessee, p1, 75,85,125.

6. Information based on author's personal observation, research and notes.

7. All information on The Ark of the Covenant was made available to the author through Ron Wyatt himself, and, Wyatt Archeological Research, Cornersville, Tennessee, some of which is available on the Internet at wyattmuseum.com. Information was thoroughly investigated by the author between 1991-99, before Ron Wyatt passed away, and is contained in the author's notes and on video.

8. Some years after Ron Wyatt passed away, part of his recorded work regarding the Ark of the Covenant was removed from public circulation. Since he passed away before he could return to the site, critics complained that he was unable to offer *proof* of his discoveries in the lower chamber, which held the Ark. I submit that his critics should have read between the lines—Wyatt's story is proof enough. After all, his discovery confirms that Christ's atonement for sin was a reality and done according to God's Law. It also proves that God's wisdom is greater than man's, and that He accomplishes things in a way not foreseen by men. To the believer, Wyatt's discovery makes absolutely perfect sense. Come, let us reason together; the discovery related in the story itself is absolute proof of the story itself—no if's, and's or but's about it.

Chapter 14

1. Information on the origin of the Bible is the result of the author's personal research on the subject, which information is also common to most Bible dictionaries.

2. Genesis 1:26, Matthew 28:18,19, Mark 1:9 thru 11, John 15:26, 2nd Corinthians 13,14, 1st John 5:7, Romans 15:13, Hebrews 9:14, Micah 3:8, Psalm 139:7 thru 12, 1st Corinthians 2:10,11.

3. Genesis 1:1,2, Job 26:13 & 33:4, Psalm 104:30, Judges 3:10, Exodus 31:3 & 35:30,31, Genesis 41:16 & 38, Numbers 27:18 thru 20, Judges 14:19, 2nd Peter 1:21, Ezekiel 2:1,2 & 11:5, 2nd Timothy 3:16,17.

4. Luke 1:35, Matthew 3:16, 1st John 5:6, Luke 4:18, Matthew 12:28, Luke 4:1,2, Romans 8:11, John 3:34.

5. John 14:26 & 16:13,14, Acts 2:5 thru 12, Hebrews 2:3,4, Acts 8:17,18, Acts 1:4,5, Acts chapter 2 thru chapter 28, Ephesians 2:20 thru 22, Acts 2:4, 1st Corinthians 2:13, 2nd Timothy 3:16,17.

6. Acts 2:37,38,41 & 47, Acts 8:12,13,35 & 38, Acts 9:18, Acts 10:46 thru 48, Acts 16:14,15 & 30 thru 34, Acts 18:8, Acts 19:3 thru 5, and Acts 22:14 thru 16.

7. Galatians 3:27, Acts 2:38, Romans 6:4.

8. John 1:1 thru 3, 1st John 5:6 thru 10, Matthew 3:13 thru 17, Acts 2:38, Ephesians 1:22 & 4:15,16, Colossians 1:18, Hebrews 10:14,18, Romans 8:28 thru 30

Chapter 15

1. John 14:6 & 6:44,45, 1st Corinthians 12:3, Romans 8:14
2. Ephesians 6:12, Ephesians 2:2, Matthew 4:8,9, Revelation 12:10, Matthew 7:14, 2nd Timothy 4:7,8
3. Isaiah 1:8, Hebrews 8:12 & Romans 11:33 thru 36
4. 1st John 1:8 thru 10, Romans 8:26,27,34, Hebrews 7:25

Also Available from Mark Stephen Taylor:

 **A High Sierra Christmas** (Fiction), an untold tale of Jeremiah Johnson. *Premier Holiday Edition.* Are you looking for a unique gift item for friends or family this year? I am hoping that you will consider, *A High Sierra Christmas*; 'an untold tale of Jeremiah Johnson.' Most everyone wants to know what happened to Jeremiah up there in the Rockies. Is he up there still? No—in fact, he later went into the High Sierras, and you can discover his illuminating fate in the pages of this new and non-traditional fiction tale of the American West.

This book is suitable for all ages, 1 to 101, and is narrated in the 'old west' style. It can be enjoyed as you sit by the Holiday fire this year and read it aloud to all of your family and friends. It is suitable for bedside reading to seniors as well. The cast of characters in the story are real folk's, and on Christmas Eve, you and yours can saddle up, ride into the majestic High Sierra scenery (full page photo at each chapter), and actually become a part of their story! (160 pages, paperback & *available on Kindle*)

 **Hiking Life's Difficult Trails** (non-fiction) A treatise on body, mind, and spirit; In this volume, Mark takes us back to the Wilderness Trail—not just to trek along its rim, but to explore its depths—to hike up its buttes, among its endless crags, and through its areas of parched desolation. He helps us to better understand and deal with the difficulties of this earthly life we journey through, and leads us along the trail of some of the most important hopes that we could ever contemplate.

This book will help you to understand the absolute necessity for your 'wilderness wanderings'—life's difficult trails. You will perhaps come to better understand your true need for God throughout life's journey. Sometimes it feels like God backs away from us when we wander into hard times, but that's just not true, as you are about to discover.

(132 pages, paperback & now (2011) available on *Kindle*)

A 'High Country Hiker's Edition' *of Hiking Life's Difficult Trails is also available,* which adds a most unique 7-day, perpetual (forever teaching, encouraging and comforting) devotional at the back of the book.

(142 pages, paperback)

 ***From the Lone Wolf Limited Mystery Series*** comes the first two installments...**The Sun, The Glass, and The Leaning Rock;** The Secret of the Lost Dutchman's Gold, is a daring tale of high adventure. The story opens in the year 1984, but centers on the 1924 discovery of the 'Lost Dutchman's mine' in Arizona, the inevitable misfortune of its discoverer, and the strange fate of the loot itself. A treasure map, an unusual necklace, and a simple nursery rhyme set the stage for double murder, betrayal, kidnapping, and unrelenting drama in this tale of the high desert!

(194 pages, paperback & available on Kindle as '*A Second Chance*')

 **The Secret of Monument Valley,** The Trail of the Anasazi, resolves the age-old mystery regarding the 1450 AD disappearance of the Anasazi people from their strongholds in the American southwest. Based on actual accounts from Native American residents of the Navajo Nation, award-winning author Mark Stephen Taylor thrusts his characters into the heart of this most interesting controversy. What they must endure is indeed most shocking. What they will find is most profoundly enlightening!

(162 pages, paperback & available on Kindle)

Also scheduled for production in the series:
Treasure of the High Sierra
The Secret of Death Valley

NEW !
Latest Release from Lone Wolf Limited! January 2011
Three Days In Lone Pine,
An Untold Tale of The High Sierra:

 Do you believe in angels? In 1873 the town of Lone Pine, California came to believe in them. Lone Pine is the home of Mt. Whitney, highest mountain in the contiguous United States, towering some 14, 497 feet. Native American legends say its high summit was the haunt of evil spirits—led by the Devil himself! But, in August of 1873, the most powerful leader of the angelic host paid an unannounced visit to the town. After his *Three Days in Lone Pine*, the mountain, the birds and the animals...even the people, would never be the same...

(202 pages, paperback & available on Kindle)

Reader's Notes:

307

8701885R0

Made in the USA
Charleston, SC
06 July 2011